WRITERS ON COMICS SCRIPTWRITING

Mark Salisbury

TITAN BOOKS

WRITERS ON COMICS SCRIPTWRITING
ISBN 1 84023 069 X

Published by
Titan Books
A Division of Titan Publishing Group, Ltd.
144 Southwark Street
London SE1 0UP

First Edition April 1999
10 9 8 7 6 5

Did you enjoy this book? We love to hear from our readers. Please email us at: readerfeedback@titanemail.com or write to Reader Feedback at the above address.

To subscribe to our regular newsletter for up-to-the-minute news, great offers and competitions, email: titan-news@titanemail.com

DEDICATION

To Dad, my superhero

Acknowledgements

Any book of this kind is only as good as its participants. I am therefore indebted to all the writers and creators interviewed herein, who graciously made time during their busy schedules to be quizzed, probed and scrutinised, as well as providing sketches, scripts and other written material for use in this book, which ultimately is as much theirs as it is mine. Of equal importance is my editor Simon Furman, who valiantly steered the ship through a difficult period, and for the duration of the journey was a constant provider of invaluable and enthusiastic support, knowledge, advice, encouragement and, of course, comics. And thanks to the rest of the team at Titan Books: David Barraclough, Gillian Christie, Vanessa Coleman, Bob Kelly, Adam Newell, Chris Teather and Katy Wild. Thank you also Sheila Eggar and Melanie Simmons at Todd McFarlane Productions Inc, Michael Martens at Dark Horse Comics, Carol Platt at Marvel Entertainment, Joe Yanarella at *Wizard*, Lorraine Garland and Richard Starkings, all of whom in some fashion helped out along the way. A special note of thanks to Dan Brooke: if anyone's to blame for kick-starting my interest in comics again, it's you. And finally my love and heartfelt appreciation to Mum and Laura, my very own Wonder Women...

CONTENTS

INTRODUCTION

In this multimedia-saturated, digital television-watching, Nintendo-playing, internet-fuelled age, comic book sales are, perhaps inevitably, declining. And, if the soothsayers' predications are to be believed, the printed word — be it the novel, the newspaper or indeed the comic — will soon go the way of the dinosaurs and the dodo. But in amongst the doom and gloom painted by comics industry analysts, there beats, ironically, the heart of a medium at the peak of its creative powers. While the Hollywood money men have turned movies into a homogenised, mass-marketed concern, comics are currently at their most innovative, coursing with a limit-less, visionary promise and a capacity for invention, intelligence, action, humour and wit that's second to none. Unlike movies or television, comics are not bound by budget or convention, a writer's creativity restrained only by his or her imagination. At their best, comics dare to explore new, undiscovered, uncharted realms of fantasy and fiction, tearing back the limits of the fantasti-cal, the political and the social, daring to question even the very three dimensions that bind our world.

It was the mid-eighties' trend towards gritty, densely plotted and character-driven stories aimed at adult sensibilities — typified by Alan Moore's *Watchmen* and Frank Miller's *Batman: The Dark Knight Returns* — that sparked a publishing rev-olution and reintroduced comics to the masses. In this new and enlightened era, comics were cool, they were hip, they were required reading. For both sexes. The rise of the graphic novel — collections of comic strip material in book form — meant you could read a comic on the train, free from embarrassment. Naturally, some of the public's newfound interest waned, the media spotlight moved on, but somehow comics never quite went back to being frowned upon as the con-cern of awkward, maladjusted teenage boys.

The role of the comics writer has long been as misunderstood as the medium itself. A common misconception is that he, or increasingly she, simply fills in the word balloons that come out of the characters' mouths, inserting dialogue into a story crafted by the truly talented individual (ie the artist). While there are a number of writer/artists operating in the medium, three of whom — Frank Miller, Todd McFarlane and Dan Jurgens — are interviewed within these pages, the majority of today's comic book scribes are first and foremost writers, blessed with remarkable storytelling skills and boundless imaginations. It's not without reason that Hollywood is continually turning to comics and comic creators' ideas for movies. There are more fantastical ideas, scientific conceits and quantum leaps of storytelling in Grant Morrison's *JLA* or *The Invisibles* than in a dozen Hollywood blockbusters put together. If you're looking for deathly black humour, droll dialogue and riotous violence as good as if not better than anything conjured up by Quentin Tarantino, check out Garth Ennis's *Preacher*. Or if it's literate fantasy as rich and profound and involving as Tolkien that you crave, delve into Neil Gaiman's epic *Sandman* saga. For crime noir to rival Ellroy, Hammett and Chandler, look no further than Frank Miller's hard boiled *Sin City* series. And if it's widescreen superhero action/adventure with bite and intelligence that you're after, you'll do no better than Kurt Busiek's *Astro City* or Mark Waid's *Captain America*. So the list goes on.

We live in a society where aspiring to be a novelist or a playwright is considered a noble pursuit, where anyone's burning desire to discover how to write a film screenplay is easily appeased by a browse through the cinema section of any bookshop. But if you've always wanted to write for comics... well, forget it. As Neil Gaiman points out later, he might as well have told his careers advisor at school that he wanted to be an astronaut when he mooted his career of choice. At least that way the guy would have known how to respond. Indeed, the art of comic scriptwriting has, up until now, been an almost top secret craft, a mysterious, magician's style code revealed to the chosen few by those in the know. If, like me, you want to write comics yourself, then maybe, just maybe, the views and opinions and tales and script extracts that follow will help you realise your dream. Because in the comics, anything is possible.

The rationale behind this book was to get some of the best creators in the business to open up and tell all. In part, I wanted the nuts and bolts; the 'how to' part of their craft. How to construct a script, the difference between writing full script or Marvel plot style, the key elements of storytelling, the beat and flow and visual sense necessary to construct a comic book. The dos and don'ts in other words. But more than that, I wanted to get inside their heads to see what made them tick, what got those creative juices flowing. Because, as I've said, comics are only limited by the imagination, and the imagination of these individuals is boundless. Candour was encouraged. I didn't want clipped, measured, politically-correct comment, I wanted the floodgates to open and for it all to pour out; the good, the bad and the ugly. These guys (and gal) *wanted* to talk, and talk they did, frankly and often explicitly. Of the interviews themselves, these were only cut for length (I had only so many pages), and are otherwise unexpurgated. There's a smattering of strong language and an open discourse on the effects of certain controlled substances, but as I said, this is warts 'n' all stuff; a ground-level portrait of how the writer's mind works. Forget comics for a moment. This is a book about the imagination and creation of fantasy, and it demands your attention.

Perhaps the most difficult thing of all was the selection process. Who to include? The initial list of candidates was enough for three volumes this size, and so pruning had to be done. It was, in no uncertain terms, impossible. How do you choose between the creative genius of one writer and another? There is simply so much talent out there. In the end, it came down to covering all bases. I wanted as wide a range of styles, approaches and work experience (or lack thereof) as possible, and so looked for specifics, something different that each writer would bring to the book. There were, of course, those I wanted to include but who couldn't spare the time from their hectic schedules. I desperately wanted input from Alan Moore, simply because so many comics writers cite him and his work as having influenced them, and because today his name still commands the sort of attention it did at the height of the comics revolution of the mid-eighties. But Alan, weighed down by sheer volume of work, couldn't commit. Maybe another time, maybe in volume two.

Mark Salisbury
London, 1999

Editor's note:

Throughout the book, references are made to two distinct styles of comic book writing, full script and (Marvel style) plot. While the line between the two often blurs, it's worth boiling each down into its simplest form so that those not already in the know are suitably prepared.

Full script: Each page (as it will eventually appear in the finished comic) is broken down panel-by-panel by the writer, and includes a description of the action with all the dialogue indented as one would in a play. In this case, the writer is called upon to judge how many pictures will fit on each page, and has much more control over the dialogue-to-picture dynamic. It is incumbent upon the artist to allow enough room for dialogue and to position characters appropriately.

Plot: In this case the writer describes — in varying degrees of detail — the action over a whole page or set of pages, with little in the way of dialogue. The artist therefore decides how the page breaks down into panels and the writer adds dialogue in once he sees the artwork. This way the artist has greater freedom and the onus is on the writer to make the dialogue fit what has been drawn.

KURT BUSIEK

It was *Marvels*, Kurt Busiek's masterful collaboration with painter Alex Ross, that elevated both a jobbing superhero writer and a little-known artist into fan-favourite, comics industry heavyweights. A densely-plotted, richly detailed and beautifully observed four-part mini-series, *Marvels* earned Busiek widespread acclaim. Ironically, the Boston-born writer had been steadily plying his craft for more than a decade previous to *Marvels*, as well as working on staff at Marvel Comics as both an assistant editor (on *Marvel Age* magazine) and Direct Sales Manager (responsible for the science fiction series *Open Space*). As Busiek himself puts it, he was an overnight success after twelve years in the business, and from humble beginnings — a back-up story in *Green Lantern* — he now writes several of Marvel's flagship titles, including *The Avengers* and *Iron Man*. Busiek's tag as a retro-writer — due in no small part to *Marvels* — is a misleading one. For while his work is thoroughly researched and steeped in comics history, he refrains from wallowing in the past, offering instead new and creative twists on the superhero genre. This trait is particularly evident in his creator-owned *Astro City*, a series that simultaneously manages to be both referential and rejuvenating, breathing inspired life into well-worn stereotypes and situations.

Were you, as your work seems to suggest, a big comics fan as a kid?

As a child I wasn't allowed to read comics. With the exception of the *Pogo* comic-strip collections by Walt Kelly and *Asterix* and *Tintin* books, my parents didn't allow them in the house. Mostly I would read comics at friends' houses or at the barbershop. I was fourteen when I picked up an issue of *Daredevil* at the drugstore; it was part one of a four-part story and I was intrigued enough to want to see the rest. By the time three months later had rolled round and I had the rest, I'd found a speciality comic book store and was reading a lot of different Marvel comics on a regular basis. It kind of steamrollered from there.

The Marvel books were the ones that hooked me. Specifically, it was their cross-continuity, the interconnections, that just hit me like a ton of bricks. When I was younger, my favourite novels were the series titles like L. Frank Baum's *Oz* books, Lloyd Alexander's *Prydain Chronicles* and Enid Blyton's *Famous Five*. I always liked the kind of book that if you read it and enjoyed it you could go back to the library and find more. So that first issue of *Daredevil* I bought, which referred back to earlier DD history in a significant way, suggested there was a whole universe out there where all of this stuff continued. That was what got me looking for the next issue more than anything. Even now, my favourite television shows are stuff like *The Practice* and *NYPD Blue*, shows that have a strong sense of episode-to-episode continuity. They're not isolated stories, they're stories in an ongoing continuum, and that's something that appeals to me very, very strongly.

Were there any comics writers who influenced you back then?

I guess I knew that people worked on the comics, even though I didn't pay attention to the credits. In one of those early *Daredevils* there was a really silly exchange within the footnotes, centring on some piece of Hydra weaponry from years ago that had reappeared. There was a note as to what the weapon was called and a footnote from the writer saying, 'Okay, it's a silly name but I didn't make it up', and there was a further footnote from the editor saying, 'Stop it with all the footnotes'. That definitely [helped me understand] that there were people working on these comics, but I didn't really distinguish between them until I realised there were certain books — anything Steve Englehart or Steve Gerber wrote, pretty much — I always liked better. I fig-

Place of birth:
Boston, Massachusetts, USA
Date of birth:
16 September 1960
Home base:
Vancouver, Washington, USA
First published work:
Green Lantern #162
(back-up story)
Education:
Syracuse University
Career highlights:
Astro City, The Avengers, Avengers Forever, Iron Man, Marvels, Power Man and Iron Fist, Red Tornado, ShadowHawk, Thunderbolts, Untold Tales of Spider-Man, Vampirella

ured out that the name in the credits had something to do with whether or not I was likely to enjoy a book.

Did you always have aspirations to write?

Pretty much from the first day I could actually hold a pencil and form words I wanted to write. My mother has the opening paragraph to an *Oz* novel I started when I was five or six, and never got further with than that. But I definitely wanted to do something in that direction. The ambition to write stories, to tell stories, long predates my interest in comic books. I wanted to be a screenwriter or a novelist, but writing a whole novel or a whole movie seemed to be such a staggeringly large undertaking that it was intimidating.

When did you realise that you wanted to write comics?

There's an issue of *X-Men*, sometime before issue 100, in which Chris Claremont* was doing the letters page. He told a story in one of his answers about how his grandfather would say to him, 'So, Chris, you write the funny books. That's very nice, but what do you do for a living?'. After reading that the penny dropped, and I thought, 'They get paid. This is a job. This is a job that people do and can support themselves with. I wanna do that'. Writing a seventeen-page comic, which is how long they were then, didn't seem anywhere near as scary as writing a novel.

At the time, my best friend was Scott McCloud and I got him into reading comics. We started talking about making up characters ourselves, and I suggested we do a comic book together. We took ten Marvel characters that we liked and divided them up into two teams and had them turn up at our high school and have a big fight. We had cameos by our friends and we destroyed all the classrooms we didn't like and we wrecked the library. 'The Battle of Lexington' it was called. We intended to do a twenty-page story, and by the time we were finished it was sixty pages and had taken us three and a half years. The first few pages are awful, but by the end of the sixty pages we'd kinda figured out how to do it. I went off to college and studied English Literature at Syracuse University, and while I was there Scott and I worked on more comics together. By the time we graduated, we'd got in enough practice for Scott to get a job in DC's production department and for me to sell a short *Green Lantern* story to a DC editor.

Can you draw, and did you ever harbour ambitions in that direction?

I can draw well enough to do a costume design or to indicate a tricky page layout, and I can get my ideas across visually. I think one of the reasons I work well with artists is that I have a pretty good sense of what works on the page and what doesn't. But while I like the storytelling aspects and the pacing, I never had the patience to teach myself how to draw backgrounds. To this day, I couldn't spend a whole day on one page, even if I had the skill to do it. I'm more interested in the story, the characters and the dialogue and where it's all going to.

---

* X-Men *writer from issues 95 (as co-plotter) and 96 (as writer) to 279, an unbroken run lasting over sixteen years!*

Was that *Green Lantern* story the first thing you ever submitted to a comics company?

Not exactly. I'd previously inundated them with letters of comment. Between 1975 and 1981 I had well over a hundred letters published in Marvel comic books, and that actually turned out to be a positive thing. When I later pitched story ideas to Len Wein, an editor who had used a lot of my letters, he recognised my name and associated me with them. So I had more of a chance because of that. The only time I'd submitted anything to a professional comics company before breaking in at DC was when I wrote up a seven-page Hawkeye plot that I submitted to Marvel. They wrote back and said, 'It doesn't meet our needs at this time', and I can now see why.

I took a course on magazine publishing at college and for a term paper we had to do an interview with the publisher of a mass market magazine. I talked them into letting me interview Dick Giordano, who was then Editor-in-Chief of DC Comics. I told him that when I finished college I had hopes of being a comic book writer and he invited me to show him some sample scripts. I went back to school and wrote four full scripts; a Flash story, a *Brave and the Bold* story teaming Batman and Green Lantern, a Supergirl story and a *Superman: The In-Between Years* story featuring Lex Luthor's eighteenth birthday. I sent them in to Dick and he passed

Scott McCloud

Unlike his former collaborator, Kurt Busiek, whose comics career could be considered 'mainstream', in the best possible sense of the word, Scott McCloud's career has — as he freely admits — been rather more 'alternative'. The titles on which he has worked, both as writer and artist, have been aimed at essentially a cult audience, published by 'small press' or independent companies, more often than not in black and white. Stand-outs include *Destroy!*, a very funny pastiche of musclebound superhero slugfests, and *Zot!*, an ostensibly science-fiction style book that was in fact far more about human emotions and feelings. McCloud's recent work includes the fully computer-generated graphic novel *The New Adventures of Abraham Lincoln*, a satirical look at the current state of American politics and the Constitution. A big Superman fan, McCloud also scripted several issues of *Superman Adventures*, a comic based on the animated television show of the same name (a collection, featuring issue number #1, written by Paul Dini, and #2–6 of McCloud's run, was published as *Superman: Adventures of the Man of Steel*). However, it is perhaps for *Understanding Comics: The Invisible Art* that McCloud is best known. This fully illustrated, witty and deeply reverential look at comics as an art form stands as both a textbook for creators and an intellectual consideration of the whole medium.

them on to the individual editors. Ernie Colon liked the *Flash* script enough for me to pitch for *Tales of the Green Lantern Corps*. I came in with something like eighteen story ideas and he picked one. I wrote it up and that was my first sale.

After that, I very cannily noted that Bob Layton was supposed to be the new writer on *Power Man and Iron Fist*, but every month a new issue came out and Bob hadn't written it; Denny O'Neil, the editor, had written a fill-in issue that looked like he'd done it in a big hurry. So I wrote up a plot for a *Power Man* fill-in and sent it in to Denny with a note saying, 'I'm writing Green Lantern stories for DC so I thought I'd pitch this to you'. I got a call from him two days later and he invited me to work up the plot and do a script, and he bought it. So I pitched him another one and he bought it, and I pitched him a two-parter and he bought it. At this time I was working freelance as the New York news correspondent for *Comics Feature Magazine*, so I would go to Marvel's weekly press conferences, back when they had them, and they announced there was a new regular writer on *Power Man and Iron Fist*. I thought, 'Oh well', and they said it's Kurt Busiek. I ended up writing it for a year and then I was fired off the book because it hadn't gone up in sales. Though it hadn't gone down either, I hasten to add.

During your freelance career you've written everything from *Vampirella* to Mickey Mouse, often at the same time. Was that difficult?

Actually, it was fun. It was engaging to stretch the creative muscles that way and do all kinds of different things. In the morning I'd do a revision on a Mickey Mouse script, trying to do what Disney wanted and give Mickey less and less personality, and then in the afternoon I'd be working on the latest chapter of *Vampirella*, where I was trying to do this absolutely compelling, creepily atmospheric horror stuff. It was useful to have different techniques, different tools in my belt as it were, that I could pull out. I'm something of a formalist; I like to play with form, and that gave me an opportunity to do so.

You write on average four books a month. Does that take some organising in terms of what gets done when?

If I'm doing four regular books then theoretically that's one a week in any given month. I have two offices, one in my home and one outside. The outside one is for solitude. When I'm dialoguing an issue of *The Avengers* I'll take the pages and go to the outside office. There's nothing else to do there, I don't even have a solitaire game on the computer, so I'll just script pages until I'm done. But when I'm plotting a story I'll be in my office at home, where I've got an entire wall of bookshelves full of old copies of *The Avengers*, *Iron Man*, *Captain America* and *Thor* to look stuff up in. Those are the times I'll be on the phone with my editor talking about ideas and puttering around until I have a structure for the story.

I'm not really a night owl, I write during the day. I get up in the morning, walk the dog, have breakfast, shower and do all the morning stuff and then I settle in

ASTRO CITY #1/2 /Nearness of You/Busiek

PAGE SIX - 6 PANELS

[1]   **MIKE** AT HIS DESK IN THE OFFICE, IN A SUIT, TALKING ON THE PHONE, WORRIED.
      1 Mike: Maybe in the <u>dorm</u>, Bob? On one of the other floors?

[2]   **MIKE** AT A PAY PHONE, A PARK SCENE BEHIND HIM, HE'S IN A "FOX-BROOME" SWEATSHIRT AND GYM SHORTS, HOLDING A BASKETBALL AS HE TALKS ON THE PHONE.
      2 Phone (elec):   -- doesn't sound like the kind of chick you <u>ever</u> chased back in <u>high school</u>, hoss.
      3 Phone (elec):   Not like it makes a difference. With me it was <u>blondes, blondes, blondes,</u> 'til Shelly showed up, and then <u>pow</u>!

[3]   **MIKE** SITTING IN HIS LIVING ROOM, A CORDLESS PHONE TO HIS EAR, SITTING IN A MOSTLY DARK ROOM, IN T-SHIRT, BOXERS AND BATHROBE.
      4 Mike: -- <u>know</u> it's late, Chet. Sorry -- I didn't mean to <u>wake</u> you.
      5 Mike: But -- look, back in <u>sixth grade</u>, I've been trying to remember all the --
      6 Mike: <u>Chet</u>?

[4]   **MIKE** SITS ON THE COUCH, HIS FOREARMS RESTING ON HIS THIGHS, THE PHONE DANGLING FROM HIS HAND. HE'S GLUM, WE'RE PULLED BACK, DISTANCED FROM HIM.
      No Copy

[5]   ON HIS **HAND**, HOLDING SOME PILLS, TAPPED FROM A PRESCRIPTION BOTTLE OUT INTO HIS PALM.
      7 Caption: The <u>pills</u> -- they stopped it, knocked him out. For a little while. Then she started to show up <u>anyway</u>.
      8 Caption: Maybe -- maybe if he took <u>more</u> of them --

[6]   **MIKE** HEARS A SOUND BEHIND HIM AND STARTS TO TURN --
      9 FX: SHK
      10 Mike: <u>Huh</u>?
      11 Mike: What's that --

[6]

Above: *An extract from Kurt Busiek's script for* Astro City #½. *Courtesy of Kurt Busiek. Used with permission.* Astro City ™ *and* © *1999 Kurt Busiek.*

for whatever the work is that day. What I'll do if I'm plotting an issue is make a bunch of notes on a yellow legal pad in enough detail so I can break it down page-by-page. Or I'll make enough notes so I have a sense that this is what happens in the story, and I'll go to the computer and type up a synopsis and then break that down into pages. Then I take my page-by-page outline and type up a full plot for the artist. When I'm plotting an issue it takes a day or two. Some days, if it goes really well, I'll rough out the story by one o'clock in the afternoon and I'll sit down and start typing it up. Once I've got it roughed out it only takes one and a half to two hours to type it up.

If it's a more complicated story, I may have the structure of it worked out by the end of the first day, whereupon the next day I'll actually do the page-by-page breakdown and look up whatever reference I need, which can be time consuming, and then type it all up and xerox the reference for the artist. That's a two-day plot, but it's very rare that it'll take me longer than that. If it's not working, I'll call an editor or a friend and we'll bounce ideas off of each other until it does. On a day that I'm scripting I'll take the xeroxes of the full-size pages that Marvel sends me, shoot them down to 8 ½" x 11" size, go off to my outside office, prop them up on an easel next to the computer, and start scripting. When I finish, I'll indicate where the balloons go, e-mail the script off to Marvel and fax the balloon placements.

Astro City is different because for that I do a full script, but it's largely the same process. I'll mess about wandering around the house thinking about things, talking with [artist] Brent Anderson or [cover artist] Alex Ross, working out a plot structure that I feel works, and then making a lot of notes until I've got a structure that makes sense. I type it up on the computer, break it down into pages, but then instead of typing up a plot I'll start typing all the dialogue for the script and captions, page-by-page. Once I've done that and I've got it all broken down into panels, I'll go back and type in all the panel descriptions. Normally I can get about eight to ten pages done in a day. So if you figure a day or two to work out the story in detail, putting together all the thoughts that have been buzzing around in my head, and then if I do eight pages a day, I'm done in a week. I also do up these little grids showing how the panels break down and then send the whole shebang off to Brent, whereupon Brent will read it and either say, 'This is really good', or 'I don't think it comes through strongly enough here, here and here'. We'll talk about what's working and what's not, and I'll do any necessary revisions.

Which method do you prefer?

I don't. Doing a full script gives me more control, but doing it plot-style gives the artist more freedom, which can be a good thing, especially if it's for the right kind of artist. If I did full script for [*Avengers* artist] George Pérez it would be terribly confining for him. He wouldn't enjoy himself and the pages wouldn't come out looking anywhere near as good as if he broke it down himself. But in something like *Marvels* or *Astro City*, where the pacing and the internal narrative — what's going on in the lead character's head — is so important, if I scripted them in Marvel plot style it wouldn't work as well.

Iron Man: The Iron Age was very similar to *Marvels* in approach. I did that plot-style, but a very, very tight plot. Even so, there were times when I had to come in with captions that were essentially saying, 'This is what he is thinking about right now'. With *Astro City* the full script approach allows me to lay in every story beat that's needed in what is a psychologically-oriented story, whereas in *Iron Age* I had to force those beats on occasion. Books like *Avengers* or *Untold Tales of Spider-Man*, which are largely plot-oriented, benefit from the artist having more leeway to visually show what is happening. Essentially, the reactive stuff is primary in *Astro City* and the active stuff is primary in *Avengers*. It's a matter of what suits what best.

Do you enjoy the process of collaborating with an artist?

To me, the connection between the writing and the art is the fun part. It's what makes comics work. So I enjoy writing comics most when I have a lot of contact with the artist, when I have a sense of what he wants to draw and what he likes best. That collaboration is one of the things that draws me most strongly to the form. I have occasionally written a full script and it's gone off to the artist and I haven't seen it until publication, but I'm usually unhappy when that happens. I did an Arsenal story full script for DC's *Showcase* series; it went off to the artist

Marvels

This groundbreaking — and career-making — series switches the perspective on established Marvel landmarks from the participant heroes and villains to that of the normal, everyday man-in-the-street, providing an uniquely human aspect to fantastic events. As witnessed through the eyes of jobbing reporter Phil Sheldon, the first appearance of the original Human Torch, the coming of Galactus, the rise of anti-mutant hysteria and the death of Gwen Stacy are represented in stunning fashion. Kurt Busiek's economical and literate script is brought to life by Alex Ross's magnificent fully painted artwork. Both words and pictures reflect an attention to detail that goes beyond the meticulous, and viewed together, the four issues (and the rather more peripheral issue #0) form one of the most well realised depictions of the Marvel Universe to date. Familiarity with the source material helps, but is not essential, as the story is less about the events themselves than their effect on the day-to-day lives of those who experience them. Originally published in 1994, the four core issues were reprinted individually in 1996. Available in one collected volume, which itself has been published in a variety of editions, *Marvels* is required reading for anyone wanting to experience 'adult' comics storytelling without any overt sex or violence.

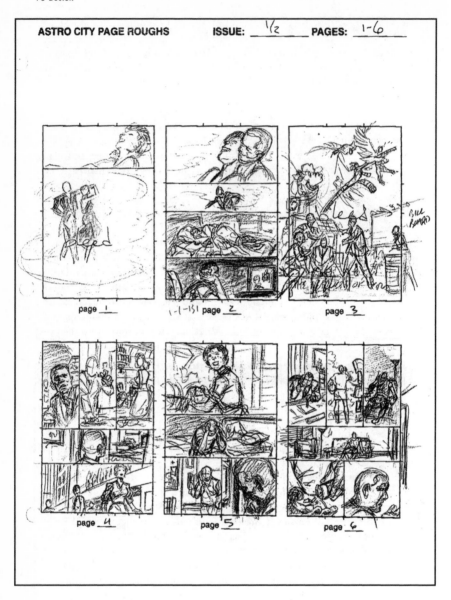

Above: *Brent Anderson's breakdowns for* Astro City *#½ over Busiek's original thumbnails. Courtesy of Kurt Busiek. Used with permission. Astro City ™ and © 1999 Kurt Busiek.*

Above: *More breakdowns from the same story, 'The Nearness of You'. Courtesy of Kurt Busiek. Used with permission.* Astro City ™ *and © 1999 Kurt Busiek.*

and when it came out I went, 'My God, this is horrible'. If I had gotten the art back I could have rewritten the story, so that all the stuff I put in the script that didn't work on the page could be made to work.

You and Alex Ross are credited as co-creators on *Marvels*. How much input did he have in the story?

Alex had ten Marvel characters that he wanted to do painted stories about, so he and I worked up this concept in which there would be a reporter, and we'd follow him through his life as he encountered each character. We envisaged these ten different stories and I wrote up the synopses for Alex to approve. Then we sent the whole package off to Marvel and they rejected it. They came back with the suggestion that instead of making up all of these new stories, why didn't we use real elements from Marvel history? I reworked it all, picking actual Marvel stories and wrote up a synopsis that I sent to Alex. He said it was real good and I sent it off to the editor. Alex has always said that at this point it became my story, because the one we had worked out together got thrown out. Alex became the illustrator of my vision.

***Marvels* reads like a labour of love. Was it something you were bursting to get out of you?**

We were telling a period piece, and for three issues out of four it was in a period I knew a lot about and loved. When I would sit down and plot out an issue of *Marvels* I would get a stack of everything Marvel published during the period we were covering and would read through the entire superhero output, noting what events were publicly seen and what weren't and what newspeople were out there. Since we were doing a series about the public perception of these events, I was researching it the way I would a historical novel, and it was indeed a labour of love. The trouble was, I was taking three or four weeks to write each forty-five page issue, so if it hadn't been 'love' I don't think I could have afforded to put in all that time. It was a very intense experience.

You mentioned that you like collaborating with artists. Does that extend to other writers and editors?

As you might have gathered, I like to talk. Normally, when I'm stuck for an idea or stuck for a transition or a story structure, I know that if I just put it away and come back to it a week later I will have solved the problem in my subconscious. If I come up with a bunch of ideas and I've got too much stuff to make sense of, when I come back to it a week later the ones I remember will be the good ones, because they're the ones that have stuck in my brain. They're the ideas that kind of settle to the top after letting them sit and simmer.

Right now, though, I'm a little too busy to do that. I can do that on *Astro City* because I'm separating it from the other stuff I'm doing. But if I'm doing an *Avengers* story, odds are I can't let stuff sit for a week. George will need the plot sooner than that, so rather than let the natural process of the subconscious take care of it, I've found I can talk to another writer and we'll pitch ideas back and forth. Usually I'll throw out every idea that's suggested to me, but the process of saying, 'That won't work' defines for me in my mind what shape hole it is I'm trying to fill. Once I know that, it's easy to fill. Karl Kesel [*Superboy, Superman and Batman: World's Finest*] lives near me and he's somebody I talk to a lot, and he does the same thing. It's a short cut to getting to where you would have gotten to anyway with enough time.

With Brent Anderson on *Astro City* I'll call him up, rattle off the latest story and he'll say, 'I like that, are you going to do this and this?', and I'll go, 'Well, no, I was going to do this and this', and we'll talk a little more and things will take shape. My name goes in the writer box and everybody goes, 'What a genius'. But we do the same thing with the art, where I go, 'I think you should change this layout this way and I think we need more of an expression on this guy's face', and Brent's name goes in the artist box and everybody goes, 'He's a genius'. It's this give and take that makes it so much fun.

When writing *The Avengers*, do you ever discuss with, say, Mark Waid, what's happening over on *Captain America*?

Technically, it's the editors' job. They're supposed to keep in close contact with each other so that Mark and I can be kept up-to-date on what the other is doing. Invariably, what seems to happen is Mark will call me up and say, 'Do you know I used Rhodey in the latest issue of *Captain America*?', or he'll call and say, 'We're giving Captain America a new shield', and I'll say 'Whoa, give me the details, I'll call George and tell him to change things'. So the system is imperfect, but because Mark and I are friends we're able to catch stuff that might otherwise slip through the net. I also talk to Dan Jurgens about *Thor*.

To my mind, doing this stuff is a lot like writing a historical novel, because there's certain aspects of it that are beyond your control. I may not like that Captain America has a new shield — I like the old one better — but by the same token if you're writing a Second World War novel you may go, 'Boy, it would be really good for my story if Eisenhower did this right now', but he didn't, so you have to deal with the reality of what actually happened. Marvel history is fictional but it's no less immutable. I cannot make the X-Men do something differently for my own purposes. Just as they can't push the Avengers around. It is occasionally frustrating, especially when another writer has what he thinks is a great idea for a character you liked the way he was. Once he's been completely changed, you never want to touch him again.

How does that compare to working on your own creator-owned book *Astro City*?

Doing something completely creator-owned is a lot of fun, because I'm the final authority. Nothing happens there without me thinking it's a good idea, but at the same time there isn't anything happening two books across the way that I can go, 'Oh, what a cool idea. I can springboard off that', something which does happen in *Avengers* and *Thunderbolts*. So it's a trade off. There are pluses and minuses and they kinda balance out. If they didn't, that's the point where you go, 'I don't want to do this any more'.

Everything I do in *Astro City*, every issue, every panel, every line of dialogue, is a brick that I add to a structure I own. Everything I do in *Avengers* is building on to somebody else's structure, with the full knowledge that someone can come along and say, 'I don't like those bricks, they didn't happen', and rip 'em out and start again. But that's the way the game is played. With *Astro City* I'm building something with Alex and Brent and it's something that will stand, that will be my own vision. *Astro City* is like a dream house. I'm arranging things just the way I like it and nobody else is gonna come in and move the furniture around on me. It's intensely satisfying in a way that the work-for-hire stuff can't match. The rule I've made for myself regarding work-for-hire is, I'll do it as long as it's fun.

What do you think of the current state of the superhero genre?

As I see it, the superhero genre is like a big field, and we've built this gigantic city in one tiny corner. Every now and then some visionary guy drives *out* of the city and goes off in a different direction, and everybody goes, 'Look, look — you can

---

Untold Tales of Spider-Man

Perhaps unintentionally, Kurt Busiek managed to present himself as something of a nostalgia writer when he followed *Marvels*, his revisionist view of Marvel history, with *Untold Tales of Spider-Man*, a series that laced new Spider-Man stories (set in the classic Stan Lee/Steve Ditko era, circa 1963/1964) into the established continuity. Busiek avoids the trap of trying to mimic the knowing tone of the era, but his wisecracking Spider-Man and insecure Peter Parker are right on the money. Likewise, artist Pat Olliffe doesn't try and imitate Ditko's style, opting instead for a more modern approach to the storytelling. The result is a very accessible series, stripped of the vast backstory and baggage that inevitably burdens the regular Spider-Man titles. The series ran for twenty-five issues and one Special, with a collected edition featuring #1–8. And while the nostalgia tag is an oversimplification, Busiek's work is often characterised by his deep affection for, and considerable knowledge of, Marvel history, as witnessed by such projects as *Iron Man: The Iron Age*, essentially an Iron Man 'Year One', and *Avengers Forever*, an all-new, time-spanning maxi-series that dips in and out of Avengers continuity. *Marvels, Iron Man: The Iron Age* and *Avengers Forever* are accompanied, for completists, with thorough notes on all Busiek's source material.

do that', and they all drive in a straight line right after him. I think the lesson that we need to learn from the likes of *Watchmen*, *Dark Knight Returns*, *Animal Man* and the *Fantastic Four* (as done by [Stan] Lee and [Jack] Kirby), isn't to say, 'Look, there's a new direction that can work', it's to go off and find your own direction. We should try and explore as much of this big field as we can, instead of building another little suburb and then overbuilding it until nobody wants to live there either.

You've tended to be typecast as the nostalgia guy. Is that stifling?

It would be if that was all I was allowed to do. In truth, the idea that I'm the nostalgic superhero guy is something of an illusion. The reason we did *Marvels* as a set of period pieces was because Alex's list of characters he wanted to paint involved the original Human Torch and Gwen Stacy, and we couldn't do either in the modern day. Thereafter, I knew Marvel was going to be doing *Untold Tales of Spider-Man*, and I was looking around for a regular series, so I called them up and told them I'd like to do it. In most cases, the nostalgia aspect, going back and telling continuity implant stories, was not something I proposed, it either grew naturally from the project or they came to me with it. The point at which I start to get frustrated is when people tell me *Astro City* is a retro book. I scratch my head and go, 'Retro to what?'. All I'm doing is creating a superhero universe with a historical sweep to it. None of it is pastiche, nor is it an attempt to recreate the past. We're telling modern stories in a modern style. In the final analysis, though, it doesn't really affect me at all, because I'm going to keep doing the stories I enjoy and every now and then people will be surprised and say that doesn't fit my image of what Kurt does. And I'll go, 'Good, got ya again'.

Do you ever feel the need to go beyond the superhero genre?

Sure. I want to do classic adventure stuff. I want to do fantasy. I want to do kids comics. I have this autobiographical story of a particularly memorable trip to Montreal as a Marvel Sales Manager. Some day I want to do an anthology series of slice-of-life stories from the Great Depression and Australian history. Just things that interest me and I'd like to turn into stories in the comics form. I certainly don't want to be limited to superheroes in the long term.

What about working outside comics? Maybe writing a novel or screenplay?

I love writing comics. The part that doesn't make me happy is the trouble the industry is in. I want to find ways to get comics to reach out to new people. The answer is not to change the audience into something that will like what we are doing today, but instead to do something they *will* like, in a format they'll pick up, and put it in places where they go shopping. I think we've got to have romance stories and action/adventure and science fiction and comedy, stuff that will be of interest to those who do not care overly about muscular men in tight clothes who punch each other in the face while they fall off buildings. I like that stuff, but I'm the last person to say it's all we need.

Someday I would like to write a novel or two. The screenplay form intrigues me, but the movie business doesn't. The same with television. I think about the non-writing part of doing it, the pitching and rewriting and having somebody else rewrite your work, and I go, 'you know, comics are really fun'. I have become so passionate about writing comics and I enjoy it so much, I don't think I'd ever want to leave it behind. If everything goes as I would like, I won't stop writing comics until I'm dead.

*　　　　　*　　　　　*

Check out:
Astro City: Life in the Big City
Astro City: Confession
Astro City: Family Album
(collects the original six-issue series and issues #1–13 of the ongoing series)

Marvels (with Alex Ross)
Untold Tales of Spider-Man (collects issues #1-8)
Thunderbolts: First Strikes (collects issues #1–3)

GREETINGS FROM ASTRO CITY

With *Marvels*, Kurt Busiek looked at superheroes and their incredible world through the eyes of ordinary people, a unique perspective he widened still further for *Astro City*. The titular metropolis, a fusion of fifties-style architecture and futuristic trappings, is the star, the cast a wide-ranging, constantly fluid set of characters both with and without superpowers. Against this broad backdrop we see how ordinary and extraordinary people coexist, highlighting their hopes, dreams and desires, which are, more often than not, uncannily similar. *Astro City* was first published in 1995 under the Image Comics banner as a six-issue creator-owned series, but such was the acclaim and success that greeted it, an ongoing series (published by Jim Lee's Homage imprint) soon followed. Lavished with praise and awards, *Astro City* is drawn by artist Brent Anderson, with covers and character designs by Busiek's *Marvels* co-creator Alex Ross. Here, Kurt Busiek opines on what sets *Astro City* apart from the mass...

The historical frame of reference I use for *Astro City* is to imagine there was a third major American comic book publisher called Astro Comics, and they published the adventures of all these characters. So, when I introduce a character that would have débuted in, say, 1968, I try and craft a name, costume and background that makes sense for that time period. Because I'm exploring the superhero genre as a whole, I need a construct that allows me to go to any period of the genre's history. *Astro City* isn't meant to have direct similarities to Marvel and DC, but rather iconic similarities that both companies and other superhero publishers share. If you boiled it all down to one basic superhero iconography, the same progressions can be seen in *Astro City* as can be seen in the genre as a whole.

There are certain characters in *Astro City* that people see as versions of other companies' characters. They think Samaritan is a Superman analogue, but he wasn't created because I had a Superman story I wanted to tell. He was created because Scott McCloud was bugging me to do a twenty-four hour comic, an exercise he'd invented in which a creator writes and draws an entire twenty-four hour comic story. It would be about a superhero who flies, but is too busy to enjoy it, so he dreams about it. I never did that twenty-four hour comic, but the story stayed in my head.

The reason Samaritan ended up in that role was because I needed a really simple, iconic character whose basic shtick is he flies and does the other superhero things: he's noble, he's fast, bullets bounce off him, etc. That just connected strongly to Superman. People also see the Confessor as a Batman-type character, and to some degree that's true. He came out of a discussion Scott and I had in junior high, about how Batman was a creepy vampire-like character and that was part of his appeal. But what if you had a character like that who really *was* a vampire? I dredged that idea up years later and turned it into the Confessor. Not as a comment on Batman, but as exploration of the archetype; the night-stalking, creepy superhero.

Occasionally I will touch on an existing comic story and play it out in *Astro City* in a very different fashion. Samaritan's battle with the Living Nightmare was written after I'd read the Superman vs Doomsday story. I said to myself, 'Doomsday can't fly, it's gonna take Superman four seconds to fly him up to the stratosphere and, if he survives Doomsday hitting him for long enough, throw him out past the moon'. So when I needed a fight scene for Samaritan, instead of having this big slugfest that destroys the city, he just throws the villain into the sun. That wasn't me saying the Doomsday story should have been done that way, that was me being inspired to do something different.

It's the multiple perspectives on superhero stories that, for me, is the key to *Astro City*. We did that in *Marvels*; take a normal person, be it a criminal, an innocent bystander or someone caught up in the events, and see what all of this is like through his eyes. But we've gone beyond that, we've gone to the question of, 'Okay, what's it like to be in a supervillain's head, or that of a ten year-old superhero, or a superhero discovering he's going to be a father?'. At Marvel or DC the main thrust of their books is to make you a spectator to the action, but I want to get into someone's head, someone's emotions. What I want to do is say: Here's the big fight. See that guy watching it, he's late for work, he can't get across town 'cause there's a superhero fight in his way. What's going to happen to his life? What's it like for him? I'm postulating that this alternate reality exists and then playing with the rules of it.

Also, to my mind, every *Astro City* story has to be a metaphor for something that has some relation to real life. The original Samaritan story connects to anybody who has ever loved what they do, but has been so harried doing it they don't have time to actually tap into the fact that they love it. Superhero stories allow you to do it in a big, broad, larger-than-life way that can make visible universal feelings. I want the superheroes to be more emotionally real than logically real. I'm interested in exploring the ways in which a superhero world is like our own, not the ways it would diverge and become unrecognisable.

As for where we're going, well, *Astro City* isn't a story like *Sandman* or *Preacher*, where I know I'm going to get to a certain point and stop. *Astro City* is a vehicle for the exploration of the superhero genre, and we jump around from place to place. Eventually, I will feel either I've run out of stuff to say or for some reason won't want to do it any more, but there is not a specific, planned ending because it's not that kind of story. Instead, we're wandering around in this universe, seeing what else we can do with the superhero story; how can we explore its strengths and what it can be and do beyond the fighting. We're building a mosaic here rather than any sort of linear construct.

PETER DAVID

Outspoken, controversial and staggeringly prolific are just a few of the terms one could easily ascribe to Peter David. Over the last ten years, David has cemented his reputation as one of the most provocative writers in the comics industry, single-handedly elevating *The Incredible Hulk*, a backwater book that nobody wanted to write, into a massive critical and financial success story. On taking over *Aquaman*, he cut off the title character's left hand, replacing it with a harpoon. In life, as on the page, David seems to thrive on confrontation, regularly analysing and critiquing the comics industry in his weekly column, 'But I Digress', in *Comic Buyer's Guide*. Having originally trained as a journalist, David came to write comics via Marvel's Direct Sales office, where he was working as a manager. David's first published work was in *Peter Parker: The Spectacular Spider-Man*, and since then he has operated as a virtual one-man cottage industry, writing movie scripts — including the fourth and fifth *Trancers* films — two episodes of television's *Babylon 5*, numerous *Star Trek* books and several original novels. His comics output is equally impressive, with long runs on *Supergirl*, *The Incredible Hulk* (well over one hundred issues) and *Aquaman*.

What originally made you want to be a journalist?

I suppose to a certain degree I was influenced by my father, who was a reporter. There were times when he would do movie reviews, and if it was something that was appropriate for kids, he'd take me along. Afterwards we would go back to his office, and while he would type up his review I would sit at another typewriter and type up mine. And when I went to college, I graduated from New York University with a bachelor's degree in journalism. However, I decided early on that making a career as a journalist was not going to be for me.

Why was that?

I had sort of an epiphany one day. While still at college, I was working for a newspaper, and one of the jobs I did was to go down to the police station and look over the police blotter, which was essentially a listing of all the various crimes that had been reported for the past week. I would look over the more interesting, more prominent ones and write stories about them. There was one week where I couldn't find anything interesting; it was all tiddly stuff. Then I discovered an item about a fifteen year-old girl who had been raped, and the first thing that went through my mind, was, 'Oh good, a fifteen year-old girl was raped', and then another part of my mind kind of stepped in, as if seeing that chain of thought from a distance, and said, 'What the hell kind of attitude is that to have?'. There and then I had an insight into what being a genuine reporter involved, that it was searching out and finding joy in the misery and misfortune of others. I became concerned that if I pursued that career I might lose my moral centre. I decided to forge myself a career in publishing instead.

How did you find yourself in the Direct Sales office of Marvel Comics?

I had gotten a job in the sales department of Playboy Paperbacks. It was just supposed to be a temporary thing, as what I really wanted was to work my way over to editorial. But I discovered I had a real affinity for sales work, and I enjoyed it, so I said to myself, 'Okay, this is the direction my life is taking me in, I'll stay in the sales department'. Playboy Paperbacks wound up being sold off and my next job was in the Marvel Comics Direct Sales department, which to me was sort of

Place of birth:
Fort Meade, Maryland, USA
Date of birth:
23 September 1956
Home base:
Long Island, New York, USA
First published work:
Peter Parker: The Spectacular Spider-Man #103
Education:
New York University
Career highlights:
Aquaman, Atlantis Chronicles, DC versus Marvel, The Incredible Hulk, Peter Parker: the Spectacular Spider-Man, Sachs and Violens, Soulsearchers and Company, Supergirl, Young Justice

the dream job, because I enjoyed doing sales and I was certainly a long-time fan of comic books. It was sort of a culmination of my various interests and hobbies.

At this stage did you have any ambition to write comics?

I don't know why, but it hadn't occurred to me. There were other people [at Marvel] who'd got into the business end of the company specifically to try and get over to editorial, but I was the first person who actually did it. I clearly remember this young guy coming up to me after he had started working at Marvel and saying, 'My name is Fabian Nicieza*, I'm hoping to be able to work my way over to editorial too'. I just said that was never my intention when I started. I was just trying to do my job in sales, because that's what I thought I was going to be doing for the rest of my life.

How did you eventually make the move to writing?

Having been there several years I thought I should try and take a few whacks at making inroads with the editors, but I was pretty much stonewalled. None of the editors were interested in giving me a shot at writing because I was in the sales department, and was therefore considered the enemy. What essentially changed all that was Jim Owsley, who became an editor on the Spider-Man titles. Jim, being something of a maverick, decided to give me a chance at writing for them. That lead to me getting the gig on *Peter Parker: The Spectacular Spider-Man*, and within the halls of Marvel it was considered a very controversial move on Jim's part. I later picked up work on *The Incredible Hulk* and came to the realisation that I could conceivably make a living doing this. So, after five years, I quit my day job and became a full-time writer.

So you were still employed in sales when you were writing *Spectacular Spider-Man*?

Yes, and I was always very, very careful not to let the two overlap. When Bob Harras† wanted to talk to me about writing *The Incredible Hulk*, he came into my office at ten to five and said, 'I'd like to talk to you about a possible assignment', and I said to him in no uncertain terms, 'I'd certainly like to hear about it, but you'll have to come back in ten minutes'. I made it a rule never to talk about editorial matters until after five o'clock, because I did not want to take the chance of putting anybody's nose out of joint.

Did you encounter much resistance to you writing?

My being put on *Spectacular Spider-Man* meant Jim Owsley first removing Al Milgrom as writer, which infuriated a number of the editorial guys, because Al is a very sweet guy and was very well liked. So not only did Owsley put noses out of joint by getting me on the book in the first place, but people were just livid because he dumped Al Milgrom in order to do so. There was intense pressure on Owsley to get me off of *Spectacular Spider-Man*, and he eventually succumbed about a year and a half later, at which point he fired me. The

---

* *Later writer on* X-Men, New Warriors *and* X-Force, *as well as Editor-in-Chief at Acclaim Comics.*

† *Long-serving editor, Group Editor and, currently, Editor-in-Chief at Marvel Comics.*

other editors felt, 'Why are we taking this guy from Direct Sales and putting him on one of our flagship characters? That's not the way it's done'. What they figured is I should be writing titles that had a far lower profile and working my way up. I would have been more than happy to do that, except I was being stonewalled at the lower levels.

Did working in sales give you any insights that helped with your writing?

I think it certainly gave me an insight into what sells, and ways to develop storylines that could be successfully marketed; things that would ideally lead to some degree of sales success. I think too many people on the creative side believe the guys in the sales department are a necessary evil, that comic books sell themselves and what the hell do we need the sales people for. However, if a book doesn't do well, invariably the first people to shoulder the blame are those in the sales or promotions departments.

Your first published story appeared in _Spectacular Spider-Man_ #103. Was that the first idea you had ever pitched?

No. I pitched a story for _Moon Knight_ to Denny O'Neil, and an Indiana Jones story. Denny said he'd get back to me. I'm still waiting. That's okay. It doesn't surprise me because, like I say, there was a tremendous amount of resistance to using somebody from sales in a writing capacity. I remember one editor saying, 'Are we gonna start hiring secretaries from subscription next?'. My attitude would be, well, if they can write a good story, why not? The way of thinking back then was if you are a sales person you are not creative, because if you were creative you'd be working in editorial.

After you were fired, did you think that was it, I've had my chance at writing comic books, or did you continue to pitch ideas to editors?

No, I thought that was it. Owsley remained, to my knowledge, the only person willing to hire me. I was fairly certain none of the other editors would be remotely interested in taking me, so there was pretty much nowhere to go. It wasn't like I could go pitching stories to DC. The only thing I had percolating at the time was _Sachs and Violens_, which I was trying to pitch to the Epic office as a four-issue limited series, but that wasn't really going anywhere either.

So how did you land the job of writing _The Incredible Hulk_?

Bob Harras was just going around trying to find somebody, anybody, to write _The Hulk_ and no one particularly wanted to. _The Hulk_ was sort of the punishment book — it was the book they _made_ you write. The character was seen as something of a dead end. Once again, it was Al Milgrom who was writing it, except this was a case of Al leaving the book via a mutual decision between him and Bob. I guess the reason Bob came to me was he knew that in this instance it was not going to engender any sort of hostility on the part of his fellow editors, because no one gave a shit about _The Hulk_.

Did working full-time in sales mean you were writing in the evenings?

I was definitely burning the candle at both ends. I would leave early in the morning, go to work and would generally be up till twelve o'clock, one o'clock in the morning. One time I was sitting at my typewriter and I fell asleep while I was typing. I woke up in the morning and discovered that the paper was covered with gibberish. What was really kind of disconcerting was that I remember at the time I had written it, it seemed to make so much sense. Once, when I was writing a *Marvel Comics Presents* six-parter, I wanted it to have the dreamlike quality of a *Twin Peaks* episode, in which virtually anything seems to go. So I would go to bed at ten, eleven at night and set my alarm clock for three in the morning. I would wake up, stagger down to my typewriter with my mind still in semi-dreamstate and then write the next instalment. I wound up with one of the loopiest six-part stories I've ever done.

You wrote *The Incredible Hulk* from #331 through to #467, and during that time missed only two issues. What happened with those two?

One of them was the result of an editorial dispute. I'd done a storyline in which Betty Banner became pregnant and after the storyline was in motion all of a sudden editorial said, 'No, she can't be pregnant', and I found that tremendously upsetting. They wanted me to do a story in which the baby dies, and I said, 'If you don't want her pregnant it's your character, I can't stop you from making her unpregnant, but you cannot force me to write the story. If you want to bring in somebody else to write that story, fine, but I'm not going to be the one who does it'. So Bob Harras came in and wrote the issue in which she loses the baby. And there was another that was a Man Thing fill-in story that was tossed in there because [artist] Dale Keown was behind on deadlines.

How much freedom did you have in plotting the book?

Not only was it the book that nobody wanted to write, it was also the book that nobody particularly cared about, so I had a tremendous amount of freedom in what I wanted to do. It was great. The rest of the Marvel Universe was going off about its business and there I was in my own little corner playing with the Hulk and doing whatever the heck I wanted. The book was getting tremendous reviews and sales were very strong, and it was pretty much that way until my last couple of years on the book, when all of a sudden the hammer came down. They said, 'We are now going to dictate what will be done on the book'. They decided they wanted the Hulk to go off in a different direction and it was not one in which I was interested in taking the character.

What did you disagree with?

They wanted to make the Hulk savage and either monosyllabic or completely unspeaking. They wanted to do big storylines that interfaced with the entire Marvel Universe and offered humungous crossover potential. I'd already had a bellyful of that in the previous year and a half and they wanted more of the type of storylines I felt were having not only a detrimental effect on the book but also on my ability to write the title. They wanted to have the Hulk split off from Banner, and that made it very, very problematic for me to write the title, because ultimately it's about Bruce Banner. The book is called *The Incredible Hulk*, but it's really about Banner.

How did you feel writing that last issue?

I wanted to write a story that would have the editors at Marvel saying, 'Oh my God, what idiots we were to let this guy go'. I was almost motivated by anger, but it was a very controlled anger. I wanted to write a story which was essentially, 'This is what I was going to do with the book. This gives you a taste of what the stories were going to be like — see what you missed, you creeps'. I wanted to write a story that was going to fill the editorial people at Marvel with complete regret over forcing me off the book, and to some degree I succeeded. I also did that story differently to any other I had written. It was constructed as a first person narrative, so there was no page breakdown and no instructions to the artist. It was like, here's the story, tell it however you want. If you want to do twenty-two pages of Rick [Jones] simply sitting there, that's fine. Tell it in splash pages, tell it in panel breakdown, do whatever you want with it. So that was kind of interesting.

Writing 130-plus issues of *The Hulk*, month in, month out, did you ever get to the point where you thought, 'I don't know what to do next'?

I always had a general idea of where I was going with the story at any given time. When I first started, and was giving some thought to the character, what I decided

---

Grey Hulk/Green Hulk

When the gamma-spawned brute and all-round tragic figure known as the Hulk first appeared in *The Incredible Hulk* #1 back in 1962 (courtesy of Stan Lee and Jack Kirby), he was grey. By issue two he was green. No one bothered to explain how or why (though the rumour persists it was a printer error that Marvel just ran with), but as the series progressed (via *Tales to Astonish*) various creative teams saw fit, whenever the 'Hulk smash' formula was looking particularly creaky, to make the Hulk grey again, by way of variety. It was only when Peter David took over as writer that a concerted effort was made to explain the different shades and hues of both the Hulk's skin and his personality. David wisely substituted the somewhat dated science at the heart of the Hulk's creation for modern psychological theories. Since the Hulk was in essence the classic split personality, it made sense to venture the theory that the Hulk's skin pigmentation was an outward manifestation of his different personas. In the classic *Hulk* #377, David indulges in a glorious (and revelatory) psychiatry session in Bruce Banner's mind, in which the grey and green Hulks are finally united.

PAGES 6 TO 7

(ADAM—this is basically an excuse for you to get to draw a big-ass double-paged spread of EVERYBODY you've ever wanted to draw connected with this title, just once. You're not restricted to the people mentioned below)

They let me in to see Bruce as soon as Marlo and I got there. I insisted that Marlo stay outside. I said, "Bruce...you want to talk?"

And he didn't even seem to be looking at me. He just said, "Hello, Rick. I think you know everybody."

I didn't know what the heck he was talking about. But he just sat there, kept on talking. And slowly, I realized that to him, the room wasn't empty. Not at all. He was...he was talking to people. He was mentioning names. Apparently, to him, the place was packed. The Leader was there, and the Abomination, and the Bi-Beast. The U-Foes. Speedfreek. Half-Life. Madman. Jim Wilson. The Pantheon. Wolverine. Jarella. People he'd known for years, people who'd tried to kill him or help him, all mingling together. It was like it was...a party. A big party that only he could see.

And I realized...that he'd cracked. Or maybe he was still in shock. That Betty's loss had damned near unhinged him. I'd talked with Doc Samson before I came in, and Doc told me that he had no idea just how much damage had been done. Whether it would ever be possible to undo it. But I figured I should go along with it, so I said that to him. "You having a party, Bruce?"

"Yes," he said. "Yes, I am. A going away party. I'm going away, you see. Nothing is forever. Oh, you think things are. You think things will last, but it's really all transitory. Nothing lasts. Nothing is forever. Do you know the poem, Rick? Do any of you?"

"What...poem?" I asked.

"Ozymandias." It's by Shelley."

"Shelley. Never heard of her...unless you mean Shelly Long from Cheers.. "

"The Leader says he knows it, but that's no surprise," Bruce said. "Percy Bysshe Shelley, Rick."

Above: *Plot extract from Peter David's final issue of* The Incredible Hulk. *Courtesy of Peter David/Marvel Comics. Used with permission.* The Incredible Hulk™ *and © 1999 Marvel Characters, Inc.*

PAGE 8

And Bruce turned from me, gesturing, as if he could see what he was talking about in his mind's eye. As if I wasn't even there. And he said this poem...

"I met a traveler from an antique land

Who said: Two vast and trunkless legs of stone Stand in the desert.
Near them, on the sand, half sunk, a shattered visage lies, whose frown
And wrinkled lip, and sneer of cold command
Tell that its sculptor well those passions read.
My name is Ozymandias, king of kings
Look on my works, ye Mighty, and despair!"
Nothing beside remains. Round the decay
Of that colossal wreck, boundless and bare
The lone and level sands stretch far away."

And Bruce stood there in front of me, his arms wide, and it was like he was standing right there in the desert, looking at that...that statue out of a poem. And he said, "I can see it, Rick, so clearly. The broken legs standing there...but you know...they're barefoot, the cuffs torn. The Hulk's feet. And that broken face, lying half buried in the desert...it's the Hulk's face. My life, a shattered ruin. Nothing left of it. Just sand. Emptiness, barren, a wasteland. Nothing. Without her...without Betty...there's nothing...

PAGE 9

And he turned and looked at me again and he kept saying, "Nothing...nothing..."

And he changed, just like that. No howl of pain. No doubling over. Nothing. He just...transformed into the Hulk. The stun guns didn't go off because his pulse never sped up. He changed as if it was the easiest thing in the world. As if the prospect of leaving humanity behind was no longer painful...but instead, a blessing.

He looked at me for a moment as the Hulk, and I tell you...I'd seen so many things in his eyes over the years. Anger, resentment, betrayal, exhaustion, any emotion you could name...but in all those years...I'd never seen him look at me with envy."

Ross blasted his way in, shooting through the glass. I hit the deck, but it was too late. The Hulk had smashed up through the ceiling and was out and gone.

Above: *More from* The Incredible Hulk #467, *highlighting David's unusual narrative style for the plot. Courtesy of Peter David/Marvel Comics. Used with permission. The Incredible Hulk™ and © 1999 Marvel Characters, Inc.*

was that the Hulk was clearly a classic example of a multiple personality disorder. I knew that eventually I was going to do a story in which he was cured, or at least believed cured, in the manner in which they usually manage to treat MPD, which is through hypnosis. What they try to do is merge the different personalities into one being. I knew I was going to be doing that story eventually, though I didn't know exactly how I was going to get there. I knew it was going to take me a while and that ended up turning into four years. I didn't have every step of those four years planned out, but I had a broad sense.

You killed off Jean De Wolff* and Betty Banner, and cut off Aquaman's hand. Do you set out to shock or deliberately provoke?

The thing is, people have a bit of trouble with my world view, because I am very aggressive in terms of trying to twist things around or say, 'Let's do this because it would make a really cool story'. I remember an occasion when I was in Jim Owsley's office and Tom DeFalco† was trying to explain to me the need to take the longer view. His feeling was, 'Don't do a story just because it's a really good story. You have to think about the long term'. He told me I could write a story where J. Jonah Jameson dies, in which there would be this final meeting of minds between Spider-Man and Jonah and there wouldn't be a dry eye in the house. It would be really great, but what do you do next issue with J. Jonah Jameson dead? Without hesitation I said I'd have the Kingpin buy the *Daily Bugle*, and Tom said, 'No, you're missing my point'. And I said, 'No, no, this would be really great, we have the Kingpin buy the *Daily Bugle* but he comes in and says he has no intention of running it as anything other than a newspaper. It puts this big split among the editorial staff, because some people quit immediately, but other people who need the job, who need the money, don't want to resign and Peter Parker's caught in the middle'. Poor Tom's going, 'No Peter, you've completely missed my point', and I'm jumping up and down, saying to Owsley, 'Let's kill off J. Jonah Jameson, this will be so great'. So Tom never really managed to make it clear to me that's not the sort of thing you should do.

Was part of that mindset you trying to make a reputation for yourself?

I wasn't thinking about trying to make a reputation for myself. My attitude was, I want to write stories that will be as entertaining and different as possible. Not different because I want people to notice me, but different because I want people to get involved in the stories. You see, a writer's job is different from the artist. The artist makes his visual stamp on the comic book and there's no way of getting around it, and if the artist is doing his job he will inevitably call attention to himself. The writer's job is to hide behind the characters, and if a writer is doing his job then to some degree he will be invisible. The characters will go through their paces and the reader will believe that these things are happening to them because this is just stuff that is going on in their lives, not because there's a writer out there putting the characters into these situations.

When you're coming onto these characters who have been around for a while

---

* *Police Captain and sometime ally of Spider-Man, introduced in* Marvel Team-Up.

† *Former Editor-in-Chief at Marvel and writer on* The Amazing Spider-Man.

but haven't really been big sellers, you have to try and lean towards the radical and do stuff that's going to grab people's attention. When you're dealing with a character like Aquaman, who was perceived as something of a second-rater, you've gotta take drastic action. You have no idea what it was like when I first took on *Aquaman*, I had both fans and retailers alike saying the same thing to me: 'Why are you wasting your time on Aquaman, the guy's a five-time loser? He's had series after series, none of which he's managed to sustain. Nobody is interested in him, he's tremendously limited'. I really got a lot of flak over it. When Eric Larsen took over recently not a single person said Larsen was wasting his time, or Aquaman's a loser. Love or hate what I did with the book, at least people started reading it and taking the character a hell of a lot more seriously.

My favourite fan letter of all time was one that was sent to *Spectacular Spider-Man*. It was from this kid, written in crayon, and what he asked was: 'Dear Marvel Comics, does Peter David write Spider-Man's jokes or are they ad-libs?'. I thought this was absolutely wonderful, the concept that to this kid Spider-Man comes up with the jokes and tells me what he said. We printed that letter and I wrote the response which was, 'They are ad-libs, everybody round here knows that Peter David has no sense of humour'.

What scripting method do you use for comics?

The most common way is Marvel style, in which the comic will read like a short

---

Aquaman

Created by Mort Weisinger and Paul Norris in 1941, Aquaman was, for many years, only ever a back-up strip in the likes of *Adventure Comics* and *Detective Comics*. Like his Marvel-based 'cousin', the Sub-Mariner, Aquaman (Arthur Curry) was the product of a union between a human and a citizen of Atlantis, thereby able to exist both beneath the waves and on dry land. Aquaman was one of the few DC superhero characters to survive the massive fall-off in interest in the genre in the early fifties, and was soon headlining his own title. Aquaman has rarely made as much of a splash (either in terms of sales or popularity) as the Supermans and Batmans of DC's world, but over the years he has doggedly persevered through various cancellations. By 1994 Aquaman was well overdue for a radical makeover, and who better for the job than Peter David? The mini-series, 'Time and Tide', set the scene for David's rougher, tougher Aquaman, complete (after losing his hand in issue two of the new series) with harpoon attachment. David's run is generally considered to be the defining one for the character, who is currently enjoying a new lease of life and popularity.

story written in the present tense. I will describe in fair detail everything that's going on, and I will have lots of dialogue in there, because I feel it is imperative to get across to the artist what is being said, so that they can put in facial expressions. I will write in both visual cues for the artist and little cues for myself. For instance, I may indicate that Supergirl is talking and her hands are gesticulating over her head while she's doing so, or I may say Rick Jones is leaning against a mantelpiece as he's speaking or Cutter* lights up a cigarette as he talks. I try and put in little scene details to guide the artist and give the plot a sense of pacing. I will break these down either on a page-by-page or group of pages basis. That way, the artist will have an idea of how much space each sequence should occupy.

There are times when I'm going for a particular type of effect that I will dictate panel layout. I'll say, 'There's a panel of dead silence as the characters react to whatever, shot from the same angle'. But in terms of the actual page construction, I leave that to the artist, because my feeling is he's the visual guy, and it's his job to tell the story from that point of view. I don't want to step on his toes too much so I don't dictate every single panel or every single bit of posture, because that's what he's got to be able to bring as his contribution. If I do too much, I think the artist is going to feel he's just a cog in the machine. The artist then tells the story visually and the pages come back to me and I script it. Scripting doesn't take all that much time for me because the majority of the dialogue is already in the plot. It takes me maybe two to three hours to write a plot. Scripting, because it's a matter of massaging material that's already there, takes less time. In terms of the physical writing, I can do a comic book within six hours, from soup to nuts.

The other way I occasionally write is full script. I might do that, say, if I'm working with one of the older generation artists who prefer to work that way, or if I'm going to be extremely tight for time or even not going to be around when they need me to do the scripting. But even when I'm doing it full script, I won't do a layout of the page. I will simply indicate everything that's being said, everything that's being done, and leave the actual layout to the artist. As long as he's got all the panels in there and all the characters and he's left room for all the dialogue, I'm a perfectly happy camper.

You once said you enjoy writing novels because it's the purest form of you. Is that because with comics you have an artist interpreting your vision?

People have asked me before to compare and contrast the advantages and disadvantages of working on comic books versus novels, and what I've always said is that when you're writing a novel there is nothing between you and the audience except the printed page. So the audience gets the purest distillation of the stories that you want to tell, and that can be tremendously gratifying. The downside of that is you're working without a net, the story's going to be only as good as the tools and the abilities that you are capable of bringing to it.

When you're doing a comic book the advantage is that you are working with an

---

* *Cutter Sharp, a supporting character in* Supergirl.

artist. The disadvantage is you are working with an artist. What I mean is, if you've got a good artist, they can take a story that is kinda mediocre and elevate it to a level that you wouldn't have been able to attain on your own. Conversely, if you're working with an artist who either totally disregards your vision or is just a bad artist, they can destroy your story, and frequently the readers will not be able to see that's what happened.

Have there been many occasions where artists have plainly sucked?

Yeah. It's very depressing. When I get artwork back and the artist has just made a complete and utter balls-up of the story it's a real drag. Because when I come to script it, I sit there and I know that it really doesn't matter what I'm writing, people are just gonna say, 'God, this is awful', and they're gonna have to fight their way past the artwork in order to read the dialogue. It can be depressing and even dispiriting, but I try not to let it bring down my scripting, and in fact I often try to overcompensate, and maybe overwork the dialogue in order to make up for what I feel is a piss poor art job. But you just have to kind of roll with this stuff.

While you've written your own characters in novels and movie scripts, in comics you've rarely gone down the creator-owned route. Why is that?

I'm not quite sure. The main exception to that is *Sachs and Violens*, although I also do *Soulsearchers and Company*, which has been coming out for over thirty issues now, and most people have absolutely no idea the book even exists. That's the thing that breaks me up. People say, 'Why don't you do a humour book that's all your own characters?', and I say, 'I do, it's called *Soulsearchers and Company*'. That's always been somewhat problematic. So I have done the same kind of things that, say, Garth Ennis has done, it's just that they're not quite as high profile.

Writing DC's *Young Justice* seemed like a strange choice. Was this an effort to break out in a new direction?

I only made a six-issue commitment to the book at first, because I wasn't sure that it was going to be my cup of tea. I mean, I was going to be writing a comic book in which I had no regular characters that, to all intents and purposes, were my own. I was uncertain whether I could pull something like that off, or even if I wanted to pull something like that off. But as I got increasingly into the title, I found myself enjoying the characters more and more. I particularly found an affinity for it once the female characters were introduced, maybe because I have three daughters rather than three sons. When I was writing about Robin, Impulse and Superboy, I was turning out stories that I thought were entertaining, and doing the best I could. But once the girl characters were brought in, I felt I had more of a window into the series, because teenage girls I'm used to; I know how they think to some degree, at least as much as any father does. I think many fans feel the quality of the series picked up once the girls arrived.

You've written a number of screenplays. How did you find the experience of working in Hollywood?

Hollywood can be problematic, but the rewards can be tremendous, both from a monetary point of view and a recognition point of view. I've got three kids I have to send to college. If I write a screenplay for WGA [Writer's Guild of America] minimums I can send my eldest daughter to college for four years. So it's not a bad direction to go in as long as you don't completely lose your mind. What I can't understand, and what I would never be able to be, is a full-time screenwriter. I read about these guys who make a fantastic living writing screenplay after screenplay that never get produced, and I know I would completely lose my mind if all I did was tell stories that nobody ever saw. Once or twice a year I'll write a screenplay, and that I don't find particularly disturbing, because at least I have other creative outlets. I can still do what my true joy is, which is tell stories and communicate them to an audience.

You've been working in comics for more than a decade now, is there anything you would still like to achieve in the medium?

It would be nice to come up with something that makes people say, 'Oh my God, this is incredible'. I don't know if I have particularly done that yet. I've certainly had my successes, I've certainly had my failures, but I don't know that I've completely blown everybody's socks off yet. I don't think I've done anything that's got

Young Justice

The success of Grant Morrison's revamped Justice League of America, or *JLA* (the first DC title for several years to stay consistently in the Diamond Distributors top ten bestsellers list), inevitably brought forth a number of spin-off series and mini-series. Of the latter, one of best received was the two-issue prestige format series, *JLA: World Without Grown-ups*, which shuffled the adult JLA off to one Earth, while the 'junior JLA' (ie. any superhero under the age of seventeen) remained behind to save the day on another Earth. Drawn in two distinct styles by two different teams of artists (Humberto Ramos and Paul Neary for the 'kids'; Mike McKone and Mark McKenna for the 'grown-ups'), *JLA: World Without Grown-ups* introduced Young Justice (though a one-shot titled *Young Justice: The Secret*, featuring the same trio, had appeared some months before as one of DC's 'Girlfrenzy!' themed run of titles) in a light but involving tale of junior superheroics and teenage angst. Comprising Robin, Superboy and Impulse (essentially junior Batman, Superman and the Flash), the team-up worked well enough to spawn an ongoing *Young Justice* series written by Peter David, who made the title very much his own.

the reaction of a *Watchmen* or a *Dark Knight Returns* or an *Astro City*. Ultimately, that's what it's really all about, getting your audience worked up, and it would be nice to do something like that. I've done series that I think are up there. I think *Atlantis Chronicles* is among my best work, and I think *Future Imperfect* rocked a lot of people. *Sachs and Violens* was also well received. I don't know if I've done my seminal project yet. I'm not even entirely sure what it would be.

Do you find writing comes easy?

There are times when it's a tremendous struggle to come up with what you want to do next issue or even the right turn of phrase. Anybody who tells you writing is always easy is either lying through their teeth or they're simply not working hard enough, because writing shouldn't be easy all the time. To a certain degree, failure is a goal in writing. You owe it to yourself to risk failure or even to fail at least once a year. If you don't, to my mind, you're not doing it right, because you've always got to be out there, you always have to be pushing yourself and the envelope. Otherwise you are doing a disservice to your readers, because it means you're not taking enough chances, and you are limiting and stunting your own growth. Only in failing do we manage to pick ourselves up and make ourselves better.

*　　　　　*　　　　　*

Check out:
The Incredible Hulk: Future Imperfect (David's alternate/future take on the Hulk)
The Incredible Hulk: Ghosts of the Past
The Incredible Hulk: Transformations (various Grey/Green Hulk variations, including David's classic issue #377)

Aquaman: Time & Tide
DC versus Marvel: The Showdown of the Century
Spider-Man: Death of Jean De Wolff
Supergirl (collects issues #1–9)

CHUCK DIXON

Known in the business as Mr Prolific, Chuck Dixon produces monthly comics at a rate that can only be described as phenomenal. Dixon's career began in the late seventies, writing and pencilling stories for an American *Heavy Metal*-style magazine called *Gasm*, and he made his mainstream breakthrough writing *Savage Sword of Conan* for Marvel. Since then he's written everything from *Evangeline* to *The Punisher*, *Moon Knight* to *Airboy*, *Lawdog* to *The 'Nam*, a selection that only scratches the surface of his prodigious résumé. Although he's worked for almost every major American comics publisher, Dixon now operates predominantly out of the DC Universe. Formerly the writer of the monthly Batman book *Detective Comics*, he has also penned stories for many of Gotham City's other denizens, including Robin, Catwoman, the Huntress and Black Canary. Heavily involved in the classic and bestselling 'Knightfall'/'Knightquest'/'Knightsend' storylines, which ran across all the Bat-books, Dixon was responsible for the creation of Bane, the venom-empowered villain who broke Batman's back. Now piloting the continuing adventures of both *Robin* and *Nightwing* (aka Dick Grayson, the original Robin), as well as *Birds of Prey*, Dixon's gift — other than his speed — is for producing fast-paced, crime-based action, laced with smart, fun, snappy dialogue... though *never* too much of it.

How do you manage to write so many comic books?

Well, I always thought you wrote comic books fast. When I was a kid, it seemed like Stan Lee wrote half the books out there, so I thought this was a medium where you just had to get it done in a hurry. I've always kind of looked up to screenwriters from the thirties and forties, who could crank out a movie script in just a few weeks. So I just thought writing was something that was done quickly, and I carried that childhood impression into adulthood.

I don't actually spend much time at the keyboard. Most of the time is just spent walking around, thinking about the stories. Some stories get thought about for months before I actually write them. I'll keep adding scenes and figuring out connections. Then, when I sit down at the keyboard, it's pretty much all in my head. It may take one or two days, with only a few hours work each day, to get the script done. There's times when I've *got* to get a script done; a fill-in issue, or a penciller needs something and another writer has fallen down on the job, so they need something in a hurry. It's not unusual for me to write an entire script, starting cold with no idea, and have it done by the end of the day.

Is it true that you never wanted to be anything else except a comic book writer?

I was never good at anything else. I never really had any other ambitions. What I'm doing now seems to be the ultimate for me. I was never interested in writing novels or screenplays. I probably started writing comic books when I was about six, and it's hard to get artists [at that age] so I had to draw my own. They were my own lame attempts at superheroes; Captain Fly was my first. I would lay the pages out on lined, loose-leaf paper. I learned early on that doing an entire comic book is tiring. In elementary school I would try to fit all the story on one page rather than having to do multiple pages. When I was older — junior high, high school — I was doing my pathetic attempts at full-length comics; thirty or forty pages' worth at a time.

I started attending [comic] conventions in high school and began to realise this was a real business. These people made a living, fed their families, bought their

Place of birth:
  Philadelphia, Pennsylvania, USA
Date of birth:
  14 April 1954
Home base:
  Pennsylvania, USA
First published work:
  Gasm #1
Education:
  Upper Darby High School
Career highlights:
  Airboy, Alien Legion, Birds of Prey, Car Warriors, Catwoman, Conjurors, Detective Comics, Evangeline, Green Arrow, Guy Gardner, Huntress, Ka-Zar, Lawdog, Moon Knight, The 'Nam,

houses and cars, all with the money they made from comics. I kinda looked at it in grandiose terms: I will either become a comic book writer or live a life of tragedy and die unhappy. I left no room for any other career. I thought I'd be one of those writer/artists, which to me is still the loftiest position in comics — Will Eisner, Harvey Kurtzman and so on — but I didn't have the discipline to do the art. Though I did do enough to help me understand what pencillers have to go through, and I write with that in mind.

You mentioned Stan Lee. Was he a major influence on you?

He was an influence, even later on, especially in terms of dialogue. Really, the strongest influence has always been Archie Goodwin. He's the first writer I really noticed and thought, 'I want to read everything this guy writes'. As a young guy I could see the quality, but it eluded me as to how he did it. I wanted to know how he could cram so much story into eight pages or how he could jump on a book mid-story and be able to go with the flow. After getting to meet him and work with him, I found out he was a big fan of movies and old movies in particular. He knew a lot about pacing and sketching a character so they seemed complete with only a few lines. I think I learned my terseness from him, 'cause he was never a very verbose writer. Also, we both shared the joy of writing for particular artists. If I find out that I'm working with Russ Heath or Rodolfo Damaggio or John Severin I want to tailor the story for them, and from talking to Archie that was the way he was.

It wasn't until the mid-eighties that you began to get regular comics work. Why was that?

I tried to get in around the time of the DC implosion* in the seventies. I kept sending scripts to everybody: Marvel, DC. If you opened up a comic company you had a package from me the next day. I would take a run at it and get discouraged and go away for a year and then think, 'Well, I've got to do it again', and take another run at it. So when I saw Comico was opening up less than an hour's drive from my house, I thought, 'Here's people I can go harass in person to get work'. That's how *Evangeline* came about.

What do you think you were doing wrong back then?

When I thought I was terrific in my twenties I probably really sucked. I didn't actually *see* a comic script until I was about twenty-nine. Robert Kanigher (*Sgt Rock*) gave me a script so I could see what one looked like. I really didn't know what I was doing. I just loved the medium and had this ability to think in terms of static pictures, which, of course, is useless anywhere but comics. I got a lot of encouragement from Archie Goodwin, people like that, who'd say, 'This is good but you're not ready'. I'd write the worst proposals in comics and I think that was hurting me. I had no idea how to get what I wanted in a comic into a short format, and so I had to show them the whole script, which is impossible. You can't get an editor to read a whole script, except Archie, he did read my whole scripts.

---

* DC drastically downscaled the number of titles it was publishing in the face of falling sales and the rise of Marvel Comics' popularity.

Do you have a set approach to writing a script?

If one of my editors ever followed me around they'd probably be horrified, because I don't seem to work much, or even sit down much for that matter. I've got two pre-school kids at home and I have an outside office I rarely get to. I do have an office here at home, so I just grab a few hours a day to actually put the stuff down. The rest of the time I'm wandering around in La-La land, thinking about Nightwing or whoever, or an opening to a story or how to close a story, or how to connect these two scenes. There are certain scenes in my head I've always wanted to do, and I'm forever wondering if I can fit them into the story. So there's no set work times, no real rhyme or reason. They have this programme in schools here where they have students follow people through their working day, and they asked me if I'd participate. I said, 'no, bad idea, they'd end up with no work ethic'.

Generally I don't sit down to write until I have the opening. To me, the opening is the most important part of a comic book story because that's what's going to drag the reader through the next twenty-two pages. With the opening I sit down cold. There's no notes, no sketches. The only thing I'll do if I'm nearing the end of a story and I'm on, say, page fourteen, I'll take a piece of paper and make little squares from fourteen to twenty-two, so I can see how many pages I've got left. That's it. And then rewrites after that if they're called for. I only do one draft. Scott Peterson, an editor at DC, used to say, 'You don't even read them before you send them out, do you?', and I'd say, 'No I don't'. I get to page twenty-two, they go in the envelope and they're gone. If there's something wrong with it, that's the editor's job.

Given the dynamism and pace of your books, don't you even do sketches for yourself?

No. That's one of the reasons I insist on knowing who the artist is, so I can picture the story the way they would draw it and tailor it for them. If I'm doing a story for Graham Nolan or Joe Kubert, I would write it a totally different way for one than I would for the other. It very rarely turns out the way I visualised it, but visualising it helps me and apparently helps them. Also, by not describing too much, most pencillers say that my scripts aren't restrictive at all, and that there's a lot of flexibility there for them to do what they have to do. When I don't know who's going to be drawing it, I just pretend it's Joe Kubert, which is strange, because the one time I got to work with Joe, his layouts were nothing like I thought they were going to be!

In my head I try and balance the art and the lettering. If there's going to be a lot of dialogue on a page I try to do something to make it visually interesting, and I'll even go back and cut dialogue if there's too much and it's interrupting the artwork. Also, I'll try and think of a gimmick page, either a silent page or something with some sort of visual hook to it somewhere. There's at least one of those in each story.

Do you ever collaborate closely with an artist?

I collaborated with Graham Nolan [on *Detective Comics*] because he insisted on my doing so, and I didn't mind that whatsoever. With Scott McDaniel on *Nightwing* I've been encouraging him to be more collaborative, 'cause it's been him and I for three years and he should have more say in the book. I encourage pencillers, but some just wanna do what they do and leave me to my job. But if they call with a change or whatever I'm very flexible. Sometimes an artist will change something and call me, and there'll be this fear in their voice, so I get the impression some writers aren't as easygoing as me. If I'm working with, say, Rodolfo Damaggio, I'll ask 'What do you want in the story?', and he'll say, 'I wanna draw a helicopter'. So I'll write in a helicopter, because that's what he wants to draw this month. It's as simple as that. Graham and I have actually written stories together, in a hotel room — we've gotta get this story done in three days — and that's been fine. He's a good guy to work with.

Do you enjoy the process of collaborating with other writers?

There are certain writers in comics who I like personally, but have a difficult time writing with. And there's other guys who are a breeze. Karl Kesel was so easy to write with it was like having two of me in the room. He would come up with whatever I didn't think of, and vice versa. We complemented each other. Karl and I did a Superboy/Robin thing together. We met briefly in New York for about forty-five minutes and then the rest we did on the phone. We split the scenes between us, which I had read they did in Hollywood in the thirties and forties and I thought that would be cool to try, and it worked out.

I understand that when writing The 'Nam you did a lot of research. Is that an unusual occurrence?

No. That's why Larry Hama hired me in the first place. He'd never heard of me, and he said, 'Why should I hire you?', and I told him I'd do the homework, that's why. If it's a Western, I'll look the stuff up, if it's a story about the Russian Civil War, I'll read four books to do this miserable little ten-page story. And when they couldn't get a Vietnam vet to write *The 'Nam*, they turned to me, because they knew I'd read the books and do the interviews. Which I did. For *Nightwing* I read a book about circus acrobats, and a lot of books about sewers and rats.

With writing so many books, do you finish one before you begin work on another?

I prefer to do that, but sometimes it's just not possible. You stall on a story and then they want another in a hurry, so you jump on that. The *DC: One Million* stories became a black hole that swallowed me up for months, and when I got back on my own books it was like I'd never written them before. Sometimes it's hard to change the mindset. My wife will tell you my mindset does change, but it's not as obvious to me. She says she can always tell when I'm writing *Conan* or *The Punisher*. Less talkative.

PAGES TWO AND THREE

BIG SPREAD
Tad, in his Nite-Wing get-up, soars through the sky above the buildings. Flying behind him are amalgams or parodies of any famous comic characters you want to throw in flying in formation. Tad holds his bludgeon the way Thor holds his hammer in flight.

FROM OFF PANEL: **NITE-WING AND THE JUSTICE FORCE!**

NITE-WING: NEVER <u>FEAR</u>, CITIZENS! MY COMRADES AND I ARE HERE TO SEE THAT THE MEEK NEED NOT SUFFER EVIL A <u>MOMENT</u> LONGER THAN NECESSARY!

NITE-WING: THE JUSTICE FORCE IS HERE TO BATTLE THE CRAVEN <u>COWARDS</u> AND COSMIC <u>BULLIES</u> THAT THREATEN OUR STREETS!

NITE-WING: KNOWN THAT YOUR HEROES WILL BATTLE TO THE LAST MAN (OR <u>WOMAN</u>)! TO THE LAST DROP OF OUR BLOOD---

SFX: (SMALL BUT GROWING LARGER AND SPILLING OVER TO THE NEXT PANEL)
beep
beep
beep
BEEP
BEEP
BEEP

LARGE INSET THAT SERVES AS OUR TITLE PANEL.
Downshot of Tad in a dim hospital room. He lies with wires and hoses running into him and life support equipment rolled up all around his bed.

TITLE: **HOSPITAL PERILOUS**

SFX: (GROWING LARGER AS IT SPILLS OVER:
BEEP
BEEP
BEEP
BEEP
BEEP
TAD: (VERY WEAK) last breath...in our body...

Above: *Script extract from* Nightwing *#22, by Chuck Dixon. Courtesy of Chuck Dixon.*

Whatever character you're writing, your style remains consistent. You always write really good, fun comics. Is that your intention?

That's what I try to do. I try to make myself as invisible as possible, as if the story wasn't actually written by anybody, the artist just drew it. I don't ever want to show off my writing talents, so no long captions with poetic stuff dripping off of them. That gets in the way. I remember as a kid reading comics and every once in a while you'd come across one where the writer was obviously flexing his muscles, and it's like, 'Oh man, this sucks!'. [In those cases, the writer] isn't remembering there's a reader out here who just wants to keep turning the pages.

So who do you aim your comics at?

Mine can be read by a ten year-old, but I kinda aim my stuff at a precocious twelve year-old, because they're more sophisticated than I was at that age. Come to think of it, they're probably more sophisticated than I was at twenty! If I write something with a little more 'hair' on it, I'll pitch it for an older audience, but I just generally aim at that twelve year-old. It's mainly, can I write a comic story that will make a kid stay away from his Nintendo for another fifteen minutes?

Do you feel the rate you churn things out sometimes compromises the material, or does it benefit from the speed?

I used to think, 'Man, let me slow down', and whenever I slowed down it wasn't any good. If I thought too much about it, it didn't come out naturally. It's like Trivial Pursuit, your first answer is usually right. I talked to Walter Gibson once, and I said, 'Did you ever write a *Shadow* story you were particularly proud of?'. He wrote hundreds and hundreds of them, and there was one he was really proud of. It's a monthly medium and I try to do the best I can.

Do you feel it's important to be able to get into the head of your characters?

In every single one of my stories there has to be a scene where the readers can go, 'Yeah, I can identify with that', even if it's *Conan*. The first time I ever did it was in *Airboy*. The cast goes to South America to visit some shaman. There's all these bones hanging from the trees and real spooky Mayan ruins, and they're going to meet this ancient Yoda-type figure, and I thought how can I turn this on its head? So, before they leave, after getting their advice from him, Airboy says something like, 'Is there anything we can do for you?'. And the shaman says, 'Yeah, next time you come down bring me a case of Dr Pepper'. I thought I should have one of those in every story, some little bit of business that's everyday. That may be the single most consistent thing in my work and I'm not happy unless it's in there.

Over the years you've specialised in writing lone vigilante characters: Conan, the Punisher, Batman. How much of you is in them?

I hate to say this, but I identify most with the Punisher. He demonstrates every negative male stereotype and I feel comfortable writing him. But I'm the guy who's always adding supporting characters to every book. I think I added more supporting characters to Batman's cast than anybody in a long time. So I don't think I've a natural bent for the loner guy. I like the character to be surrounded by people, but when you're writing about masked vigilantes, how many people can they hang out with? So no, I don't think [there's much of me in them], it was just the nature of the comics business when I got into it. Everybody wanted to be on the team books, so the loner characters were left to the new guys to come in and write. Nobody wanted to write Conan, but I did. He's a great character. They always used to say the Punisher was one-dimensional, but I don't think so. I saw a lot of depth to the character. He's the classic Marvel tragic figure, they just wrote him in a one-dimensional way.

Your work seems to reflect a real fascination for crime fiction. Are you a fan?

Oh yeah, especially police procedural mysteries. But whodunits I have no use for. Richard Stark's *Parker* novels are just incredible to me because they're solely about criminals. The greatest challenge that I offer myself in this business is to come up with a new twist on a heist, a new kind of robbery. I read the *Wall Street Journal*, which has a whole lot of crime in it — they have an art crime update every month — looking for what is a crime now or could be a crime in the future. And good books on crime, though good true crime stories that aren't about

---

The Punisher

Originally created as a supporting character (in *Amazing Spider-Man* #129) by Gerry Conway and artist Ross Andru, the Punisher continued to guest-star for the better part of a decade. Almost a vigilante-by-numbers (Vietnam vet, sees family murdered by mob, starts killing criminals), Frank Castle (aka the Punisher) finally turned headliner courtesy of a defining mini-series by writer Steven Grant and artist Mike Zeck. He became one of Marvel's most popular characters, featuring in two ongoing series (*The Punisher* and *Punisher War Journal*), a host of graphic novels, a mini-series or two, and eventually a third ongoing title (*Punisher War Zone*). With his single-minded, non-ethics - cluttered approach to justice, the Punisher epitomised the late eighties' trend in comics for cold, violent anti-heroes and heavy body-counts. To be fair, the various writers — including Mike Baron, Dixon, Larry Hama, Dan Abnett/Andy Lanning — flesh out the character well, and provide at least a modicum of moral framework, but eventually it all becomes a little deadening. As sales dropped away, Marvel cancelled all its Punisher books. A second series came and went fairly soon after, and the character disappeared until the recent Marvel Knights relaunch.

PAGE SEVEN

PANEL ONE

Punisher in an upshot is looking up as he stands in the basement with the rifle in his hands.

CAPTION: FIREFIGHT ABOVE ME.

CAPTION: THE MOOKS RAN INTO SOME TROUBLE.

PANEL TWO

Punisher runs for that gap in the wall that leads out of the building.

CAPTION: BE EASY TO JUST LET THEM CHOP EACH OTHER DOWN.

CAPTION: BUT CALL ME A PERFECTIONIST.

PANEL THREE

Vic and Sid are cornered in that room and firing from the doorframe which is chopped full of holes by now.

CAPTION: BUT IF YOU WANT A JOB DONE RIGHT...

VIC: I'M DOWN TO MY LAST CLIP, SID.

SID: WE MAKE A BREAK FOR IT THEN. SHOOT OUR WAY OUT.

PANEL FOUR

Shoe Box is looking up in alarm as Shopping Bag and the others return fire.

CAPTION: ...SOMETIMES YOU HAVE TO DO IT YOURSELF.

SHOE BOX: I HEARD SOMETHIN'!

SHOPPING BAG: YOU ALWAYS HEARIN' SOMETHIN'!

Above: *An extract from 'The Condemmed', a ten-page Punisher story by Chuck Dixon. Courtesy of Chuck Dixon/Marvel Comics. Used with permission.* The Punisher™ and © 1999 Marvel Characters, Inc.

some guy killing his whole family and getting away with it are rare. Carl Hiaasen, Donald Westlake, George MacDonald Fraser, Hammett, James M. Cain, Charles Willeford. Hiaasen's good; he should do comic books, 'cause he writes such tremendous villains.

When you're writing a Bat-book, how much input and guidance do you receive from Batman Group Editor Denny O'Neil?

At the beginning, there was [quite a lot], but once I got more comfortable, there was less. I initially wrote a three-issue Batman arc and told Denny I probably only had this one Batman story in me. He said he didn't think I was right and I guess I wasn't. The first one I did was exhausting, 'cause it's Batman and it's intimidating. Most intimidating of all, though, is writing a Joker story, because if you write a lousy Mr Freeze story everybody will forget about it in a few months, but if you write a lousy Joker story it's with you the rest of your life. Batman I eventually got into a groove on because I had so much to do with the Tim Drake Robin. That sort of became my inroad. I would look at Batman and his world through Tim's eyes, and that gave me a more comfortable handle on all the stuff. He was a new character entering the story and I was a new writer entering the story.

I was surprised when I got on the Batman books how little had been written about Gotham, and how little was established. I've probably established more Gotham landmarks and streets, and named more buildings, than just about anybody. I thought, for these books to work the city has to be a character as well. So I kinda established the geography as mine and then got more comfortable with the characters. There was also a surprising amount of free rein to create gadgets and stuff like that. Graham Nolan and I created the Subway Rocket and a bunch of other things, and Denny was always surprisingly open to suggestions. He did resist the Batboat for the longest time, but I gave Nightwing a boat so I was happy. *Nightwing's* different because it's all mine. Except for Nightwing himself, it all started with me from the ground up, so that's an easier book to write. I've got a real sense of the city, the avenues are all names of hard boiled crime fiction writers and the streets are named after whaling terms; Blüdhaven was a whaling town. In Gotham City there's way too many Gotham Stadiums and Gotham Art Academies.

How did it work with the other Batman writers?

When it was Doug Moench, Alan Grant and I writing the books, we would plan a year or sometimes more in advance and then figure out how each of our books was going to work into that continuity. We all had our own take on Batman, and yet it worked; all of our versions were somehow right, even though they were all different. Alan's *Shadow of the Bat* was more psychological, more cerebral; Doug's was more your straight-ahead 'classic' Batman book; and mine was a detective book: more police procedural, more investigation and delving more into how the criminals worked. Whether it was by design or happenstance, those are the books we fell into and they were what we wanted to write. I couldn't have written what Alan wrote or what Doug wrote.

Have you run into much opposition from the Bat-office in terms of what the character can and can't do?

Denny has a lot of Batman stuff stored in his head. At almost every Batman conference he would drop a bombshell; something about the character he thinks we should already know. Batman is so and so, and we'd all go, 'What?'. It wouldn't be like, 'You're wrong' or 'You're crazy', but 'I didn't know that', or 'I never thought of that'. Denny's thought about aspects of Batman that no one else has thought about, because he's had more time to think about it. These aren't horrible secrets, just the everyday mundane details about Batman that we don't necessarily need to know, but that Denny has hard and fast rules in his mind about. Everybody who works in comics has these rules, but Denny's about Batman can be very restrictive. When we did 'Knightfall', and Batman breaks his back, we spent half an afternoon begging him at a conference to have Superman come and ask about him. At least maybe have Clark Kent call Tim Drake on the phone and say, 'Is he all right?' But no, never. We couldn't have Superman in the story.

Denny's also very uncomfortable with Batman going into space. I share some of that, because when Dan Jurgens was doing *Teen Titans* and he wanted Robin to make an appearance, I said, 'That's fine, but if you're meeting space aliens or creatures from the bottom of the ocean, Robin can't be there, Robin can't see them'. If he does, he has to be like Scully [in *The X-Files*], he has to have an explanation for how this could be, without it being supernatural or alien. If and when Robin meets somebody from outer space, I'd really like to be the one who writes it, not have it

The Bat-Books

At Marvel it's the X-books, at DC it's the Bat-books; a high profile, money-spinning franchise that exists as its own fiefdom within the editorial geography of the company. Beyond the core Batman titles — *Batman, Detective Comics, Batman: Shadow of the Bat* and *Batman: Legends of the Dark Knight* — lies an ocean of one-shots, prestige format books, spin-off titles and graphic novels. In any given month there may be as many as ten Batman titles, not counting the Bat-related books such as *Robin, Nightwing* and *Catwoman* and the many titles in which the character guest-stars (Batman is a regular in *JLA*). One might be forgiven for thinking that with this plethora of Batman product, the law of diminishing returns would inevitably set in, watering down what is essentially a solo character, but — in large degree due to the efforts of Batman Group Editor Denny O'Neil — that is not the case. O'Neil, a writer and editor with some thirty years in the business, much of it spent on or around Batman, maintains tight controls on how and where the character is used, and (as the recent 'Cataclysm'/'No Man's Land' storyline ably demonstrates) is constantly reinventing the wheel.

as sort of a cast-off in someone else's book. I've written Batman with a gun, and I've had Batman firing a gun. But that's within the Batman group and Denny approved. I think every editor is this way and let's face it, Denny's controlling the big guy. It's Batman. It's not like everybody's wanting to have the Atom in their book, but you've really *gotta* have Batman in your book. So Denny has to be careful that Batman isn't diluted. He's seen it happen to other characters. Look at how Marvel ruined the Punisher; they had him visit Archie for God's sake!

So outside the Bat-office, say in *JLA*, there are likely to be more restrictions?

In my opinion, some of the problems Grant Morrison has met with [on *JLA*] are deserved. When he wanted the Huntress to join the JLA I was a little incensed. It starts to sound fanboyish, but some of my first Batman stories involved the Huntress. I was the one who brought her back, and who insisted she be Helena Bertinelli, the character she was before. They wanted a new Huntress and I said, 'No, we can do plenty with this character, there's a lot there'. For years I was the only guy writing Huntress stories. I threw her into my books every chance I had, and I kinda saw it as a saga. Each time she appears we see a little bit more of her, learn a little bit more about her. The biggest hook for me was that Batman *knew* she had a problem, but he didn't know how severe it was and the readers did; they knew she was definitely out of her mind. And then she goes and joins the Justice League! I loved it when Green Arrow joined, but I didn't like this at all. Denny tried to block it as much as possible but the powers-that-be wanted her in there. She's still not a good fit. Maybe Grant has something down the line where the JLA realises she's crazy and she ruins something... but the idea that Batman put her up for membership, it's like there's *no way.*

Do you find it necessary to read and keep up with all the other Batman books, as well as those featuring subsidiary characters?

No. See, whether superhero comics writers want to admit it or not, they have their own universe. I write in the Dixonverse and someone else writes in their 'verse, and within them the characters act the way the particular writer wants them to act. I don't worry about what everybody else is doing. This is what I want to do and if I run into major continuity glitches the editors will catch it and do rewrites. But I can't sit there thinking about all that when I'm writing. This is my take on a character, and it's usually simple. Catwoman, for example; I love Catwoman because she enjoys what she does. So few comic characters do, they're an unhappy bunch. She's not, she loves life and likes what she does, and she's a joy to write. So that's my take and I don't stray far from it. Now other people will say she has this in her background, and that. Well, not in the Dixonverse she doesn't.

With *Birds of Prey* you've defied the odds by writing a successful book which stars two female lead characters — Black Canary and Oracle — neither of whom are big comic book names.

Yeah, they keep their clothes on, one's in a wheelchair, they think a lot. One

ANATOMY OF A COMIC BOOK STORY
THE OPENING ACTION

This can be the inciting incident of the story, or it can just be a sequence that shows how good our hero (or villain) is at what he does. I can't tell you how many faceless thugs have been shot, beaten or humiliated in the openings of my stories just to give the readers a re-cap of how bad my title character is. It's a challenge to come up with new ways to accomplish this. This scene can also be used for exposition, recap, characterisation or humour. Sort of like the pre-credits sequence in a James Bond movie. You can also use it as a springboard to flashbacks. I once opened a story cold with the Punisher leaping from a plane at 35,000 feet without a parachute. The next eighteen pages told, in flashback, how he got to be there. Todd, you remember this one, right?

THE MINOR ACTION

This can be supporting characters in some kind of action that parallels the main story. It can be the villain beating up one of his own henchmen (my personal favourite), or the hero encountering conflict as he moves through the story. Any excuse for this scene's appearance is a good one. So long as someone's being thrown through a plate glass window on page nine you're on the right track.

CLOSING ACTION

If it's a cliffhanger it can be a short action piece that leaves our hero in a dilemma, making your next issue opener real easy to write.

If it's not a cliffhanger, then it should be your main action set-piece and take up the most pages. Don't rush the ending. The readers are looking for a pay-off and will disappointed if the final conflict isn't a zinger.

None of this is meant to denigrate the plot aspects of your story, but plot must be hammocked between action. If you're reading this there's nothing you need to be told about plot.

There are other formulas:

THE ALL-ACTION ISSUE

This one is a killer to write. The action set-piece starts on page one and roars through to the conclusion. You have to carry the plot through dialogue between the combatants or witnesses, or the internal dialogue of the hero. But if you can write a good one of these you've got my respect. One act.

TWO BEAT ACTION

A brief inciting incident and a little exposition that just sets up an extended action sequence that takes us to the last page of the book. The classic revenge plot structure. Two acts.

Above: *An extract from 'Anatomy of a Comic Book Story', a writer's guide. Courtesy of Chuck Dixon.*
© *1999 Chuck Dixon.*

of the reasons it's successful is that it's garnered a female audience. It's not just the female leads, [editor] Jordan Gorfinkel and I have made sure there's a lot of story in each issue. I think the way to attract female readers is to put as much story in there as you can fit, because they don't want two guys hitting each other for twenty-two pages. They want something more. That's helped us out, because any time you can attract female readers it bumps up the sales, *and* they tend to be more loyal. And more generally, because it is densely plotted people tend to stay with the book; they wanna see what happens next. *Birds of Prey* has more subplots than even *Nightwing*, which was my most subplot-laden book. There's just dozens of things to think about: when is this or that going to pan out? Who is this person going to turn out to be? I didn't create Oracle, I didn't create Black Canary, but the two of them together, they're kinda mine.

What you write is fundamentally superhero stuff. Do you foresee a time when you might move on to something along the lines of _Preacher_?

I'd like to do other genres. I'll do a Western any time anybody offers it to me, even if it has superheroes in it. The most fun I had in comics was at the very beginning, working on *Savage Tales*, writing Western stories. So while I would like to write other genres outside of superheroes, superheroes are the game here. But no, something like *Preacher* isn't in me. I've had offers from Vertigo but I

Birds of Prey

It's a sad but true fact that female lead characters don't sell comics and thereby rarely endure in their own titles. There have been notable exceptions (Catwoman, Witchblade, Wonder Woman, She-Hulk, if only while John Byrne was writing/drawing her), some noble tries (Elektra, Ghost, Silver Sable) and a few more alternate takes (Tank Girl, Death, Martha Washington), but apart from the brief flirtation with 'bad girl' books (Glory, Avengelyne, Lady Death et al), which were aimed squarely at the raging hormones of teenage boys, there really hasn't been a success story for some time. Until *Birds of Prey*. To be honest, on paper, it's not the most immediately obvious candidate for success: wheelchair-bound former Batgirl, Barbara Gordon — now calling herself Oracle and using her computer skills and contacts to supply information to fellow heroes — teams up (though they never meet) with Dinah Lance, Black Canary, a freebooting martial artist. Published originally as a series of one-shots and mini-series, Chuck Dixon's intelligent, fast-paced, multi-layered plots (which work almost as self contained, mini action movies), combined with generally above average artwork, turned *Birds of Prey* into a sleeper hit. An ongoing series quickly followed.

don't *get* Vertigo, I don't understand what that imprint means. At what point do they go, this is no longer a DC Universe book, this is a Vertigo book? That they use four-letter words is the only big difference I can see, and the violence is more graphic. I'm not putting them down, but that stuff is not to my taste.

So what comics do you actually read?

Not a whole lot, to be perfectly honest. I actually don't like that many other comics, they're not my kind of thing. I generally write the ones I wanna read. I'm in the medium 'cause I like the medium. Clint Eastwood once said, 'Take your job seriously but don't take yourself seriously', and that's kind of a guideline for me. I take the work very seriously. I love the comics medium, nothing excites me more. A good comics story done well is a killer. And the real beauty of it is that it's a monthly medium. I'll talk to Hollywood people every once in a while — they'll approach me about writing something — and when they start talking about seventh drafts and treatments I just run away screaming. Because, hey, I can write a story today and in a few weeks I'll see artwork, and a lot of people will be reading it a few months after that. To me that's better than any other writing gig out there.

*   *   *

Check out:
Batman: Knightfall pt 1: Broken Bat
Batman: Knightfall pt 2: Who Rules the Night
Batman: Knightsend

Batman: Contagion
Batman: Legacy
Batman: Prodigal

Birds of Prey
Catwoman: The Catfile
The Joker: Devil's Advocate
Nightwing: A Night in Blüdhaven
Robin: A Hero Reborn

WARREN ELLIS

Like his fellow imports Garth Ennis and Grant Morrison, Warren Ellis has been insidiously plugging his uniquely twisted, subversive sensibilities into mainstream American comics for several years now. Ellis is a writer who literally knows no limits, constantly challenging the status quo and pushing the medium to the boundaries of decency and taste. Take Ellis's superhero comics work — *Stormwatch*, *Ruins* and the recent *Planetary* among them — and marvel at his ballsy, no-nonsense approach. In Ellis's universe superheroes may well wear spandex and possess superpowers, but they operate like real people with real desires and real flaws: his characters smoke, take drugs and have sex, even die. Indeed, Ellis is no respecter of convention. If it makes good story sense to wipe out lead characters, then they're toast, plain and simple. Since his first work — *Lazarus Churchyard*, which centred on a 400 year-old cyberpunk hero — Ellis has bounced around the industry, writing everything from *Batman: Legends of the Dark Knight* to *Thor*, *Dr Strange* to *Excalibur*. Currently the regular writer on Vertigo's *Hellblazer* and creator of the highly acclaimed *Transmetropolitan*, the tales of journalist and embittered, miserable bastard Spider Jerusalem, Ellis, like many of his comics creations, pulls few punches.

Did your interest in comics begin when you were a kid or were they something you discovered later in life?

The first comics I remember were the ones my dad brought home for me when I was four or five, things like *Countdown* and *TV21*. I saw a few of the American comics, then *2000 AD* launched around my ninth birthday and that was it. I was hooked from then until my teenage years, when everyone goes through the same thing of, 'These comics are pretty good, but *that's* a girl'. I didn't really develop any major interest in comics again 'til late teens, twenty maybe.

What was it about *2000 AD* that had you hooked?

It was the intensity of the fiction. You saw these little Superman comics, which I guess are passably interesting to a six or seven year-old — he's flying around, moving the Earth out of orbit and stuff — and then you open *2000 AD* and there's people falling out of a spaceship into space and their stomachs are exploding, flip back a few pages and there's a big dinosaur opening his mouth to show you a gobful of chewed-up cowboy, and then there's this bloke who looks like the Six Million Dollar Man, only he's just splattered three terrorists under a ten foot high steel door. This was a bit more interesting to me than Superman. You're a nine year-old kid, you want to kill the world anyway, and there was *2000 AD* doing it for you. Then, of course, there was Judge Dredd, who achieved a bodycount of somewhere in the region of twenty in just six pages.

What got you interested in comics again?

I was running a bookshop and we started stocking comics, and comics were essentially anti-magazines. I'd been vaguely paying attention to things, I had followed *Watchmen* and *Dark Knight Returns*, and they were probably what brought me back. In terms of *Swamp Thing* and *Watchmen* it was the sheer quality of Alan Moore's writing. With Frank Miller's stuff it was the energy and the intensity of *Dark Knight Returns* and *Elektra: Assassin*. I was reading Eddie Campbell* at much the same time, and he'd found this completely natural, organic idiom to work in and I had seen nothing quite like it; utterly relaxed, conversational pieces straight out of the social novel being made to work in comics. Bryan Talbot was well into *Luther Arkwright* by then and no one was telling stories like Bryan. It was

Place of birth:
  Rochford, Essex, UK
Date of birth:
  February 1968
Home base:
  Southend, UK
First published work:
  Blast #1
Career highlights:
  The Authority, Batman:
  Legends of the Dark Knight,
  Druid, DV8, Excalibur,
  Hellblazer, Hellstorm,
  Lazarus Churchyard,
  Planetary, Ruins,
  Stormwatch,
  Transmetropolitan

* *Writer/artist on* Bacchus *and* Deadface; *artist on* From Hell *(with writer Alan Moore).*

that whole eighties renaissance — Jaime Hernandez and Gilbert Hernandez, for instance, they were trying to reclaim social fiction via the comic book.

How did that lead you into writing comics?

I'd been writing, and I certainly messed around with comic scripts an awful lot. What brought things to a head was that we were selling comic-related magazines in the bookstore and one of them was just so frighteningly bad I sent them a filthy letter about their review section, because the standard of journalism was so poor, and ended up sending them a couple of reviews, which they then ran. Another comics magazine called *Speakeasy* contacted me on the strength of those and said you can do this for us, only we'll pay you. So I ended up doing reviews, interviews and general journalism part-time for them, for six months, a year, at which point they decided they wanted to get into the comics publishing business and basically said, 'If you think you're so bloody clever, why don't you write a comic?', which, as challenges go, wasn't one I could walk away from. So I wrote my first *Lazarus Churchyard* story, sent it in and they bought it. It was kind of as simple as that.

You mentioned you were already messing around with the comics form. How did you know how to write one?

Years and years ago, when I was a kid — and I remember this quite vividly — there was a *2000 AD* annual released that had a section in the middle — and it's really sad that I remember — which explained how a *Judge Dredd* comic strip is put together. It went through all the stages from initial idea to script to pencilling to lettering to inking, etc, and had examples of each, and there was a page of John Wagner/Alan Grant *Judge Dredd* script* in there.

Those early scripts you wrote, were they for yourself or did you send any of them off?

A lot of them were for myself because the comics form always interested me even when I wasn't reading comics; there had to be a way to make it do things that comics weren't doing at the time. I liken it to the artists who say they have to get a thousand bad drawings out of themselves before they get one good one. You just had to find a way to write all the shit out of you before you got to the good stuff.

You wrote *Lazurus Churchyard* for *Speakeasy*, which later became *Blast*, and when that folded you went to work for Tundra UK. How did that come about?

The editorial director at *Blast* was a man called Dave Elliott, who left just before *Blast* collapsed to form Tundra UK, the British arm of the company run by Kevin Eastman, he of the *Teenage Mutant Ninja Turtle* millions. When *Blast* went down, Dave rang me up and said he would commission another eighty pages of *Lazurus Churchyard* stuff and let's see what else you've got. I wrote a forty-eight page one-shot called *Sugar Virus*, which is a vampire story, and several shorts based around a character called Harlequin Bones, which was a spin-off from the *Lazurus*

---

* See also Garth Ennis, p75.

Churchyard environment. I believe only three ever saw print, but I wrote over one hundred pages of it. I came up with another three forty-eight page stories, and co-created a superhero universe for them.

Most British writers have had some dealings with *2000 AD*. Did you?

I did one six-page strip for them. The benefit of my generation, and certainly of having done a little bit of journalism in the comics industry, was that you knew the horror stories of the previous generation who had grown into the business with *2000 AD*, so frankly I knew to avoid them.

Was it then that Marvel Comics moved in and picked you up?

Actually no. What happened was Tundra UK collapsed, leaving me high and dry, and a week later Archie Goodwin phoned from DC. Over a year earlier I had sent him a pitch for a two-part *Batman: Legends of the Dark Knight* and never heard anything back. He phoned up saying he had just gotten round to reading the story and asked if he could buy it, which kind of saved my life. Because there was a certain prestige associated with your first sale to an American company being to Archie Goodwin on *Batman: Legends of the Dark Knight*, I began being offered work at Marvel.

During the next few years you wrote a wide variety of books — *Hellstorm, Excalibur, Ruins* — seemingly dabbling in a number of different areas. Was there any reason for that?

If I had been in a position to get the sort of work I really wanted to do straight away, I may have found myself settling on a particular book or two. Despite Archie Goodwin's interest, DC as a company had no interest in me at all, so Marvel was obviously where I was going to stay for a little while. They cancelled *Hellstorm*, they cancelled *Druid* — not because they sold badly, but because they didn't sell as much as the X-Men books. The situation for creators has always been much less stable at Marvel, because Marvel have always been that much more willing to cancel books. The books at DC that have low sales but critical acclaim survive because of that, even though they would have been cancelled years ago at Marvel. So because Marvel didn't have anything to offer me that really engaged me strongly, emotionally, as a creator, I found myself dabbling in lots of different things to keep my interest level up — which ultimately meant learning how to write superhero comics, of which I've never been a fan. I ended up having to do an awful lot of research, because I really hadn't read many superhero comics. I spent a long, long time reading just masses of material on the superhero and I found the underpinnings of the genre much more interesting than the genre itself. You do tend to find me going for the base of it.

One of the first things I realised once I was writing superhero comics was that I was very much working in a pulp idiom and environment. I was writing fantastic — as in, fantasy — comics very, very quickly, much as was done at the height of the pulp business, so I tended not to have much time to think through what I was doing in any great, analytical detail. Whatever was in my head about these things came to the fore or bled through subconsciously, simply because I was working at such an insane speed, and that's why I eventually quit working on the X-Men books. Creatively, I was kind of emptied, and basically I was exhausted. Two years on the X-books was the hardest work I've ever done. Things like *Ruins*... well, by that time I'd worked up a healthy loathing for the superhero and needed to vent.

Whereas someone like Garth Ennis shows his distaste for superheroes by having Hitman throw up on Batman, you seem to take a more realistic, hard-edged, cynical view. Do you agree?

I'm doing the reader a disservice if I don't attempt to present superheroes as real people, no matter what the situation or environment is. Presumably, that's what people come to fiction for, they want to understand, relate to and empathise with the characters they're reading about, and you can't do that unless there's an element of reality to them. So I just try and present them as real people as far as I can, no matter if they're wearing spandex or not. I remember hearing that someone at DC read *Ruins* and called it the most cynical and mean-spirited comic that they'd ever read, which amused me no end. I really wanted to put that on the back cover. What comes out as distaste with some people and a certain disappointment with people like Alan [Moore],

Ruins

Originally presented as a *What If?* proposal, *Ruins* explores an alternate Marvel Universe in which superhuman abilities are, in all cases, a curse rather than a blessing. In principle, it sounds like standard *What If?* material; a skewed take on established Marvel 'history', but when you get down to the specifics — diseased, dying superheroes; a prostitute Jean Grey (not to mention other scenarios that Marvel just wouldn't weather, including Doctor Strange smoking dope, — you begin to realise *Ruins* is anything but standard, hence its stand-alone, two-issue status. This savage deconstruction of the Marvel Universe (which bizarrely features journalist Phil Sheldon from *Marvels*) in many ways typifies Ellis's superhero writing, underlining his complete and utter disregard for established conventions and mythos. As a springboard, of sorts, it took Ellis to Jim Lee's Wildstorm Studios (then part of the Image Comics group), where he wrote first *DV8*, designed, it seems, primarily as an antidote to the company's lighter-toned team books. Certainly, in those terms at least, Ellis's run can be deemed a success. Far better was Ellis's literal deconstruction of Wildstorm's *Stormwatch* book, wherein he single-handedly (in an *Aliens* crossover) killed most of the team, paving the way for *The Authority*.

just comes out in me as pure, bloody hatred, and I suspect that's why the cynicism burns so brightly in my work. I got to the point where I just hated superheroes. I hated this false reality they presented. I hated the fact they present a society where nothing can change because it takes superhuman effort to keep things the way they are, which is just frightening bollocks.

And yet you continue to write superhero comics. Why is that?

At the moment, yeah, I'm still writing superhero comics. But *Planetary* I'm only expecting to run about three years, and that will be the last superhero project I do. Once *Planetary* is complete, that's it, I'm out of the genre. *Planetary* is designed to say everything I have left to say about superheroes.

I remember an interview in which you flippantly said you wrote superhero comics for the money. Is that still the case?

I'm not saying there's no truth in that. Certainly, I have a family to support and sometimes the work you want to write is not the work anyone wants to buy. There was a period where no one would entertain anything but superhero work from me, which I find quite bizarre, bearing in mind that a few years earlier they were actually leery of giving me superhero books.

Sounds like editorial pigeonholing. How did you find that?

Hugely annoying. Any kind of pigeonholing is annoying, because it's only due to people using labelling as a short cut to thinking. They didn't actually bother to read the work, they just looked at the pretty covers and the sales figures and just went, 'Oh yes, he should only be doing superhero books'.

Did you ever consider giving up superhero comics and taking your work into other mediums?

I knew things would come full circle. I knew, provided I did the best work I was capable of on these things, that eventually an opportunity would present itself to get back to writing the sort of projects I wanted to do, which it did. I just knew I would have to do superheroes for two or three years first.

What's your method for writing a comic?

I carry around a notebook and a handheld PC with me. It fits in my jacket and has a cut down version of Windows on it and a cable that allows me to zip stuff into the main computer. I'm a gadget freak, I can't help it. Monday, I'll often leave the house, go out with the handheld and make a few notes; get down what I want the job to do, what I intend to have happen in the story. I'll try to keep the theme up front, find the spine of the piece. Dialogue, if it occurs to me, gets jotted down; just random note-taking I'll eventually sort into some kind of order. Tuesday I'll import all that into the machine and I'll start writing, connecting the notes together and making them into scenes. If I'm lucky, by the end of

PAGE ONE

Pic 1;
All right then... let's crack into this and see where it goes, eh?

There are four pics on this page; three page-wide pics, and one small inset shot dropped in on the bottom right hand corner. I'm going to be dealing in page-wide pics, letterbox shots, quite a lot — they approximate Cinemascope, and that's a useful connection to make.

Anyway; here's our opening shot. We're up a goddamn mountain, people, and it's cold and bleak, just tough little patches of wet green grass jutting out of cracks in rocks or areas of damp earth to brighten it up. A huge blue empty sky above us on this plateau area set into the mountain — we see the mountain continue on above — and a large ramshackle house compound in the plateau, its back to the ascending rock. Are you with me? Am I making sense? Somehow, I doubt it... oh, and whack the fucking thing out to bleed at top, left and right... just to confuse things, that's right...

CAPTION;   **Up a goddamn mountain;**

CAPTION;   SO THAT IGNORANT, THICK-LIPPED, EVIL
                              WHOREHOPPING EDITOR PHONES ME UP
                              AND **SAYS**,

JAGGED VOICE (no tail);   DOES THE WORD **CONTRACT** MEAN
                              ANYTHING TO YOU, JERUSALEM?

Pic 2;
Cut; to a close up on **Spider Jerusalem**.

We're inside the shabby house, but concentrating largely on Spider, giving us a good look at our protagonist up front. Of course, his visual will have changed by the end of the issue, but what the fuck... At this point, Darick, Spider is in his hermit phase, and he bloody well looks like it. His hair's dead black, I should note. Long straggly beard, long filthy hair, full of lice and rat's-tail tangles. Here and there, spent bullet casings are tied in his hair. I'm also tempted to have other stuff tied in there, too — a small Native American dreamcatcher, maybe, a couple of runestones, a dead lizard, I dunno... see what you think, I'm wondering whether adding more stuff would make that great mane look too crowded and busy...

Anyway, we're close in on Spider, as he holds the cracked and perished receiver of what is actually one of our current-day phones to his ear, and looking shocked, disgusted and nauseous all at the same time. One eye bulges uncomfortably.

Above: *Part of the script for issue one of* Transmetropolitan, *by Warren Ellis. Courtesy of Warren Ellis.*

Wednesday it looks a bit like a screenplay, mostly just dialogue and setting. Thursday and Friday is when I go in and turn it into a script, expanding the setting, looking at the storytelling, breaking it down panel-by-panel and by page. So normally, by the end of Friday I've got something that looks like a comic script.

Do you think visually?

I've got this rule that I won't ask an artist to draw anything I can't draw myself and I can't fucking draw. I keep a notebook by the machine and I will actually sketch out a page if need be. Time was I'd sketch out an entire issue to make sure I wasn't doing anything wrong but I can hold a lot in my head now. I can actually see a page in my mind and move panels around, so it's not often that I have to resort to the notepad, but I still keep it there. You just learn the vocabulary, you learn how to communicate the pace, you learn where the beats fall and you learn when you need your widescreen moments.

How much collaboration do you like to have with the artist?

It all depends on who I'm working with. If I'm working with someone for the first time I will envision the book very clearly and in some detail so they can understand how I see things, what my visual sense is like. Once I've been working with them for a while the scripts become more pared down. With Darick [Robertson], who I've been working with for two years now on *Transmetropolitan*, I write fairly lean scripts — unless I'm after a specific effect or I'm describing something that must be imagined in absolute detail — because I know how he thinks and he knows how I think. We understand each other's eyes, and so I can write a scene knowing how he'll stage it. To be honest, I find it more interesting at the start. It's almost like the first few weeks of a love affair, where your new girlfriend is just so new and you're still exploring and learning and are fascinated by anything that they do. Working with John Higgins on *Hellblazer* has been like that, just watching him come out of himself on the book and achieve a real clarity to his images where he hadn't before. That was just fascinating. And John Cassiday on *Planetary*, finding this sudden intensity has developed to his line and added a real urgency to the work.

Have you any artist horror stories?

Yeah, there was one guy who decided he didn't like the back four pages of an issue so he drew something else. He was fired. I'm sorry, I'm all for collaboration and the magic fairy dust of working on comics together but don't fuck with me. If it was wrong, I wouldn't have written it down. I'm kind of militant and dictatorial on this point. If you've got a problem with a story, you've got my phone number, it's on the front of the script, talk to me, don't just change it and then expect me to be happy about it, because it's my name going on the front of the book as writer, not yours.

Your work seems truly inspired by the seedier, seamier side of life. Any personal experience of it yourself?

I lived in this little red light district [in Southend] for eighteen months, waking up every morning to find broken glass in the front garden and used syringes in the back garden, and being lulled to sleep by the sounds of gunfire. I've always been interested in the underside; seeing how things look from down there, and seeing how you end up there.

Does your personal life filter into the work? Are you, as your works seems to suggest, a cynical bastard in real life?

Oh, by Christ yes, ask anyone. I think Grant Morrison once called me the man with a snarl for every occasion. If there's one thing I hate, it's people. Certainly personal life does filter in, it can't help but colour your work. I'm not the same man I was when I was writing *Lazurus Churchyard*, that was something only someone in their early twenties could have written.

Given the intensity of your work, have you encountered much editorial interference and/or censorship over the years?

Not as much as I used to. When I was working at Marvel it was a fight every month on some jobs, to the extent where often the problem was not with my editor but with my editor's supervisor, who was just attacking the book line by line as being too nasty, or too this, or too that. It got to the point where myself, my editor and other staff members were colluding to get the book to the printer without the editorial supervisor seeing it. *Hellstorm* we had terrible problems with, *Druid* we also had trouble with. When I was doing *Satana*, which of course never saw print, the problem was that one Marvel publisher had given me a promise that they wouldn't fuck with the work, and that it would be put out as an adult comic book. Then Marvel changed hands, a new publisher came in and said no previous promises count any more, all Marvel books will be for kids. That sort of thing happened to me all the time at Marvel.

Nowadays it doesn't happen so much. I recently had a couple of sticky moments with Vertigo. There is a scene in my first issue of *Hellblazer* [issue #134], in which John Constantine is having a conversation with a woman called Clarice, who is at least sixty years old, and with whom he has had a previous relationship. That's made quite plain when, in the original script, Clarice says, 'I know what you are, I've known what you are since I sucked your cock in Highgate Cemetery when you were twenty-five years old'. There were huge arguments over this, which essentially boiled down to the people at Vertigo saying this is completely beyond the pale, and me wondering what their fucking problem was. And there was a short *Transmetropolitan* script in *Winter's Edge 2*, in which Spider [Jerusalem], just possessed by hate, grabs himself in the middle of the street and screams while on live television, 'I killed Santa Claus, I killed Santa Claus with my cock', which I was told was unacceptable. But when I suggested we stretch the panel so we could see Spider actually grabbing his own penis through his trousers while shouting, 'I killed Santa Claus with this', that was quite acceptable. In the original version you couldn't see his hand.

Did Vertigo give you any idea what was acceptable and what wasn't?

Only afterwards. I was already writing *Hellblazer* when I was told that certain things would not be acceptable on this book. In general terms, there's a level of violence, of vulgarity and of horror that they will deem unacceptable for *Hellblazer*. I'm sure these people have their reasons and I'm sure they believe they are being perfectly reasonable, but I don't think they understand the amount of annoyance and time-wasting it causes on my part to have to deal with this inconsistent shit. I assumed on *Transmetropolitan* and certainly on *Hellblazer* that these things will be taken as read. *Hellblazer* is a horror book, it is set in London so people are going to do nasty things and say nasty words, words that you wouldn't ordinarily use in America. Like cunt, which is a word of frightening power in America and in London is punctuation. And no matter how I try, it is still an unacceptable word in *Hellblazer*.

Nevertheless, your first issue contains some pretty strong stuff. The description of the death of Constantine's former girlfriend is one of the nastiest things I've come across in a comic.

That was my intention, and some changes had to be made to that. There was a fairly graphic description of the killer fucking the wound in her thigh. It just finished off that piece quite nicely. I brought it to a point where it made me feel ill, and I had to pull back, and it still annoys me now that I had to pull back at the ending.

Hellblazer

Created by Alan Moore during his run on *Swamp Thing* (issue #37 features the character's first appearance), John Constantine is a trench-coated, self-serving and manipulative mystic. The 'Hellblazer' tag exists in cover title alone, Constantine's never referred to as such in any of the stories — it was originally intended to be 'Hellraiser', but Clive Barker got there first. The 'American Gothic' story arc in *Swamp Thing* led into *Hellblazer* #1, by Jamie Delano and [artist] John Ridgway, both British creators. Delano's take on the character was dark and guilt-ridden, the horror rooted in social realism. Very few concessions were made for the American market, either by Delano or his successors. Grant Morrison and Neil Gaiman dabbled briefly with the book before Garth Ennis started a long and acclaimed run that upped the blood and guts content considerably, and imbued the character with much of the writer's own personality (repeated trips to the pub became a feature of the book). Ennis was joined on *Hellblazer* by artist Steve Dillon, and when both left with issue #84, Eddie Campbell and then Paul Jenkins took over. Ennis returned for a five-part story, 'Son of Man', before Warren Ellis came on board with issue #134.

The whole description needed a crescendo, it couldn't just peter out, only it did.

Is that you purposely trying to shock?

Not to shock, to disturb. That is very, very different. I could shock you by wringing a cat's neck in front of your eyes. I wanna disturb you, I want you to go away from the book still thinking about it, I want you to live in that guy's mind for a little while. I want it to resonate afterwards. If I'm writing a scene of horror then I want it to fucking disturb you. I'm not interested in doing something half-baked, so I could shake my head and smile when someone asks me if I only did that to shock. Of course I did it to shock, it's a horror book. I want you to feel ill. This was the point of picking *Hellblazer* up. When there are moments of horror in *Transmetropolitan*, I want them to horrify. When Vita Severn gets shot at the end of 'Year of the Bastard', I want you to drop the book, otherwise it wasn't worth doing the scene like that. I want to excite a reaction, I want you to walk away from that book still thinking about it. I'm not consciously trying to write something disposable.

Are you trying to push the envelope of what's acceptable?

I don't think about it that closely. I just write my stories as best as I am able. Sometimes I've tried to make comics do things I haven't seen before, but I'm just trying to tell my stories as best I can. And you can do anything with words and pictures; there are no narrative limitations upon it. There are creative limitations, but that's only due to the way the medium exists right now.

In one interview you said you used to take drugs. Did you ever use them to enhance or influence your writing?

Most of the drugs I took were in the spirit of healthy exploration, the only drug I enjoyed for any length of time was speed because it meant I could work more. It probably added a healthy edge of paranoia to the work, but it was a tool. Those were the only drugs I was interested in, the drugs that could make me work faster, work better. I wasn't interested in the effects they could lend the work. I used to just sit and smoke forty cigarettes and drink a gallon of coffee and then start writing, but now I'm old and broken and have even quit cigarettes, which was interesting in itself because that initial week of not smoking induced the first hallucinations I'd had in eight or nine years. Now I have no stimulants, so it's simply by the force of my own mighty will that I come to the keyboard every morning. I will punch out that keyboard until one of us spits out the story I want.

I know you're friends with Garth Ennis; do you, like many other comics writers, have another writer that you call to talk out ideas and use as a sounding board?

No. No one. I lock myself in this room and I don't come out until the damn thing's written. That to me is what being a writer is. You sit there and you solve the damn thing yourself. I had this conversation with Mark Waid a couple of years ago and he just kinda stared at me: 'You do *what?*'. And I was the same with him, because I just couldn't conceive of phoning these people and saying, 'I've got half an idea...', it's just not me. I lock myself in a room and I write and that's how the job's done.

Your work is, by and large, deeply political. Do you think comics, as a medium, make for a good political soapbox?

Well, it's one of the last mediums you can get on a soapbox in. It's one of the last media to not have had all the interesting quirks and creases ironed out of it by corporate control and the demands of a mass audience, because the mass audience doesn't want to hear about politics. A mass audience wants its football and its tits. This is one of the bonuses, if you like, of working in comics. We address a relatively small and relatively literate audience. We're not addressing the culture as a whole, so we get to do things like be on a soapbox or write our comics on drugs and be quite open about it. It's nothing you could do with television or film any more.

Do you see the subversive side of you living in England writing all this deeply political stuff that mainly Americans read? Are you trying to screw up their culture from afar?

Certainly there is an appeal to the idea of throwing a monkey wrench into the ongoing cultural colonisation of the world by America. It's almost like having sex with Minnie Mouse behind Walt Disney's back. There's an appeal to that notion,

Helix

No doubt hoping to recreate the critical and, to a large extent, financial success of its Vertigo imprint, DC launched Helix (originally billed as Matrix), a creator-owned line of science fiction comics with a Vertigo-like adult sensibility. Among the opening salvo of limited and ongoing series were Garth Ennis and Carlos Ezquerra's *Bloody Mary*, Howard Chaykin and Don Cameron's *Cyberella* and Tim Truman's *Black Lamb*. Helix's intention, in broad terms, was to demonstrate that science fiction in comics could be done in a way that was 'fresh, original and totally up-to-date'. And while a noble aim, this was never going to be easy to accomplish. For some strange reason, science fiction and comics have rarely gelled (*Alien Legion* is perhaps one of the exceptions to the rule), and previous attempts to fuse them had generally met with failure. Given that, to all intents and purposes, Helix is no more, it would be easy to write the imprint off as yet further proof that science fiction fans aren't comics fans and vice versa, but Helix, if judged a failure, was a heroic one. Though now a Vertigo title, Warren Ellis's *Transmetropolitan* remains Helix's one major success story,

PAGE TWENTY

Pic 1;
Watford dips to the bag again, pulling out another two photos, still reading from his sheet as he does so.

WATFORD;   FIRST, HE CUT OUT BRACKNELL'S IMPLANTS. HIP AND TRENDY THING TO DO THESE DAYS; STICK SHIT UNDER YOUR SKIN. FUCKING SCUM...

WATFORD;   HE LEFT THEM ALL AT THE FOOT OF THE BED. THE HIGHLIGHTS OF THE LIST; STAINLESS STEEL BALLS, RODS, ETC (APPROX. TWO POUNDS). PRE-WAR MASONRY NAILS (3).

Pic 2;
He shows the top photo to John, who leans in, not quite believing this one.

WATFORD;   ABORTED FOETUS (1), PRESERVED.

WATFORD;   REASONABLE SUPPOSITION WAITING FOR CONFIRMATION FROM THE HOSPITAL IS THAT SAID FOETUS IS THE ABORTED CHILD OF BRACKNELL, I.

Pic 3;
Watford strips away the top photo — and John stops moving entirely.

WATFORD;   THEN HE THOUGHT FUCK IT, AND WENT FOR HER FACE.

WATFORD;   'ERE.

Pic 4;
Rest of the page.

This is the black and white photo of Isabel Bracknell's head in death. Because it's about time we showed something nasty — we could afford to let the audience's overheated imagination do the work up until now, but it's time to swing for the bastards.

She was a beautiful brunette, not yet thirty. Dark eyes, pretty lips, snowy white skin. Now, her left temple is a jagged hole. Her mouth, ajar, has been widened by inches at either side. Her cheeks have been all but slashed off. One side of her face is so badly cut up that you can see her tongue through it. One of her eyes has been slit across, and the thick soft white has pushed out through the slit a little, all else in the eye is dark. Dead as hell. Dead ugly, dead with inhuman hate. Dead Isabel. Horrifying. If it doesn't make you feel sick while you're drawing it, then it ain't ugly enough. It's got to hit hard, got to make you want to puke and weep.

(no dialogue)

Above: *Ellis's graphic description of murder victim Isabel Bracknell, from* Hellblazer #134. *Courtesy of Warren Ellis.*

and also to standing behind them and shouting loudly, 'This is what voting was about for you, you were supposed to be the revolutionary society, why the fuck do I have to stand here and remind you of it?'.

So how did Transmetropolitan come about?

It all began with [editor] Stuart Moore asking me to submit something to Helix, which led to me spending a week locked up in this room trying to work out what the hell I wanted to do in a science fiction piece, which is all Helix was doing. I started by thinking about the kind of science fiction I had always liked when I was reading it, which was easy because it was the science fiction that approached social fiction; a tradition that came from H. G. Wells, of using the future as a tool with which to explore the present. All of which in my mind led to journalism, which I've always read an awful lot of. It seemed to me to be the clearest and easiest way to explore the present through the future. Then I thought, I need someone to buy this damn thing, which would mean the book would have to be character-driven, so I needed a compelling journalist, a journalist who it was entertaining to watch. Of course, if there's one man who's made the watching of journalists into a spectator sport, it's Hunter S. Thompson, so Thompson certainly started as the inspiration for Spider Jerusalem. Spider Jerusalem doesn't write anything like Hunter S. Thompson, but Thompson was the original and obvious inspiration.

How much of the embittered journalist Spider is you?

Not much. The sense of outrage, perhaps, but there's not much. Less than you'd think.

Do you have any ambitions to take the comics medium into any new direction?

My ambition for the medium is much the same as any other sane person's, which is to take off the limitations that are provided by the commercial arena. There should be the money and the space and the inclination available to do things other than superhero comics, and frankly we should be able to use any language we want and any depictions we want in the service of our stories. We should not have to be limited by someone else's idea of what is acceptable. There is no reason for that.

Do you foresee a move into other forms of writing?

Yeah. I've already signed the contract to do a spin-off Daredevil novel for Marvel and there has been talk of a *Transmetropolitan* movie, which I'm involved in right now. I'm in the middle of the first draft of the script.

How about going the Hunter S. Thompson/Spider Jerusalem journalism route?

I must confess there's a certain appeal to it. Certainly I like the idea of buying a castle somewhere. Have you ever wanted to do that, buy a castle and walk the ramparts with a shotgun? Just culling the peasants and livestock occasionally. Maybe get a cannon up there. That'd be nice. I'd like a cannon.

See, you're more like Spider than you know.

Oh come on, who wouldn't want a cannon.

*   *   *

Check out:
Transmetropolitan: Back on the Street (collects issues #1–3)
Transmetropolitan: Lust For Life (collects issues #4–12)

Thor: World Engine (the acclaimed four-issue story arc by Ellis and artist Mike Deodato Jnr)

WildC.A.T.S./X-Men

GARTH ENNIS

Garth Ennis is no stranger to controversy. From his first published work, *Troubled Souls*, an account of a Belfast teenager pressed into service with the IRA, right through to his audacious masterwork, *Preacher*, the Belfast-born writer has managed to provoke shock and outrage in fairly substantial measure. While his scripts are characterised by their unflinching depiction of violence and its shocking after-effects, Ennis's world is not without morality, and mixed in among the body-parts and twisted protagonists is a Kevlar-coated streak of black, *black* humour. Nor is Ennis shy about tackling fundamental issues of religion and faith. *Troubled Souls* was followed by the equally controversial *True Faith*, which took a sharply satirical stab at Catholicism and earned him the wrath of his publisher, who ordered every copy pulled and pulped. In 1991, while writing strips for *2000 AD*, Ennis was recruited by DC Comics to take over from fellow British writer Jamie Delano on *Hellblazer*. Since then, Ennis has eschewed traditional superhero traditions, choosing instead to embrace a blood-spattered rogues' gallery of anti-heroes and mavericks, continually pushing back the boundaries of comics storytelling. In both *Hitman* and *Preacher*, Ennis has crafted some of the most memorable characters of recent years.

What kind of comics did you read as a kid?

I was a fan of British comics. I read *The Beano* when I was little, and then came *Battle* and *2000 AD*. They were both very, very influential. I look at my stuff now and see how stories by people like Pat Mills and John Wagner have filtered down into my work; that appalling violence mixed with really black humour. American comics never appealed — the whole superheroes thing, men dressed up in tights, running around fighting crime — compared to the stories in *2000 AD* or *Battle*, where justice was delivered in a very final and usually gruesome way. To see Batman drag the Joker up to Arkham Asylum for the umpteenth time so he can escape once again soon rings hollow. Judge Dredd blowing away some law-breaking swine had a finality about it that I appreciated at a very early age.

At what point did you think, 'I'd like to be a comic book writer'?

Around about fifteen or sixteen I got into the idea of wanting to write, although initially I thought about journalism. I'd always enjoyed reading and writing fiction, but the idea of writing comics didn't really come about until I was seventeen or eighteen. A friend of mine turned me on to things like *Dark Knight Returns*, *Watchmen*, *Swamp Thing* and *Elektra*. Those, combined with *Crisis*, when it was first launched by Fleetway, gave me the idea that you could tackle any story in comics. But I didn't have a serious stab at it until I was at university, having the worst time of my life, and I began to send off scripts.

How did you know how a comic strip was written?

2000 AD Annual 1981. Tharg the Mighty very kindly reprinted a script from *Judge Dredd* and took you through the process of scripting, pencils, inks, lettering and production. With this page of a John Wagner script for *Dredd* I was able to work out pretty much what a script was. It wasn't a bad script to learn from, either. It was sparse as hell, stuff like, 'Dredd on bike' and dialogue, and my scripts are not unlike that.

What writers influenced you back then?

Pat Mills, John Wagner and, to a lesser extent, Alan Grant. To me, Alan Moore was just this guy who wrote *The Ballad of Halo Jones* and those really funny

Place of birth:
  Belfast, Northern Ireland
Date of birth:
  16 January 1970
Home base:
  Clapham, South London, UK
First published work:
  Crisis #15 (Fleetway),
  part 1 of *Troubled Souls*
Education:
  Queen's University, Belfast
Career highlights:
  Bloody Mary, The Darkness, The Demon, Goddess, Hellblazer, Hitman, Judge Dredd, Medieval Spawn/ Witchblade, Preacher, Pride and Joy, Troubled Souls, True Faith, Unknown Soldier

'Future Shocks' in *2000 AD*. And while I really enjoyed that stuff, to me it wasn't the meat of the comic. It was only when I discovered American comics that I saw what Alan was really, really capable of: *V for Vendetta*, *Swamp Thing* and *Watchmen*. And although they weren't credited, I found out later it was Mills and Wagner who were writing the stuff I was reading when I six and seven in *Battle*, all that blackly humorous, excessively violent, dramatic, character-driven stuff.

Extreme violence seems to characterise the majority of your work. Growing up in Northern Ireland, did you witness much violence first hand?

Absolutely none. I grew up in a little town a couple of miles outside Belfast called Holywood, which is in the suburbs, and really it was the kind of suburb that people all over the world could relate to. I have no real memories of violence on the streets, or of a major army presence. I think the strong level of violence in my work is probably a combination of having read and watched a lot of fictional stuff like that, and a desire on my part to be as honest about violence and its effects as possible. But it doesn't come from anything in my childhood.

So *Troubled Souls* didn't reflect aspects of your own youth?

To be honest, it was just opportunism. When I started sending off scripts I met Steve Macmanus [Managing Editor of Fleetway and editor of *Crisis*] at a signing and got his office number. A while later I phoned and suggested, out of the blue, a story about Northern Ireland, because no one had ever done that. It was in no way a reflection of my own childhood or upbringing. It was the way I thought a story like that should unfold, and what it should say. The only genuine honesty in *Troubled Souls* was the reflection of what I felt at the time and continue to feel about Belfast. Johnny McCrea [the artist on *Troubled Souls*], who I met when he opened Belfast's first comic shop, hates it more than I do. He's horrifically embarrassed by it.

Religion has always been an integral component of your work. How much importance was placed on religion when you were younger, and were you raised as a Catholic or a Protestant?

Neither. My family's of Protestant descent, but growing up in the suburbs with a middle-class background meant religion could be, if you chose, largely irrelevant. So I was brought up with no religion at all, didn't even go to church. Obviously you're aware of it, but it's a choice that other people had made and something that never really impacted on me to any great extent. When I went to school I ran into organised religion for the first time, and I suppose I became aware of its influence a lot more. So while religion is not something that had any direct relevance on my life, it's something that always fascinated me; the Church, faith, the idea of the keepers of that faith and of the abuses of it. Faith, I suppose, is a fairly harmless thing. It's when people see ways to manipulate other people's faith that the trouble starts.

Also, the Christian Church is absolutely stacked with iconography, particularly the Roman Catholic side of things, so you've got great special effects for your horror stories. You can trot out the demons and the angels and the Holy Ghost and God and Jesus Christ, pour them into your story and it looks great. So it helps with the actual mechanics of the storytelling. As to my own interest in it, I don't know exactly where that came from, probably running up against it, not being comfortable with it and being interested in the way other people reacted to it and accepted it. So it's an interest of mine, the same way that Westerns are and America itself; her myths and her legends and her romance and her dreams. It all goes into the mix.

I remember the first time I ran across religion. I have this memory of the teacher sitting us all down and telling us about God, who was a special friend who lived in our heart and who knew what we were doing always. He loved us and watched us, and if we loved him back — this was put in terms that a five or six year-old could understand — and did right by him, then he would reward us. Exactly what would happen to us if you didn't was glossed over at that point. Outside in the playground afterwards all the other kids were going, 'Do you love God?', 'Yeah I love God'. And I remember when they came to me, I said 'No, I think I hate him', simply because I was so freaked at the idea of him being in your heart and seeing everything you do. I didn't like that at all. I went home from school and told my mum, and I have this sense that it didn't trouble her much, because she just said to me, 'What do you think of that then?'. I replied, 'Well, it all seems a bit stupid', and she said, 'There you are', and that was it. That was my first exposure to the idea of religion and I suppose it's never made more sense than that. I was able to use that experience in *Preacher*, in issue nine, where grandma tells little Jesse about God. When she says, 'Isn't it nice to have a friend like God?', he says, 'No... it's kinda scary'.

Troubled Souls led to work on 2000 AD, where you wrote Judge Dredd for a while. How did you find that?

The wisdom of the time was, if you sent in some short stories to *2000 AD*, eventually they would pick you up for an ongoing series, and, all being well, the Americans would then notice you. And once the Americans noticed you, they were going to give you an old superhero character to reinvent, and from that you were going to be handed some great superhero epic, and then the sky's the limit. While it sounds slightly facetious, that's exactly what happened for Alan Moore and Grant Morrison.

But for me, working at *2000 AD* proved to be a wee bit of a backwards step in the long run, because although it got me plenty of work and a lot of money, creatively it didn't do me any good. I did a bit of *Strontium Dog*, and when John Wagner needed someone to take over scripting *Dredd* they settled on me. I think it was mainly because I had a better sense of story construction — just moving from A to B to C — than some other guys who were around at the time, who were going for crazy, wild stuff before they really should have. My mistake with *Dredd* was because I loved the character so much I didn't bring anything of my own to the strip. A lot of my stories probably read like ones John Wagner would have thought of and then thought better of doing. There are ones I'm pleased with, but ultimately it wasn't for me. I have to put my hands up and say I fucked up. My future lay with coming up with my own stuff and my own characters. Once I started working on more personal stuff, I was putting more of myself into the work.

You made the leap into American comics with *Hellblazer*. How did that come about?

Jamie Delano was getting ready to quit the book in early 1990 and they started casting around for someone to take over. I believe [Executive Editor] Karen Berger had seen *True Faith* and *Troubled Souls*, and she asked me to send in a proposal. Out of all the various people who sent them in, mine was chosen.

Were you a fan of the comic?

And of the character [John Constantine]. Very much. When I started getting into Alan's stuff, Constantine was a big player in *Swamp Thing*. So when he got his own comic it was an absolute delight. There is something about that character that makes you want to stick with him. What Jamie gave you was a guy who was hanging on by his fingernails, who was this far ahead of the Devil every month and fucked up regularly and his friends suffered terribly because of it. While I thought Jamie's [take] was grim to the point of disbelief, I really admired that he hadn't gone the most obvious, most commercial route. He said, 'I have

---

2000 AD

The list is long and prestigious: Alan Moore, Dave Gibbons, Brian Bolland, Garth Ennis, Grant Morrison, Alan Grant, Pete Milligan, Steve Yeowell, John Higgins, Barry Kitson, Simon Bisley, Dan Abnett... a veritable who's who of British writers and artists who made it big in America. The linking factor? *2000 AD*, an originally black and white weekly science fiction comic launched in 1977 by IPC Magazines. The brainchild of competitions writer Kelvin Gosnell and writer Pat Mills, *2000 AD* was an antidote to the sterile, squeaky-clean future of strips like *Dan Dare*, and introduced the British comics-buying public to Judge Dredd, a fascistic policeman dispensing instant and brutal justice on the streets of a massive, over-populated, dystopian city. Other notable strips included *Harlem Heroes*, *Strontium Dog*, *Slàine*, *Zenith*, *ABC Warriors* and *Rogue Trooper*, all of which provided British creators with an opportunity to impress their American cousins. In the late eighties/early nineties, *2000 AD* (now published by Fleetway) and the more 'politically-aware' spin-off *Crisis* virtually became talent catalogues for American editors, especially those working on DC's Vertigo imprint. Suddenly, thanks in no small part to Alan Moore and Dave Gibbons' *Watchmen*, British creators were in. And how!

to write this book every month and I'm going to do it the way I want, otherwise what's the point?'. And I suppose that's what I did as well. I also figured that because people had stuck with Jamie so long they'd all be ready to jump ship as soon as the new writer came on board, so I thought, 'Christ, better grab them by the balls from day one', which is why Constantine got lung cancer in the first issue.

What did writing for American comics mean to you?

I was already starting to see that *2000 AD* was not the promised land I'd hoped it would be. It may have been a fucking great comic to read as a kid, but as a place to work it was not particularly nice. So there was a sense of stepping up a gear, working on a comic that allowed you to do stuff that was a little more relevant to yourself, rather than adventure fiction. You could write about ordinary people in an ordinary setting. Occasionally the vampires and things have to come out the woodwork, but largely it's this tosser in a trenchcoat walking around London smoking forty a day, getting drunk, getting into trouble, and getting involved in and worried about the kind of things I suppose a lot of people were at the time.

It was also a foot in the door, to a place where you were treated so much better, where you were paid well and on time, where there was a proper royalty and benefits structure, and where the people you worked with were totally professional. That made such a difference. To work with editors who were dedicated to getting as good a book as possible out there was a joy. I never want an editor who just rubber stamps stuff. Stuart Moore rejected the first two drafts of the first issue of *Preacher*, and quite rightly because they were bloody awful. It was only on the third go that I hit it.

How do you go about the actual process of writing a comic?

What I tend to do is, I have these wee notebooks. Every idea I have, no matter what, no matter when, goes into them; every line of dialogue, every cool scene, every idea for a character, even ideas for whole new stories go in there. Then, when it comes down to write the particular episode of whatever I'm doing, I trawl through the notebooks. It's my own dopey wee system and I'm loathe to change it, you know. I note down all the ideas, the lines of dialogue, and then I divide it into scenes, which I'll letter, say, A to J for that issue. Then it's a question of working out how many pages per scene and then you just link the ideas you've got to the letter of the scene and get stuck in.

I don't see a script in terms of pictures and word balloons, I see it in terms of people and, ridiculous and mad though it sounds, I hear them saying things. It's like I hear Jesse drawling away in that Texas accent and I hear Cassidy's kind of lilt, and I see them moving about. They're not like frozen pictures to me. That's not to say I regard them as real people or anything like that, but it's like I'm seeing the scene unfold and it's up to me to try and capture it. When it comes to actually writing a particular panel, I'll do my best to freeze the action in my head and describe what they're doing for [*Preacher* artist] Steve Dillon. That's the point at which I have to try and write down the dialogue, describe where the emphasis goes and how the punctuation works.

So you end up with the script written out in longhand, and then I'll take a lazy afternoon to type it up. It comes in at something like a script a week, which includes maybe a day and a half off. Sometimes it's a lot quicker. I've written whole episodes in two days because I've been enjoying them so much I haven't wanted to get away from the pen and paper. It's also taken two weeks, just because it's a real fucking drag. At the moment it's an average of five days per script.

My main inspiration when I'm sitting down to write is the story itself. Let's see where it goes, let's move the characters on, put them through their paces, let's see what happens when so and so runs into so and so. Let's see what happens when that idea you've had for the strip for so long actually goes into the mix. It's curiosity, about what's going to happen next. I just love stories.

How much visual information do you put in your script for the artist to work from?

I keep my scripts as sparse as possible. Partly that's because I trust the two guys I'm working with [Steve Dillon and *Hitman* artist John McCrea] implicitly. Partly it's probably laziness. As I mentioned, I always admired something about those John Wagner/Alan Grant *Dredd* scripts, which had minimal exposition. When you think of some of the great shots that have been drawn from 'Dredd on bike', you can see that vast amounts of explanation are not always necessary. I remember Jamie Delano telling me he makes his scripts kind of 'artist friendly', almost like a letter from himself to the artist. Personally, I prefer to get the collaboration aspects out of the way before the work begins, so when the artist comes to draw it they have as little information as possible in front of them. That way they can process it in their head quickly and get down to work.

With *Preacher*, do you have to send your scripts to your editor, Axel Alonso, first?

I send scripts to Axel at the same time I send a copy to Steve. If there is anything that Axel wants Steve to watch he'll mention it to him. We all trust one another, and we are all friends. No one wants to get anyone else fired by drawing something particularly hateful, and we all have a good idea of exactly how extreme the book should be.

Do you ever send a synopsis to Vertigo outlining the direction of the story?

Occasionally Karen Berger might like to see half a page of where *Preacher's* going, and I've no objection to doing that. But a half-page projection of two years' worth of *Preacher* and where it eventually ends up don't bear much relation to one another. When I wrote the initial *Preacher* proposal, I wrote that part of the appeal of this book is that it's going to be pretty extreme, the violence is going to be kind of nasty and there are going to be some pretty far out characters in there. While a lot of the stuff I don't find anywhere near as extreme as other people might, I'm aware of the fact that the publisher will. I've been told on numerous occasions that *Preacher* has been able to go a wee bit further than any other Vertigo book simply because I put that in the proposal. I had no idea. I just thought I'd better cover my arse. But it seems they've allowed us to go a bit further than *Hellblazer* or *The Invisibles* simply because I warned them in advance.

You've tended to remain very faithful to your artists. Do you feel more comfortable working with friends?

Long term, I'm more comfortable working with people who I have spent years working with. Short term, working with someone who I've never met before, where I have no idea how they work, can be very rewarding. Killian Plunkett on *Unknown Soldier* springs to mind; I think I've met him twice. On the other hand, it can be bloody miserable. I did this *Shadowland* mini-series, and it wasn't very good. I didn't do a particularly brilliant job, and the artist was one of these guys very influenced by Dave McKean and Simon Bisley; heavily textured, shadowy, dark pages, and not a very strong storyteller, and the whole thing just went down the toilet. You couldn't tell which character was which, you couldn't tell what was going on half the time. So yes, while it can be rewarding to work with new artists just for short periods of time, for a long haul it's got to be Steve Dillon or John McCrea. Those two guys I count among my best friends, and workwise we just click.

Wagner/Grant

Of all the famous writers associated with *2000 AD* and particularly the *Judge Dredd* strip, the names that spring most readily to mind, often in the same breath, are those of John Wagner and Alan Grant. Wagner had written for *2000 AD* since its inception and, with Pat Mills, was largely responsible for the renaissance of British comics in the 1970s (also writing strips for *Battle* and *Action*). When Pat Mills stopped scripting *Judge Dredd*, Wagner picked up the reins in earnest, crafting some of the best-remembered and defining Judge Dredd stories. In 1980 Wagner was joined by Alan Grant, a former sub-editor on *2000 AD*, and the two (often under the singular pen name T. B. Grover) made the character very much their own. American stardom soon beckoned, and via an Epic series titled *The Last American* (drawn by former *Dredd* artist Mike McMahon) the pair began to make inroads. A DC maxi-series, *The Outcasts*, followed, but then the route forked for the two creators, with Wagner writing for Dark Horse's *Aliens* and *Star Wars* titles, as well as *The Crow* for Kitchen Sink, and Grant joining DC, where he became regular writer on *Batman: Shadow of the Bat*.

PAGE TWENTY-FIVE   (SAME)

1.
Couple of minutes later. The tank is nearest, ~~stuck~~ out in front of the U.S. position roughly where John and Space fell. It's sitting sideways on to the V.C's last position, turret turned for the main gun to crack off a round. The crewman up top blazes away with the turret mounted MG; a couple of infantrymen take cover behind the tank and open fire too. Clem - the b/n actually comes from behind the tank.

Tank: ~~THEY'RE~~ WHO? ~~THE MEN ARE~~

2.
Behind the tank, safe in cover, half a dozen medics are hurriedly working on John and Space (NB - no red crosses). Not much of a sense of what they're doing; bandages going on, blood slopping around, clothing being scissored away. Further back, Bolden confers with a Corporal. shading over the foreground Other G.I.s keep firing from behind the tank. Everyone stays low and tense, no-one's relaxing out here.

Corporal: I SAID I THINK THEY'RE MARINES, SIR!

Bolden: WELL THAT FIGURES —

3.
Close in on Bolden, grimacing as a shell lands in the background. The Corporal ducks, holding his helmet on.

Bolden: WHO THE HELL ELSE'D BE DUMB ENOUGH TO WALK THROUGH A GODDAMNED MINEFIELD?

"   "   OKAY, GET 'EM OUT OF HERE! GO!

Above: *An extract from Garth Ennis's handwritten first draft script for* Preacher #50. *Courtesy of Garth Ennis.*

PAGE THREE

1.
Exterior shot on another large building. At the far end in the distance, trucks back
up to a loading bay, pull away when they're full.

From in: NOW...

2.
Big. Inside, sides of beef- cleaned of blood now- hang from the ceiling, rank upon rank.
Sausages are piled in great heaps, twenty feet· high or more. Side of bacon and hanks
of ham are stacked on benches. Its a room full of meat- walls of it, towers of it. A
pink, red and brown landscape, a disturbing, sliding, glistening world of flesh that
rolls back into the shadows and gloom. Keep it dark.

From in: SAY THE NAME...

3.
Two men stand flanking a doorway somewhere inside the building. Darkness beyond. They're
in a storage area lined with workbenches and bust machinery, rusted meathooks and so
on. One stares emotionlessly ahead. The other glances warily back into the darkness.

Door(big):   SAY THE NAME

4.
Close on the two guys, the nervous one facing front sharpish.

Doorway: ...MORNIN', BOYS.

Both: MORNIN', MISTER QUINCANNON.

PAGE FOUR

1.
Odin Quincannon strides out of the darkness towards us. He's about 4½ feet tall, aged
75, a scrawny little reptile, with no chin and no hair. Clean shaven. Nasty, mean little
face, curiously emotionless here, eyes staring ahead. Limbs like sticks. Loose skin
hangs at his neck like a wattle. Skin riddled with liver spots. Little pot belly. Big
ears. He wears oversized, black-framed glasses, giving him a goggle-eyed look. He wears
long undershorts, black shoes, socks and those little suspenders people used to wear
keeping them up. Apart from that his vile body is there for all to see. He's been
smeared- not splattered- with blood from head to foot, like he's been rubbing up against
or rolling around in meat- which he has, in fact.
His two bodyguards stand at the doorway he's just emerged from, carefully impassive.

Title: THE MEATMAN COMETH

and credits

(W e need big, impressive lettering for this to work best- as of issue 41, I'd like
to go back to the pre-"War in the Sun" style)

Above: *Part of Garth's typed script for* Preacher *#42. Courtesy of Garth Ennis.*

Can you describe how you 'click' exactly?

With Steve it's his sense of story, and particularly his sense of characterisation. I think Steve can communicate a lot with his artwork. He has a consistency to his characters. You can always tell who's who, and although that sounds fairly basic, it's actually very important. Once you have that, you can start using those characters' faces to tell the story, just with their facial expressions. There are very few people you can do that with, because it's rare artists can achieve that consistency. Jesse [in *Preacher*] always looks like Jesse and nobody else.

Steve and I did a few things together on *Judge Dredd* and a few fill-ins on *Hellblazer*, but it wasn't until we started working regularly on *Hellblazer* that it really clicked. I remember, I said to him, 'What sort of things do you wanna draw?', and he said, 'Just give me a good story'. Now that doesn't sound like a particularly momentous statement, but it bloody was for me, because it meant, 'This is fucking great, all I have to do is entertain this guy and he'll provide me this beautiful artwork. He'll tell these stories *for* me'. I remember feeling particularly elated and liberated by that. Ask most people the same question and you'll get a particular topic; big robots, action scenes, plenty of crumpet, and while I don't object to writing those things in moderation, it's better if they happen naturally within the story rather than being forced into it because that's what the artist wants to draw. Steve and I do share, pretentious as this sounds, an almost telepathic ability to tell a story together. There are times when I put stuff in the script, just a line, an off-hand remark about how a character feels so and so, or has that look in his eye, and Steve will just draw it perfectly.

With John McCrea you're talking about pretty much the same thing, except with John and I it's a sense of humour that we share above all else. John will ask me to put particular things into the story, but because he and I created *Hitman* together and because we've been working together for so long, going back to *Troubled Souls*, we know that we're going to find the same things funny. I'll put stuff in there to amuse John and he'll put stuff in there that will tell the joke the way he knows I intended. This one time we created the Bucket Burger franchise in Gotham [for *Hitman*] that has burgers the size of footballs. John drew all these really fat bastards around the place and eventually came up with the idea of a firefight in a Bucket Burger and a fat guy exploding. I wrote that in, and I remember how beautifully that scene unfolded in the artwork; where the fucker explodes and the skull flies out of the explosion and this tidal wave of gore slooshes down the corridor and carries our heroes out into the back yard*. This was obviously stuff Johnny had had in his head for ages and he knew I would find it just as funny.

How specific are you in regard to the way the comic should look?

I am fairly specific, but I'm aware with Steve I'm dealing with a guy with immense experience, a master storyteller. There's no one I would pick out as being better at that side of things than him. So I know pretty much I'm in Steve's hands. I can make all the suggestions I want, but ultimately that side of the storytelling is his.

---

* *The story ('Who Dares Wins' part two) appeared in* Hitman #24.

Fortunately we see eye to eye, we trust each other. He knows what to expect and I know what he's going to do most of the time. So, although the layout of the page sometimes differs from what I expect, largely I can anticipate where he'll put characters and how he'll shoot a particular scene.

You're listed as the co-creator of both *Preacher* and *Hitman* with the respective artists. How much input did they have on the books originally?

Hitman came about because Johnny and I were the new team on *The Demon*. At the time we were really into John Woo movies. We still are, but it was early 1993 and we really loved all that two-fisted gunplay stuff. So that was where Tommy Monaghan came from. I suggested the kind of world he moved in, the little old Hell's Kitchen part of Gotham City, and the character of an Irish gangster on the wane that was a part of that kind of life, and Johnny gave Tommy his look; that kind of bad-ass leather overcoat and the twin guns and the shades, while at the same time giving him these raffish good looks; which are, in fact, John's raffish good looks. So Tommy is just John with dark curly hair and a pair of shades on.

When *Hitman* became a comic of its own and Tommy was going to have a regular cast of guys that move around him, I would describe them a little bit but mostly it was down to John to really bring them across. If you look at Ringo Chen, he's really Chow Yun-Fat, he's like our direct tribute to those movies. For the Mawzir, who was like the big villain in the first couple of issues, I just said to John, 'he's this ten-

---

Hitman

Now here's an oddity, and certainly for DC something of a risk-taking enterprise that paid off. Tommy Monaghan is an assassin; essentially he kills superpowered beings for a living. Not the most immediately commercial proposition, especially when you consider Monaghan resides firmly within the mainstream DC Universe (and in Gotham, no less), potentially rubbing shoulders with such iconic figures as Batman and Superman. No Vertigo escape valve here for the somewhat confrontational talents of writer Garth Ennis and artist John McCrea. Nevertheless, by reining in the expletives somewhat and tempering the violence with real (black) humour, *Hitman* thrives. Citing the films of John Woo as a major influence, Ennis and McCrea go for gunplay and splatter in a big way, mixing it with gross-out bad taste (Tommy throws up over Batman during the first issue; the crime boss is Siamese twins, one of whom is dead, the rotting corpse still attached; Tommy uses a dead cat and a torch beam to try and attract Catwoman's attention... and so on). *Hitman* has, perhaps against the odds, carved out its own little anarchic niche in the DC Universe, where it continues to regularly thumb its nose at superhero and comic book convention.

PAGE SEVEN

1.
Big. Rear view on Ringo as he strolls along. The Huey is coming straight for him, already opening fire.
BRRRRRTTT   BRRTTTTTTT

Off: CLOSER- LITTLE BIT CLOSER-

2.
Tommy is squinting down the sights of his 203, butt tight to his shoulder, barrel leant on the rock for extra support. Natt looks past him.

Tommy: ALMOST-

Natt: TRUST THE FORCE, LUKE...

3.
Close. Tommy turns to look at Natt, crushing. Natt whistles innocently.

Natt: (musical note)

4.
Wide. Ringo stands still. The gunship is still blazing away, racing straight for him. Bullet trails kick up the dust, converging- their point of convergence is Ringo, and they'll reach it any second.
BRRRRTTTTT   BRRRRRRTTTTT

5.
Tommy fires a grenade. FOOOMMM

PAGE EIGHT

1.
The gunship's windscreen shattered and it blows itself apart in a firey detonation. The tail flies off aft of the cabin, a doorgunner is flung out in bits, the flexguns on one side separate, still firing.

2.
Ringo stands still as the whole mess crashes to earth in a fireball, not fifty yards from where he stands.

3.
Ringo turns and smiles over his shoulder at us, a hint of dark amusement on his face, lit by the fireball that rises amidst a pillar of smoke behind him.

Ringo: BRAVO.

4.
Hacken gapes. Tommy and Natt watch quietly, grimly, very impressed.

Natt: THAT DUDE GOT ICE WATER RUNNIN' IN HIS MUTHALOVIN' VEINS.

Above: *From* Hitman *#32. Courtesy of Garth Ennis.*

armed demon', but John takes that stuff and runs with it and gives you these crazy fucking visuals.

Do you collaborate with the artists on the ongoing story direction?

It's pretty much down to me in terms of how the story unfolds. I'll tell Johnny what's coming up because he wants to know, and if there's anything he objects to strenuously it will come out, although I can't remember any instances of that happening, simply because we are on the same wavelength and have the same sense of what's right for the book. I like to think that the ongoing evolution of the book is a more organic thing. When I'm telling him this stuff there are several times when he goes, 'Yeah, that's great, but what about if...?', and that'll take me down another pathway. He'll help me define ways to make the story better. One example of me providing him stuff is I know he likes drawing dinosaurs, probably because I love dinosaurs too, so pretty soon there are dinosaurs in *Hitman*. But I'm not going to ask Johnny to do something he doesn't want to do and he's gonna do things that I guess he knows I like. And that's what *Hitman* comes out of, that sense of mutual trust.

Is there much discussion with the artist once you've handed over your script?

Incredibly rarely, and then only if someone at DC has raised an objection to the material. I'll give you an example. In issue forty-five of *Preacher*, the Klan put a burning cross in the front yard of the sheriff's office and Jesse goes out and pisses on it. Axel, who always has one eye on this kind of thing, suggested that he might have to get Karen [Berger] to look at it. He pointed out that as the piss extinguishes the cross, once the fire goes out he's pissing on a symbol of the Church. When we became aware of that, Steve and I started to talk about how he might shoot that particular scene. Should we put a bit of smoke coming off the cross to indicate that it's still alight a little bit? Because, although in context the panel would make perfect sense, all it takes is some bastard to pull that one shot of a man pissing on a Christian symbol and stick it in the middle of a big article about the new deviancy in comics and we're fucked. As it turned out, it was okay*. Really, the only places we directly collaborate is when we're trying to pre-empt trouble, and that happens maybe once every six months.

While *Preacher* is creator-owned, *Hitman* is a part of the DC superhero Universe. How do you approach the latter?

Because superheroes are essentially for kids, if you're gonna have the kind of affection for them that lasts till adulthood you have to come to them young. I came to them as an adult and just thought, 'Come *on*!'. At the same time, I understand why people like them and I have a pretty good understanding of how each character works and appeals. So it's fun for me to take those characters and drop them into *Hitman*. Heroes who usually stand for very high-minded ideals come up against a bloke who's in it for the money, who wants the easy life and really doesn't want to fuck around with nonsense like this. Once he sees people like that, he'll take the piss, and I think that is probably my biggest single reaction to superheroes; it's a

---

* In the published version the cross was never shown fully extinguished until Jesse had 'zipped up'.

bloke in a bodystocking — take the piss. There are exceptions: Catwoman is a great character and Superman I treated with a lot more respect, because he's the original and an American icon.

I see *Hitman* as operating in a weird little corner of the DC Universe that occasionally the regular DC people infringe upon, but really it's just someplace the others will occasionally rub up against, and come away from not too sure what happened to them. Take a guy like Batman, a great superhero icon, and have Tommy throw up over him. Feature Green Lantern and just make an idiot out of him. Really, it's a question of having your cake and eating it. I get to play with these characters but I don't have to really give much away in return. I don't have to tie myself in tightly with this very involved superhero continuity that people who are into those books seem to think is so important.

Do you deliberately set out to shock? I'm thinking specifically about the *Hitman* story in which they club baby seals, albeit zombie baby seals, to death and the *Preacher* issue in which Starr is forced to wipe a cannibal's arse. Or is it simply a case of British toilet humour taken to extremes?

I think the latter. But rather than identifying a common theme running through all this, it's more a case of individual motivation for each of those scenes. For instance, that *Hitman* story came from visiting Seaworld with my then girlfriend. We were walking around the exhibits, having a great day out, and there was this one little enclosure where they were looking after these baby seals that they'd rescued from some oil slick, and they were the most adorable wee things on earth. It just popped into my head, 'What if they were zombies?', and from there came the whole idea of the aquarium. Then you just pop it into *Hitman* and it makes a kind of weird, fucked up sense. The business with Starr relates to a couple of things. One, we're doing an ongoing series of mutilations that Starr suffers because he's the bad guy and because he deserves it. And two, I like putting the boot in to Starr. He's humiliated beyond reason, the most powerful man on earth — which he more or less is, as he can instigate Armageddon just like that — having to wipe this guy's arse.

*　　　　*　　　　*

Check out:

IT WAS THE TIME
OF THE PREACHER

Whereas many writers have explored the theme of a man in search of God, few have presented it quite as literally as Garth Ennis in *Preacher*, his sprawling synthesis of road movie and Western. The Reverend Jesse Custer, a small-town Texas preacher losing his faith, is merged with a half–angel, half–demon hybrid and — accompanied by his gun-toting girlfriend, Tulip, and an Irish vampire, Cassidy — sets out to find God, who has abrogated his responsibilities. Against this broad and measured backdrop of a story, Ennis and artist Steve Dillon present an unflinching, unrelenting cocktail of violence, sexual deviancy and horror. Although always — and knowingly —offensive, *Preacher* is characterised mainly by its wonderfully fleshed out and absorbing characters, a deep vein of often hilarious black humour and dialogue so real it fairly leaps off the page. Lavished with praise and awards, the series is remarkable for its consistency, both in terms of Steve Dillon's cinematic visuals and Ennis's ability to shock and surprise on a regular, monthly basis.

How did *Preacher* come about? Many people have pointed to the demon/angel affair that appeared in *Hellblazer* as being the genesis of the story.

That was really just one of the many ideas that were drifting around and I suppose got caught in the net when I was looking for stuff to use in *Preacher*. The series came about because Steve Dillon and I needed something to do next after *Hellblazer*. We both agreed that it would be best to leave the book on a high note rather than drag things out and do the title a disservice by plugging away at it and taking the money month after month. We kind of bought ourselves enough brownie points on *Hellblazer* for [Vertigo] to trust us to do something of our own.

The basic idea was some kind of modern American Western, inspired by movies really; stuff like *Wild at Heart*, which was a big, big influence on *Preacher*. We also seized on the idea of America itself, which is such a fantastic backdrop and just so huge. I've travelled across it myself and I know how vast it is, I know how easy it must be to get lost out there. Whereas I think Britain, England, is a place where smaller things happen. Though ultimately if you're going to disappear, you're going to disappear.

Why did you fix upon the notion of a contemporary Western?

The idea of a Western was important to me because it allows you to have arche-typal characters: the hero, the girlfriend, the roguish sidekick, the comic relief, the villain who's a total, horrible shit. There's no point messing around with those. And, of course, the Saint of Killers himself is a direct representation of the Old West, and has kind of stepped out of those mythic times to reach the present. As soon as I came up with the title, I always kind of imagined I heard it in a Texas drawl, and that added to the Western quality of it all. I also wanted the thing to have a religious element, and the idea of a man hunting God, looking for God, came in at that point. That religion figured so heavily meant I could draw upon things that were relevant to both *Preacher* and *Hellblazer*, and one of those things was the demon/angel crossover.

How much of you is in the characters? Is Jesse the kind of person you'd like to be, and Cassidy a reflection of your flaws?

You're not far off there. Jesse's kind of an ideal. I wouldn't say he's a guy I aspire to be, because I'm realistic enough to know that's totally out of the question. But the idea of a guy who is so hard he can snap anyone in two who dares to fuck with him, even before he'd ever think about using his word of God, is certainly an attractive one. Also, he's a modern-day John Wayne, one who has an element of cynicism and realism about him, and I suppose has one eye on taking the easy way out if it comes to it, but will still struggle like hell to do the right thing. For Jesse, honour and loyalty are the most important words in the world. So that's an ideal for me.

Cassidy is a sort of a miserable failure, and the kind of guy I hope I'll never end up like. Just how bad Cassidy has become will become apparent as *Preacher* continues. Again that's one of the big themes of the book: the idea of redemption, of just how far into Hell can you go and still be worth saving. As a matter of fact, the character I always identify with the closest is Tommy Monaghan [from *Hitman*]. Forget about the superpowers, the incredible fucking reflexes, the gunplay and the fact that he's both a lazy fucking slob and pretty fucking brave, forget all that; I could just see myself getting into Tommy's little world quite well. Just sitting in the bar with your mates, bullshitting. It's not a hard existence to empathise with, and when I'm writing Tommy his reactions are never a problem. With Jesse, it's more like, 'What's the right thing to do here?', but most of the time with Tommy it's, 'What would *I* do here?', because Tommy's moral choices are rarely difficult ones to make. He's a very easy character to write.

How did you and Steve come up with the cast of *Preacher*?

That was somewhere where Steve very much made the running. I did write a little bit about what the characters would be like, and he would generally fit their looks to my description of their personality. Jesse is Steve. I always think of Jesse as an idealised version of Steve, although he denies it. I think if you saw a picture of both, you'd see it. For Tulip I suggested Anne Parillaud in *La Femme Nikita*, and I think he largely seized on that. For Cassidy I suggested that he be short and look like [singer] Shane MacGowan. Steve went for something a bit better looking than that, and I think it worked that he did, because you couldn't really imagine him having quite the same way with women. Starr is your archetypal movie bad guy, just a shit. He just looks like a fucking villain; he's bald for one thing, and he's got that eye. Arseface is based on one of those stupid bastards who shot himself after listening to music backwards. The Saint was a pretty interesting example, simply because that was a direct bit of collaboration. I said Clint Eastwood, specifically in his later movies, the long coat, the wide brimmed hat, the old Colt revolvers, but Steve preferred Lee Marvin, and that's why you've got this character who I always think moves, speaks and has all the mannerisms of Eastwood but has that kind of handsome ugliness that Lee Marvin had.

Jesse has John Wayne looking over his shoulder. Were you a fan too? Or is Clint Eastwood 'The Man' as far as you're concerned?

Pretty much. I remember being ten and seeing *A Fistful of Dollars* for the first time and being struck by how in control the guy is. With John Wayne, stuff happens to him and he reacts to it, whereas Clint always seems to be one step ahead. What he's good at is sizing up the situation and then reacting to it. As well as that it's just bloody enjoyable to watch him do what he does best. In *Where Eagles Dare*, for instance; the scene on the stairs where he's just machine-gunning hundreds of them. But as a little kid I can remember watching John Wayne films and really liking the character, particularly the older John Wayne figure in films like *True Grit*, *The Cowboys* and *The Shootist*.

There's an interesting dichotomy in *Preacher*; you treat America itself with great reverence but take the piss out of Americans. Did you ever wish you'd grown up there yourself?

Rather than wanting to have grown up there, I like the idea of coming to America, the classic immigrant experience of kind of joining the melting pot. One romantic dream of mine is to visit New York on an ocean liner so I can have the same experience as all those people must have had in the twenties and thirties; seeing all those skyscrapers rearing up on the horizon and swinging past the Statue of Liberty to whatever the future held. I do like the States very much, I respond very strongly to it as a romantic dream, while at the same time being under no illusion as to the reality of America and the harm it has done. But the dream, the romance of it, the idea of a country where ideals like liberty and freedom and justice are so much a part of the very documents that began the country. Of course, whether those things are acted on is another matter. The fact that there is a statue to Liberty herself in New York, that kind of provides a dream to live up to. Not really something we have in Britain.

Preacher has provoked controversy with its depiction of violence and its sexual content. How much further do you intend to push the envelope?

Contrary to popular belief I don't want *Preacher* to be just the vilest, most horrific fucking thing out there. There is a morality to the book and if we turned it into a total gorefest I think that would be lost. We're aware of just how far we can go, which I'm glad to say is not far behind as far as I wanna go anyway. They're very cagey about sex, particularly kinky or perverse sex, down to the way various positions are shot. There was a bit when Jesse had gone down on Tulip and she made some remark like, 'According to a magazine article I read, ninety per cent of American men won't do that', and Jesse replies, 'Ninety per cent of American men are dumb as posts'. We wrote that, it got published and I thought no more about it. Then a week later in the DC office some of the non-Vertigo editors were coming up to Axel saying, 'I can't believe you got away with that', and it slowly dawned on him they were talking about the 'ninety per cent of American men' line. They couldn't believe we'd been able to put that in. I just thought it was a good gag, a good one-liner. You can't get anywhere near hardcore pornography, but that's okay, I don't want to anyway. Sex is not a big part of what *Preacher*'s about. I guess I would like a bit more freedom to stick my foot into the Church, frankly. The business with the cross [see page 87], and any kind of image of crucifixion, is something they're incredibly wary of. But that's okay, there's always ways around it.

I'm told that one of the senior guys at DC didn't read *Preacher* until the seventeenth issue, and when he did he got a big shock. He got the seventeen issues, took them home, read them all at once, and had a few incisive comments to make the next day, one of which was that if he'd been aware of the chicken fucking scene in issue eight there's no way it would have got through. I'm really glad that didn't happen, 'cause I would have been well pissed. We all understand that a certain amount of give and take is necessary, but there are things that I would be prepared to put my foot down and quit over, things that Steve and I had agreed we will not allow to happen to the book. It's a case-by-case thing, we don't have a definite line, but if they come back and say to me you definitely can't have something, and Steve and I have agreed that it's important or we definitely want it to be in there, then we'll quit and fuck 'em. We'll just walk away. So far that hasn't proven necessary, and fingers crossed it never will.

NEIL GAIMAN

Infused with mythology and magic, horror and humour, Neil Gaiman's epic *Sandman* saga elevated comics to a literary art form. The sprawling, wildly ambitious tale of Morpheus, Lord of Dreams, *Sandman* presented an intense, intellectual alternative to the more typical comics vision of caped superheroes duking it out with masked supervillains above city streets, and helped find the medium a place on bookshelves alongside more conventional fantasy fiction. People who hadn't previously looked at a comic found themselves inexorably drawn into the world of Dream and his extended family, The Endless, and the series received serious and positive critical evaluation from academics, mainstream publications and literary giants alike. Witty, barbed, sly and superbly spun, the *Sandman* stories, together with Gaiman's other work — including *The Books of Magic* and his many collaborations with the artist Dave McKean: *Violent Cases, Mr Punch, Black Orchid, Signal to Noise* — revealed the former journalist to be a sublime storyteller on a par with Angela Carter and Clive Barker. While the Hampshire-born, Minnesota-based Gaiman has, of late, made the transition into other forms of writing — novels, movie scripts and the television show *Neverwhere* — his influence on the comics medium remains undeniable and still reverberates today.

You were a journalist and short story writer before you began working in the comics industry. Why the change of tack?

I was a journalist to make money and short stories were something that I did on the side. If I sold one, I was happy. Journalism did teach me a great deal, though: how to write to deadline and, more importantly, a certain economy of words. In an average comics speech balloon you need to be able to capture a whole personality and/or indicate vocal patterns in maybe a dozen words. From that point of view, it was tremendously helpful, but I never wanted to be a journalist. I wanted to write comics.

Had you harboured such ambitions from an early age?

As a kid, one of the biggest mysteries to me was how you wrote comics. But I knew they were written by someone, and I knew that was what I wanted to be. When I was fourteen or fifteen my literary heroes were Roger Zelazny, Samuel R. Delany and Harlan Ellison, but also comics writers like Len Wein — I was a fan of his *Swamp Thing* and *Phantom Stranger* stuff — and Archie Goodwin. And at the top of my list was Will Eisner. I remember at school in Croydon, an outside careers advisor came in to discuss what we wanted to do, and I said, 'I want to write American comics'. I might have well said, 'I want to be an astronaut'. In fact, if I had, he probably would have had some kind of idea of how to reply. This was obviously something that no one had ever said to him before, and eventually he said, 'How do you go about doing that then?'. And I said, 'I have no idea, you tell me'.

Many of today's comics writers grew up reading the characters they've subsequently gone on to write. What kind of comics were you interested in as a child?

If I list my favourite comics you can begin to triangulate the genesis of *Sandman* somewhere in there. They were the Len Wein/Bernie Wrightson *Swamp Thing* issues, *The Phantom Stranger*, and maybe Jack Kirby's original run of *The Demon*. Plus all of the old DC *Witching Hour, House of Mystery, House of Secrets...* though these also kind of disappointed me, because I felt there was some wonderful potential there. Also, Barry Smith's *Conan* and Eisner's *The Spirit*. The superhero stuff I enjoyed but even as a little kid it felt kind of fundamentally pointless, in that if it's a hero versus a villain I know who's going to win. I figured that out early on. I liked *The Brave and the Bold*, where they'd team

---

Place of birth:
Porchester, Hants, UK
Date of birth:
10 November 1960
Home base:
Minneapolis, Minnesota, USA
First published work:
'Future Shocks' in *2000 AD*
Education:
Ardingly, Whitgift
Career highlights:
*Black Orchid, The Books of
Magic, Mr Punch, The Sandman,
Signal to Noise, Stardust,
Violent Cases*

Batman up with someone unlikely. They'd be weird, and that was definitely the stuff I liked. It was all well written and all a little odd. Mostly it was about storytelling, it wasn't about the costumes.

When did you finally crack the mystery of how to write a comics script?

If I'd had any idea exactly how to sit down and write a comic script I might well have started writing them at fifteen or younger. That was how they finally talked me into printing the script to *Sandman* #17 in [the graphic novel collection] *Dream Country*. On the one hand, I didn't like the idea of taking people backstage and showing them how it was done, but on the other I thought, 'What if there's the equivalent of a fifteen year-old Neil out there going, "How do you do this?"'. In the end I learned because Alan Moore showed me. We met at a convention, and after we'd been friends for a while I said, 'I've always wanted to know how you write a comic script', and he just pulled out a piece of paper from a notebook of mine and said, 'Well, I start with page one, panel one and put everything in it that you could possibility want an artist to know'. He basically went on to show me how it was all done and I went home and wrote a short comic story. I sent it off to Alan, who said it had some problems but it also had potential. Then I wrote another one and he said it was good, that he'd be pleased to have written it himself. Then I more or less left it for a couple of years until fate plunged me back into the wacky world of writing comics.

So how did the big break come?

I was sick of journalism and I ran into a man in a pub, a friend of a friend, who asked me what I did. I said, 'I'm a journalist, what do you do?', and he replied, 'I write comics'. I expressed my own interest in comics and he called a couple of days later. He was working on a new comic and was interested in working with fresh young talent. It never came out, and the reason the guy was interested in working with fresh young talent was because nobody who had been around the block would work with him. But through it I met Dave McKean, who was a young art student, and we were introduced to Paul Gravett from *Escape*. He liked what I was writing and what Dave was drawing and asked us if we were interested in doing a five-page strip for him. It is much to Paul's credit that when we went to see him a week later and said, 'Would you mind terribly if instead we did a forty-eight page graphic novel called *Violent Cases*?', he thought about it for a minute and said sure. That's how I wound up working with Dave, which was easily the most important thing that ever happened to me.

Didn't you also do some work for *2000 AD*?

I did about five 'Future Shocks' and was not impressed. One time I got saddled with a Spanish artist who didn't speak any English, and had obviously had some kind of rough translation of the script placed in front of him, and he hadn't quite drawn it as written. And then the people in the *2000 AD* office went back over it and rewrote what I'd written to try and make it match what the guy had actually drawn. And then they took out all the jokes.

Page 8 panel 1

THIS IS OPPOSITE AN AD PAGE. OKAY. NOW, FOR THE FIRST TIME
WE SLIDE OUT OF REAL-TIME AND INTO AN ALMOST MONTAGE
MODE. OVER THE NEXT FEW PAGES WE'RE GOING TO COVER A FEW
YEARS IN REAL TIME. WE'RE ALSO OPENING UP HERE, SO THE
FEELING OF CLAUSTROPHOBIA, WE SHOULD HAVE GOT FROM THE
LAST FEW PAGES, SINCE WE ENTERED FRY'S HOUSE, SHOULD BE
RELIEVED. WHITE PANEL BORDERS HERE AGAIN, FOR THE FIRST
TIME SINCE PAGE 4. WE'RE LOOKING AT THE TOP, ATTIC ROOM OF
A HOUSE -- MADOC'S HOUSE, -- FROM OUTSIDE. WE CAN SEE THE
BRICKWORK, AND A WINDOW, BARRED WITH A METAL GRILLE.
THROUGH THE WINDOW WE CAN SEE, ON THE INSIDE, CALLIOPE,
LOOKING AT US SILENTLY. SHE'S NAKED AGAIN, BUT WE CAN
PROBABLY ONLY SEE HER HEAD AND BARE SHOULDERS, AND THE
SIDE OF HER ARMS.

Caption:And Madoc took Calliope back to his home, and locked her in
the topmost room, which he had prepared for her. *WHITE INK ON BLACK FOR FIGURE of CALLIOPE*

I changed "bare wooden floor" to "musty old camp-bed" when I saw the art-work.

Page 8 panel 2

NOW I WANT TO TRY TO GET ACROSS THE RAPE, AND THE ~~HORROR~~ *obvious reasons)*
AND THE DOMINANCE, FAIRLY SUBTLY, DOING ALL THE WORK IN
THE READER'S HEAD. THE WHOLE THING SHOULD BE REALLY
UNDERSTATED. WHAT WE'RE ACTUALLY LOOKING AT IN THIS PAGE
ARE BARE WOODEN FLOORBOARDS. AND COMING IN FROM THE
RIGHT, WE CAN SEE CALLIOPE'S LEFT ARM AND HAND, PALM
UPWARD, LAYING FLAT ON THE FLOOR. COMING DOWN FROM
ABOVE IS RICK'S RIGHT ARM; HIS HAND IS CLAMPED AROUND HER
WRIST, HOLDING IT DOWN TO THE GROUND. THAT'S ALL WE CAN
SEE.

Caption:His first action was to rape her, nervously, on the ~~bare wooden floor.~~ musty old camp-bed.

Caption:She's not even human, he told himself. She's thousands of
years old. But her flesh was warm, and her breath was sweet, and
she choked back tears like a child whenever he hurt her. *I sent Kelley some photos I took of my*

Page 8 panel 3

WE ARE NOW DOWN IN HIS STUDY, FROM PAGE ONE, AND HE'S *space, to give*
SITTING DOWN IN THE CHAIR NEXT TO HIS WORD-PROCESSOR, *an idea of the*
SMOKING A CIGARETTE. HE LOOKS VERY PLEASED WITH HIMSELF, *place I*
SMILING A LAZY SMILE, HIS FEET UP ON THE DESK. THE SMOKE *had in mind. He*
FROM THE CIGARETTE DRIFTS UPWARD. HE'S NOW BAREFOOT, AND
JUST WEARING JEANS AND A SINGLET.

reproduced it

Caption:It occurred to him momentarily that the old man might have *amazingly accurately.*
cheated him: given him a real girl. That he, Rick Madoc, might
possibly have done something wrong, even criminal... *[Although he left out*

Caption:But afterwards, relaxing in his study, something shifted *Groucho Marx*
inside his head. *statue.]*

Above: *Script extract from* Sandman *#17. Courtesy of Neil Gaiman.*

Not long after that you made the move to American comics with DC's *Black Orchid* **and** *The Sandman*. **How did that come about?**

[DC editors] Dick Giordano, Karen Berger and Jenette Kahn came to London on a talent scouting expedition, the one on which they recruited Grant Morrison and Pete Milligan. Dave and I walked in and pitched a Phantom Stranger idea, and they said no. I got desperate, picking forgotten characters, but somebody was doing everybody, it seemed. Finally I said Black Orchid, and Karen Berger looked up and said, 'Black Hawk Kid, who's he?'. And I thought, 'Yes, I've got one they don't know'. We did an issue of *Black Orchid* and the people at DC really liked it. But then I got a phone call from Karen, who said they were worried because they'd got two people nobody had ever heard of working on a character that nobody had ever heard of, and a female character at that. So she said, 'What we're gonna do is put Dave on this Batman book that Grant [Morrison] is writing and give you a monthly comic. That way we will raise your profile, so by the time we release *Black Orchid* people will know who you are'. And that was why, at the end of the day, Dave got to do *Arkham Asylum* and I got to do *Sandman*. Six months earlier I had mentioned to Karen and Jenette that I was thinking of reviving the seventies Sandman, the Joe Simon one, because I loved the idea of someone who lived in people's dreams, and Karen suggested I go ahead and do it. Then the next day she phoned up and told me, 'Roy Thomas has already revived that character for *Infinity Inc.*, so can you make up a new Sandman? Just keep the name and go have fun'.

Do you consider what you write to be literature, as opposed to just comics?

I would hope so. The lovely thing about comics, because it's words and pictures together, is that people come to them from different traditions: from the written word, from films and from comics. What I was interested in most of all was words, because they were the one thing that I had complete control over as a writer. I sometimes worry, looking at some of the comics that are now on the stands, that I may have done some bad things there. I see comics that are desperately overwritten, where you never get a silent panel and everything is captioned almost to the point of redundancy. They'll show something in the panel and then there will be a long caption explaining it in florid, sub-literary terms. That may be my fault, and if so I'm really sorry. It certainly wasn't anything I set out to do.

I came from a very booky tradition. I love words and the things you can do with words. And it always seemed to me that, with the exception of a very few writers like Alan Moore and Will Eisner, words always seemed to come in second in comics. I wanted to get them up there so they could come in at least equal. And it was interesting to see some of the things you could do if you decided to break the rules and just play. Like in *Season of Mists*, in the opening chapter, just to stop and do these little pen descriptions of each member of The Endless. That was enormous fun and worked terribly well.

The thing about *Sandman* was at the end of the day my intended audience was me. I remember the thrill of discovering Alan Moore's *Swamp Thing*. There I was, twenty-four or twenty-five, and every month I'd go down to my comic store and get the new *Swamp Thing* and it was wonderful. It was a great feeling to be twenty-five and have somebody writing a comic for you, something that was as well written as anything you were going to find in the prose section or the poetry section or the play section of a bookstore. So what I wanted to do with *Sandman* was write a comic with me as the target audience; the kind of thing that if I wasn't writing it, I'd like to go down and read every month.

Your work has always been steeped in mythology, magic and fairy tales. Are these particular obsessions of yours?

Oh yeah. You can probably write about something you're not interested in, but not with any level of conviction. It's like writing *Star Trek* books, you have to care or at least be interested in those characters or else the magic isn't going to be there and the readers are going to know. There was a science fiction fan and occasional writer whose real name I've forgotten, but who wrote under the pen name of David McDaniel*. He wrote two, maybe three *The Man From U.N.C.L.E.* books. There were dozens of these books that came out during the sixties and early seventies, but the only ones that anyone who has ever read them remembers are titles like *The Vampire Affair* and *The Dagger Affair*, which were written by David McDaniel. They were the only ones where the author obviously cared about adding to the mythology and was having this wonderful time with it. I think that's true with more or less anything; you follow your obsessions.

Sandmen

Over the years, there have been three distinct DC characters to bear the name Sandman, with most of the connect-the-dots continuity filled in retroactively. The first Sandman was Wesley Dodds, a crimefighter who débuted in *Adventure Comics* #40 (1939). Dressed in a gas mask, a purple opera cape and a snap-brimmed fedora, his trademark was to sprinkle sand over each defeated villain to let the underworld know that 'the Sandman was watching'. After a stint in the forties superhero team The Justice Society, Dodds was given a spandex makeover and a sidekick, Sandy the Golden Boy (!), and began battling more fantastical menaces. In the seventies, a completely new Sandman was introduced, courtesy of Joe Simon and Jack Kirby. This new, also spandex-clad Sandman supervised the dreams and nightmares of children from his headquarters, the Dream Dome, located in the Dream Stream. Taxing stuff it was not. Much later, this second Sandman was given an origin and an identity (that of Doctor Garret Sandford, an UCLA sleep researcher), which Gaiman neatly debunked in the third incarnation of the character, revealing Sandford and his successor, Hector Hall, to be creations of two of the Dream King's rogue subjects.

---

* *Bizarrely, David McDaniel was the author's real name. He used his pseudonym, 'Ted Johnstone', in real life.*

So are you incredibly well read or do you tend to make stuff up?

There are areas where you know your shit and there are areas where you fake it. The art of writing is the same as the art of convincing a teacher that you really did do your homework or you studied something that you didn't. It's the art of lying convincingly and it's amazing how much you can learn from a little. Having said that, it's also huge quantities of stuff that one simply knows. If you are a writer, you tend to have sort of a magpie head. You store away all sorts of weird and wonderful trivia, which pops out when you need it. A lot of the mythology stuff, maybe ninety-five per cent of it, I know fairly well and I'm interested in. And then there's stuff that you'll read for pleasure. I remember this book called *Funeral Customs Around the World.* It was wonderful. I kind of picked it up on a whim and started reading and got completely fascinated by the different ways different cultures — based on different environments — have of disposing of unwanted corpses. There are cultures in which you can't bury them, so what do you do? Sometimes you drop them in a river, to be eaten by crocodiles. In Tibet, where they don't have any wood to burn them with, and don't have any rivers to throw them in, and the ground is too hard and rocky to bury them, they wind up grinding them up and feeding them to the birds mixed with a little corn as a way of getting rid of them. It's called sky burial. I remember reading that and going, 'that's an issue of *Sandman*', and doing my funeral issue set in a necropolis, with this huge graveyard and all the different burial methods get demonstrated and discussed, just because I thought that was so cool.

I also think that if you're writing magic, anything that sounds right is right, or it may as well be. In fact, I figure that on the whole you're better making it up convincingly than going out and researching it, because I always find the real magic that you research is always so unconvincing. I also remember very early on in *Sandman*, I put in some genuine Enochian magic words, really just to spice things up, and a number of times over the following couple of years I was taken aside by people who needed to know where I had been initiated and how dare I betray the profound secrets of the Order by using words that are not to be written down.

How much of you is in the character of the Sandman?

They're all me. The mistake that people tend to make with any of this stuff is, 'Is this character you and the rest of them not you?'. No, no, no — when you think that way you've lost it. Is the Sandman me? Yeah, he's kind of me-ish. He doesn't have a sense of humour, which I think I do, and he's thinner and taller and much, much older. But I gave him my dress sense just because it made it easier for me to write him as a more sympathetic character. But Death is me too, and Delirium, and Merv Pumpkinhead. In fact, Merv very often wound up being almost the voice of the author. Writing *Sandman* I'd get to the point, looking at a certain character, where I would go, 'I can't believe you're doing this. Come on!', and that's normally the point I would bring Merv on and have Merv say, 'I can't believe you're doing this. Come on!'. The way you make up characters — for me at least — is you very rarely go and find them outside. Normally you take a little bit of you, even with the bad characters — the Corinthian, say — and you go and find that side of you in them. And if you find it with any conviction, you'll be writing something that will convince.

So how much of your life have you documented within the pages of *Sandman*?

A lot of it is not exactly one-to-one correspondences. But things would happen and I would put them in the comic, but I would put them in the comic probably in a form that only I would ever recognise. If there is a code, it's private and normally they become starting-off points for things.

Yet that's you narrating *Violent Cases*, isn't it?

Definitely, but that was Dave McKean's idea. I wrote the story and I remember Dave saying, 'I think I'm going to make you the narrator'. At the time I was very kind of, 'hang on, but then people will think this is true', and he said, 'oh shut up, I don't have anyone else as a model so it may as well be you'. And I said okay. It's kind of cool and a lot of the memories in *Violent Cases* are mine anyway. Just as a lot of the memories in *Mr Punch* are mine. Those books are very unreliable works of autobiography.

I remember an interview in which you said that in a comic the writer is the director and the screenwriter, while the artist is the cameraman. Does that still hold?

Yep, and in Dave McKean's case it's normally a lot more than that. I'll write scripts for Dave that I don't write for anyone else in terms of their looseness. Very

---

Dave McKean

It is somehow insufficient to describe Dave McKean as a comic book artist. Even back in the days of *Violent Cases*, and despite, by his own admission, being influenced by the work of Bill Sienkiewicz (artist on *Moon Knight* and *Elektra: Assassin*), there is more 'artist' than 'comic book' in his work. Certainly McKean's output since then has never fallen easily into categories. There is *Arkham Asylum*, a very uncommon graphic novel written by Grant Morrison, CD covers for the likes of Tori Amos and Michael Nyman, launch images for Sony Playstation and Kodak, a comic book adaptation of the Rolling Stones album *Voodoo Lounge*, and every single *Sandman* cover (including collections, reprints and one-offs). It was the *Sandman* covers that revealed the true artistic depth of McKean's work; combining painted artwork with models, sculpture, computer-generated images and photography, often using whatever bric-a-brac and ephemera were to hand at the time (a spider stuck to a piece of sticky tape, where it remained and ossified, adorns *Sandman* #15's cover). McKean's work is quite literally of gallery status, and he has exhibited to great acclaim. A collection of McKean's *Sandman* work can be found in *The Sandman Dustcovers*.

often with Dave I'll just give him the words and occasional little stage directions. With anyone else I'm going to be very, very precise. I'm going to tell them exactly what I want and hope they can basically get something out of my head and onto the paper. I look at Dave's work and as far as I'm concerned he has a better storytelling sense than I do. In fact, he has a better storytelling sense than pretty much anyone I've ever met. So I tend to give him very much a free rein.

Normally if we're doing something, we've probably been talking about it for six months to a year first. *Signal to Noise* was slightly less than that, just because it leapt out at us. With *Mr Punch*, we'd been talking for two years about doing this book, gathering reference material together. So when I finally wrote it — and *Mr Punch* went through three very solid drafts — there was a level where I felt all I had to worry about was the words and the story. I knew that the pictures would take care of themselves, that was all Dave. I knew the kinds of things he would be doing with puppets, with photos and with art, but I didn't dictate and I don't think I even suggested. When I came to write it, I simply sat down and wrote the words.

Have you ever had a situation with an artist where you've had to ask them to do something again? Or do you trust the artists you've collaborated with?

I trust my scripting and writing skills enough. I know my storytelling skills are not the greatest in the world. On the other hand, I also know that what I suggest will work, so what I always say at the beginning of any script when working with a new artist is, 'look, I'm the writer here, you are the artist, if you can see a better way of doing it then do it that way. Not a different way, but if you can see a better way, then do it that way'.

Do you think working that way gives an artist enough leeway?

Well it depends. It depends on the artist and what I'm doing. On *Sandman*, with a very few exceptions, I didn't want to give people leeway. I wanted to make sure they got it right. I feel when you're telling an artist, 'Do this', or, 'This will work', what you want is for them to do that and for that to work. And mostly it does. When you give an artist leeway, unless you trust them implicitly and know what you're going to get, you can very often wind up with something that bears no relation to what you did. I've heard too many horror stories from too many friends of mine who write comics, where what actually came out bore no resemblance to anything that was in the script and then they had to desperately try and cover it over by rewriting.

So is there ever any interaction between you and the artist?

Oh sure. For a start I won't write a script unless I know who's drawing it, and then I'll want to talk to them. Sometimes you really hit it off with an artist as friends, sometimes you don't. Working with Bryan Talbot was wonderful, because Bryan would always fax me stuff as he was doing it and very often what he was drawing would find its way immediately back into whatever I was writing. I've never been able to understand how writers can write scripts not knowing who's going to draw it, because you write *for* the artist. The most important thing to know about that *Dream Country* script is, at the end of the day, it's a letter to Kelley Jones, telling him what to draw and how to do it. But if you compare the script and the finished comic you'll also find places where he went off on his own and did something that wasn't what was suggested.

Stylistically, you're closer to Alan Moore, who also describes in detail what he wants in a script, than, say, Garth Ennis, who favours the stripped-down approach. Do you agree?

I suppose. Philosophically I think the place I'm coming from is closer to where Alan is coming from but also to some extent closer to where Grant Morrison is coming from. An Alan script for a twenty-four page comic will probably be about eighty pages long. A Grant script for a twenty-four page comic is normally twenty-four pages long. With me, a script for a twenty-four page comic would normally come in at about forty-eight pages, maybe 10,000 words. I think part of it was influenced by Alan, yes, but I think mostly it was wanting to be able to call the shots. If I say, 'Dredd comes in room', I want to know what kind of room, what kind of angle is he coming in at, is this important, and what else do we need to know? Very often with artists I've been working a long time with, or I trust and who have obviously got it, I may well be giving them panel descriptions that are no longer than, 'Dredd comes in room'. With an artist I don't know or haven't worked with before, you'll get much, much longer panel descriptions because I'm trying to cover all the bases.

What was fun with *Sandman*, though, was that if it was anything, it was a kindly dictatorship. In that it was my story, dammit, these were my people and the artists were playing in my sandbox. I was also trying to work it in such a way so everybody had the most fun, and make sure the artist had a cool experience they could look back on. But at the end of the day I wanted it to be my thing. This was not a 'plays well with others' kind of thing. No. You're playing my game, you have to play according to my rules.

Do you think that's why, despite the fact you had many different artists working on *Sandman*, with differing styles, it still feels like a coherent whole?

I think so. The storytelling, the panel-to-panel storytelling, is mine all the way through. It's the way I tell stories. There are only two episodes in the whole of *Sandman* where I didn't do them full script. One of which was 'Ramadan' in *Sandman* #50. Because I wanted to get that 'Arabian Nights' effect I wrote the first half of the thing as prose, because I wanted to get that sweep. I thought I'd go back in and break it down into panels later, and when the time came I phoned [P.] Craig Russell and said, 'Craig, what kind of panels do you like? Big ones? Little ones? How many panels do you like putting on a page? What are you comfortable with?', the kind of stuff I normally ask an artist. I always like to ask an artist first what they like drawing, which very often nobody's ever asked them, but which can make an enormous amount of difference to the story. They can say, 'I always wanted to do a blah', and you go, 'That's a great idea for a story'. In Craig's case, he answered, 'What have you written so far?', and I read it to him and he said, 'Let me do this, please, just give me the story as is and let me do it'. And that's how we did it. I had read Craig's adaptations of Rudyard Kipling and operas in the past, so I knew he'd do a wonderful job. The other time was with John J. Muth, who did the penultimate *Sandman*, which I wrote more or less as a poem. I just wanted to see what he'd do with it.

How long does it take you to write a script?

When I started writing it was about a week and a half to two weeks at the most. Occasionally I'd get lucky and write one in a weekend, even at the length my scripts run to. Then, as I went on with *Sandman*, it got harder, mainly because there was so much that I'd done before. I'd go, 'Okay, I've done that panel transition already, I've done that scene, so think of another way of doing that'. When you're starting out there's a huge gulf between one panel and the next. How do you get from this panel to that panel? There comes a point where it stops being very hard and becomes very easy for a little while. Then, for me, it started getting hard again because I really don't like repeating myself. If there's anything that characterises me as a writer, it's probably that. By the time an audience turns up I've already gone and decided to do something completely different. In the beginning I could write a *Sandman* script a month and have half a month left over to do other things in. And by the end of it I was taking eight weeks to write a twenty-four page script. The last two *Sandman* arcs, *The Kindly Ones* and *The Wake*, took ages to write, and the book only maintained a vague semblance of schedule because I started *The Wake* while I was still writing *The Kindly Ones*, in order for [artist] Michael Zulli to get a head start. Even then it must have taken two years to bring out the last thirteen or fourteen issues.

I remember being told off by one writer who writes a comic in a day. We were talking and I was saying, 'I've just finished this last *Sandman*, and it took me about three weeks to write', and this person looked at me and said. 'I bash them out in a day. How can you afford to do it?'. Because at the time we were only making $1,500 to $2,000 a script. On the other hand, the ten volumes of *Sandman* are still in print, and they still sell more than anything else does. We've done roughly a million of them in the US alone and well over a quarter of a million in the UK, and over the years they've paid me back for the amount of effort I put into them. There was no guarantee that they would in the beginning, it was just how I felt they had to be done. Looking back, I'm not sure why I was doing it. I definitely wasn't doing it for the money. It was partly the fun, the joy of creating art, and a lot of it with *Sandman* was just the joy of doing something I didn't feel anyone had done before, which is not something that you get very often in any field of art or literature.

Is it true you make a mini version of a comic before you begin writing?

I take twelve pieces of paper and fold them over so you have the cover, and everything including the ads. I'd irritate DC because I'd always want to know where the ads were going to be placed. They hated that, but it's kind of useful for knowing where to put double-page spreads. I'd draw a little cover for it and then turn it over and on the back page I'd write the numbers one to twenty-four. I'd jot down the high points; the things that I knew were definitely going to have to happen at some stage, roughly where they were going to happen, and more or less on what page. Then I'd probably draw page one for myself and sometimes I'd draw and write as I went along. Sometimes I'd draw the whole thing and then I'd write it. Often I'd know I had four pages of conversation and I'd just note 'page of conversation here'. I'd use the little booklet almost as a problem-solving device. If I was stuck, I would just sit and draw something. If it got to the point where I couldn't figure out a way to make the story seem interesting, I'd go in there and just draw it. It would also stop me doing silly and irritating things which I would occasionally do when I was writing on the road, like accidentally writing a twenty-five page comic without noticing and then have to try and talk everyone into letting me have my twenty-five page comic and only do twenty-three pages in the following issue, which occurs at one point in *A Game of You.*

I understand that you listen to music when you write, and that issue three of *Black Orchid* was heavily influenced by Frank Sinatra. Was that the case with *Sandman* as well?

Very definitely, and very often I'd have to figure out what the right music was. The worst time was during one of the 'going to hell' episodes where I just had Lou Reed's *Metal Machine Music* on in the background and kept it there for three days while writing. Not something I recommend for anybody's health. Lots of

Stardust

One of the 'obsessions' that can be traced through Neil Gaiman's work is the realm of Faerie, a magical domain inhabited by all manner of elves, sprites and other mythical creatures. Owing a debt to William Shakespeare's *A Midsummer Night's Dream* (indeed, *Sandman* #19 features an award-winning presentation of that play by Gaiman and artist Charles Vess) for its cast (Auberon, Titania et al), Faerie features heavily in the *Sandman* series, *The Books of Magic* (the first volume of which was written by Gaiman, with the Faerie section again drawn by Vess) and most recently in *Stardust.* The tale of a union between a mortal and a princess of Faerie, *Stardust* was notable for its mix of elegant prose and illustrations (by Vess), as opposed to being a straightforward comic strip, and perhaps forms the bridge between Gaiman's comic and literary goals. Indeed, *Stardust* the novel (minus illustrations and with revised, embellished text) appeared soon after. But while Gaiman may have moved on, his career as a writer of 'serious' fiction blossoming, the legacy of his comics work continues in titles such as *The Dreaming, The Sandman Presents, The Books of Magic* and *The Books of Faerie.*

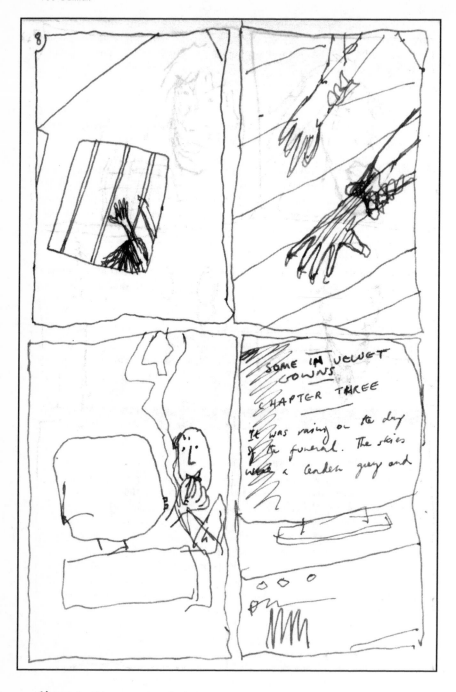

Above: *Detail from page eight of Neil Gaiman's mini-version of* Sandman #17. *Courtesy of Neil Gaiman.*

Above: Sandman *thumbnails by Neil Gaiman. Courtesy of Neil Gaiman.*

Sandman was written to Iggy Pop and Talking Heads. I like having appropriate music. When I was writing *Stardust*, which is not actually a comic, I wound up loading the CD player up with English folk music, which I don't normally listen to, but seemed completely right for the mood. It's the magic of mood and you want to be in the right kind of place and have the right kind of stuff. It's one of the reasons why, when I'm writing a lot of fiction, I don't read fiction. Instead I read non-fiction, because you want to keep your palate clear. If I'm reading an author you'll find them in what I'm writing, the flavour of them. It's like milk in a fridge takes on the flavour of whatever it's sitting next to. I'd also choose music that will keep me sitting there, because when you're writing the easiest thing in the world is to stop writing and find an excuse to go and do something else instead. I remember the joy when random play came into my life, because there were all these albums that I couldn't play any more because as each track finished I'd start humming the beginning to the next one.

You've written a number of screenplays for both television and film. Was comics a good training ground?

Probably. It's definitely harder writing a comic script than writing a movie or a television script, because in those there are decisions that will be taken by the director, the cameraman or the editor that you don't have to worry about as a writer. Say you have a scene where somebody rings a doorbell and your guy gets up and answers the door. If you're writing that in a movie script you say, 'The doorbell rings, Joe gets up and answers the door'. In a comic you say to yourself, 'I have two panels to do this door answering scene, so how I am going to do it?'. You have to decide essentially where you are going to shoot it from; are you going to shoot it from outside? Are you going to have a shot of him walking down the corridor? Is the door going to open from outside? Are you going to cheat and have a very small panel of a finger pushing a bell and the door opening? These are problems you're going to have to solve while you're writing a comic. Having said that, I get very puzzled watching people move or fail to move from one medium to another. It seems to me so natural that anybody who writes comics could also write novels, television or movies. And yet one watches famous novelists coming to write comics and running badly aground, and comics people are likewise going off, trying another medium and making an unholy mess of it.

Do you still see a future for yourself in comics?

With comics right now I'll do occasional little things if somebody waves an artist at me that I've always wanted to work with. I did this little Vertigo story because Jeff Jones wanted to do his first comic in twenty-five years. I loved the idea and I didn't even care if it was any good or not. I will probably go back one day and write some more, but the thing is, I feel now like I've written a few good comics — *Mr Punch*, maybe three or four issues of *Sandman* I was fairly satisfied with — whereas I feel there's lots of things out there that I haven't done to my satisfaction. I haven't yet made a movie I'm pleased with. I haven't made a television series I'm happy with. It's quite possible in five or ten years' time I'll do some stuff that has to be comics, and I'll come back and spend a few years just doing more comics. But I did comics because I loved them and I stopped because I felt it was right to leave while I was still in love. I never got to the point where I had to get up in the morning, stare into the mirror gloomily and go, 'Oh God, I've got to write a comic today'. I'm pleased, proud and slightly baffled that comics seemed to have brought me a modicum of fame and a modicum of fortune, but I didn't go into it to do that, because when I started writing nobody got famous and rich from writing comics. Do it because you love the medium. Do it because there's stuff to be said. Do it because it's fun.

*   *   *

Check out:

The Sandman: Preludes & Nocturnes
The Sandman: The Doll's House
The Sandman: Dream Country
The Sandman: Season of Mists
The Sandman: A Game of You
The Sandman: Fables & Reflections
The Sandman: Brief Lives
The Sandman: Worlds' End
The Sandman: The Kindly Ones
The Sandman: The Wake
(collects *Sandman* #1–75 and *Sandman Special* #1)

Black Orchid
The Books of Magic
Death: The High Cost of Living
Death: The Time of Your Life
Mr Punch
Signal to Noise
Stardust
Violent Cases

DEVIN GRAYSON

In the space of a few short years Devin Grayson has established herself as a leading light in comics' next generation of influential young writers. What makes the San Franciscan's lofty position even more amazing is that until her early twenties Grayson had scarcely even picked up a comic book, save for a copy of *Archie* when she was nine. Her sudden and life-changing interest in the medium kicked off when she happened across an episode from the first season of *Batman: The Animated Series* while channel-surfing. So immediately enamoured of the characters and their interaction was she, a love affair with comics began that is still ongoing. Following that chance encounter, Grayson undertook a crash course in comic book education, reading back issues voraciously and immersing herself in both the culture and mechanics of the business. She initiated a dialogue with several editors at DC Comics that, after two years of correspondence, finally earned her a story in *The Batman Chronicles #7*. Grayson's gift for rich characterisation and perceptive dialogue landed her a number of high-profile monthly assignments — including *Catwoman*, *The Titans* and the new Marvel Knights makeover of *Black Widow*, cementing her position in the comic book lexicon.

What was it about that episode of *Batman: The Animated Series* that proved to be so revelatory and appealing to you?

There was this relationship happening between the Batman character and the Robin character that was very resonant for me. It reminded me of a lot of parent-child relationships where there was this sort of incredibly competent but very workaholic and distant father figure and this very loyal, eager-to-please and somewhat rebellious younger person. I felt like I knew the relationship, but I didn't yet know the characters. In order to understand Batman and Robin I had to chase them back through their own medium, which led me to a friend who worked in a comic store, and suddenly this whole new world opened up. And it struck me that Robin really *belonged* to the comics medium, more so even than to the animated series or the movies, and it seemed like the appropriate place to get to know them both better.

I was working on a novel at the time, and I really lucked out. The friend, Arnold, who was working in a comic store in San Francisco, gave me just the best of the best. He sent me off that day with a bunch of Alan Moore stuff, the Neil Gaiman *Sandman* run and Frank Miller's *Dark Knight Returns*. Frank Miller made the character real for me, and I knew there and then I wanted to write Batman. I digested all those stories within a week and it just seemed like a fantastic new creative outlet that had a lot of potential. And it looked difficult to me; it looked challenging and exciting and new. You had to learn to think concisely and clearly in terms of story structure, and to think very visually. In a sense, these were all my existing weaknesses as a writer. I picked up Scott McCloud's *Understanding Comics* and his enthusiasm just really got to me.

After that I read just tons of back issues of *Detective Comics*, *Batman* and *Batman: Shadow of the Bat*. *The Batman Chronicles* had just started coming out at that time, and that lead me to *Nightwing*, and suddenly I bounced over to *The Titans*. I was reading them out of order and trying to put these stories together in my head and to figure out the continuity, which was sort of a fun way to do it because I was trying to construct the history of these characters rather desperately, with almost enough resources but not quite. So my involvement was an absolutely necessary part of making it make sense.

Place of birth:
New Haven, Connecticut, USA
Date of birth:
19 July 1970
Home base:
Brooklyn, New York, USA
First published work:
The Batman Chronicles #7 ('Like Riding a Bike')
Education:
Bard College/UC Berkeley
Career highlights:
Catwoman, 'Fear of Faith' (in the Batman titles), *JLA/Titans*, *The Titans*, *The Weinbergs*

You mentioned you were writing a novel. Was that your ambition, to be a novelist?

Absolutely. I graduated from college and was taking creative writing classes at UC Berkeley. Writing novels is a very lonely and solitary pursuit, and if you're interested in having any sort of communal support you have to really seek that out. Your best option is a class or workshop environment, both of which have their own limitations. In some ways, writing comics comes down to the same thing — there is a point where you have to be completely alone with the material, engaged in it — but it's much more of a communal activity than novel writing. For instance, I would never call another person I knew to be writing a novel and go, 'Let's talk this through', but with comics you do that quite often. There's much more of a sense of a community and passing ideas back and forth. Then the minute you finish with a comic script, it goes on to the artist and there are editors involved, and so on.

I would still love to finish that book some day, but since discovering comics I've stopped dead on page 273. I actually thought that when I finally went freelance full-time to write comics I would have more time to work on the novel, but it just doesn't work that way. The deadline pressure is so intense with comics that I couldn't be writing all day in one medium and then go, 'For fun I'm going to switch to another'. I suppose there are some people who have the energy for it, but I haven't quite got there yet. Right now I really feel like I'm learning so much from the comics medium that it can't help but make my writing in other mediums better, and so as long as I'm learning it seems completely worthwhile waiting on the novel.

What have you learned from writing comics?

A lot about story structure and how to express theme and nuance through action. With the novel, what you choose to describe and not describe is very much a stylistic choice. With a comic, if you're not thinking visually it's just murder, it simply won't work. Also, learning how to meet a deadline, to be quick on your feet and just a generosity with ideas. With a novel you get your one good idea and you're kind of set for two years. With comics, every week it's like, 'Next!', it never ends. So you learn not to be stingy with ideas, you learn to take risks and to trust your imagination a little bit more and tease characters into revealing things about themselves through questions and actions and odd situations.

Wasn't it daunting, coming into comics cold like that?

In its own weird way, that lack of knowledge was my greatest asset. I really came in understanding that I didn't understand, and wanting to learn. Out of anything I've ever been good at in life, number one is I'm a natural student, and I approached comics as one. Editors get a lot of submissions from fans who think they know everything about the business, and approach it like they're gonna come in and fix things. But I was like, 'I have no idea what's going on here. This is so cool. Teach me'. People were very generous with their time and their attention, both the editors at DC — especially in the Bat-office — and, later, other creators. They were surprisingly willing to sit down and say here's what I know about the craft and about story structure. I also did a lot of reading, I took the Robert McKee story structure class, I hung on every word that came out of Denny O'Neil's mouth, I read memos that Chuck Dixon had written up about structuring scripts, I studied Mark Waid's composition in his comics, and looked at the way Neil Gaiman shapes character arcs. There was a lot of information there, ready to be mined, and I really dove into it fairly obsessively. But that's what worked, and people seemed to like that I was willing to listen.

Didn't you, by your own admission, 'pester' DC for a job over a period of two years?

I say pestered, but the editors were really nice about it and didn't seem to mind my enthusiasm. I would call and say, 'What should I read this week?', and they were real good at recommending stuff like Christopher Vogler's *The Writer's Journey*, and all the great comics that were out there. It reminded me of being fourteen, and falling in love with a rock band and trying to learn everything you could about them from *Vox* magazine. Because you're actively filling in all the gaps in your knowledge, you feel very involved.

I got to know the material quite well, although the best way to learn about characters is to write them. So I started doing what I guess is referred to as fan fiction, and I joined a little Amateur Press Association. In this way I was just exploring the thematic content of these characters over and over again, fully realising that they were all under copyright, so if I wanted to do this seriously I'd actually have to work for the company in question. That was exactly how I came to them: 'I have a need to do this, you're clearly in control of whether or not I can, so teach me how to do it'. I think if I'd had any idea who I was calling, if I'd understood who Denny O'Neil was, I would have been much more shy about it. Denny was enormously helpful with story structure, but it was [*Nightwing* editor] Scott Peterson who first took me seriously. He started sending me reading lists and critiquing my fan fiction.

How did you land your first assignment?

Some of the editors got a hold of examples of my fan fiction. Though clearly not in comics format, I think they showed I was very attached to the characters and that I did have skills as a writer. I just didn't know the medium, though they were aware I was willing to learn. I'd already been in this relationship with them for two years, where I would periodically call, fax and e-mail or send the occasional short story with a little Post-It attached saying 'Did you like it?'. My interest was clear, but I still hadn't turned in anything like an official proposal. They knew I wanted to write for comics, and the best way to learn is to do it. Darren Vincenzo was the editor at DC who gave me my first work. It was a ten-page Dick [Grayson, Nightwing] and Donna [Troy, ex-Wonder Girl] story in issue number seven of *The*

Batman Chronicles. I was naturally thrilled, but when I hung up the phone I realised I had never seen an actual comic script. One of Neil Gaiman's *Sandman* collections had a sample script in the back and I grabbed that. A friend of mine convinced me you had to sketch stuff out and send in what I guess are thumbnails, and as I didn't know any better I was gamely trying to do that as well.

How long did you have to write it?

One of my favourite things about the Bat-office is that by the time you receive the assignment you are already late. I believe I had a week, but I had this day job at the time, so essentially it was written in a weekend, with a little polishing late at night. I sent it in and I think it pretty much went straight through. Then it all just escalated from there. The second story I got given was thirty-eight pages, and that was very intimidating and took a while longer. But it came together pretty fast. It's a monthly industry and you've gotta be able to work quickly, so that was part of the training too. My work ethic is that things are due when they're due, and you need to be cooperative and on the ball in order to get them in on time. That way you don't slow anybody else down who's waiting behind you. It's one of the greatest challenges of working in this field.

How do you begin the process of writing a comics script?

I usually start by having a 'conversation' with the main character, in which I'm try-ing to figure out a good question to ask them or a good situation in which to put

Nightwing

Well, he couldn't be Robin the *Boy* Wonder forever, could he? Dick Grayson, 'youthful ward of Bruce Wayne' and trusty sidekick to Bat-man, finally grew up, and flew the coop — as Nightwing. In one of the major shake-ups of the established Batman mythos, Dick Gray-son hung up his Robin costume and stepped out of the shadow of the bat. As Nightwing, Grayson headed up what was then called the *New Teen Titans* (see page 121), and forged a relationship with Donna Troy, Wonder Girl, which ended up very, very briefly in mar-riage. Via several one-shots and mini-series, Nightwing eventually found his way into his own regular series, written by Chuck Dixon, in which he relocated from Gotham to Blüdhaven, an even more crime-ridden city. Naturally, the departure of Grayson left some-thing of a void in the Robin department, and eventually this was filled by newcomer Jason Todd. However, the change did not sit well with fans, and in the face of growing discontent, DC ran the 'Death in the Family' storyline, which enabled readers to vote on Robin's fate. They did, and he died. A third Robin, Tim Drake, proved much more popular and survives to this day.

them that's going to force them to tell me something about themselves I don't know yet. That's what is essentially going to end up being my theme or my driving point. I understand the economy of laying the story out before you start, but I guess I'm a little too lenient with my characters, because they tend to sort of run off in different directions no matter how carefully I plan. Some of my friends tease me, saying that it's really not necessary to write the same script three times, but I often find that I start with the idea from my outline and something else comes up, and I end up rewriting to accommodate it. It feels like it should take a very long time to write that way, but it doesn't. It happens quickly and passionately, although there's always that point where you're at page seventeen for the third time going, 'I must finish this, I must finish this'. Then something magical happens and it comes together. I wish I sat down with a very strict structure and laid every page down according to that — I have done it once or twice — but it is actually the surprise and mystery of diving in there and seeing what happens that really excites me.

When you say you start off by having a conversation with the character, what do you mean exactly?

It's not like I address Nightwing via a picture of Nightwing or anything like that. It's essentially trying to be a conduit, letting the character come into your mind and then giving them the keyboard. You sit there and try to disinvest your own persona and go, 'Okay Selina, I'm ready to write a *Catwoman* script, this is about you, what do you want to say? What do you want to talk about?'. I try and give her room to come out. Of course, often she's very antisocial and uncommunicative, and sometimes she doesn't want to cooperate. But other times I really hear her like a chattering in my head.

These characters have stories they want to tell, though I'm sure if you analyse what you end up writing it's actually your own subconscious, and themes and issues in your own life that are coming through. Later on, when you look back at the work, you can go, 'Oh, this is what was going on in my life at that time', but when it's happening, the characters' voices are very distinct and it feels almost like a possession or something. It's like there's this fictional entity coming to speak to you and you try to be quiet and listen and help guide them through the structure of your own story. I think there's something, call it the universal unconscious, which we can all tap into and draw on, especially when dealing with such archetypal characters. You *know* Batman, everyone's got Batman in their soul, and everyone carries some Catwoman around with them. If you can subconsciously imbue those archetypes with your own issues then you are really going to get some exciting material.

Do you have to relate to the characters you write or do they find their own way in?

I have to be sympathetic to them. I have to be able to understand what their motivation is by the time I am shaping the structure of the story. For instance, I find villains very easy and enjoyable to write, because we're in a pretty chaotic, dark world and a lot of times their goals and motivation make as much if not more sense to me than those of the heroes. It's more difficult to continually think

CATWOMAN 56   Devin Kalile Grayson
August 9, 1997
Prepared for Denny and Gorf
Script – 22pp   working title: AND THE EARTH DID MOVE;
                                                            Claustrophobia

PAGE 1, SPLASH

Interior, a crowded department store. We're in the electronics department, with at least twenty different kinds of digital and analog clocks on a back wall display proudly announcing that it's (TEXT:) **7:00 PM.**

A salesman strolls calmly by the display, failing to notice, as does everyone in the store, Catty, lip bit and eyebrows lowered in concentration, hanging halfway out of an open air vent in the ceiling (a loose screw or two still evident), her arms and torso resting on top of the display shelving unit amid the clocks, very much in shadow. She has a thin, stiff wire line in her hands that ends in a hook, and with the hook-end she's carefully snagging a display pair of expensive, new binoculars which is set up near the clock display. The binoculars are very slim and compact, small enough to fit in her boot.

There's an elevator nearby, with a screened air vent just above the elevator doors.

Title and credits on this page; there's also a sign with the display binocs (and credits):

COMING SOON!
WAYNE TECH COMPACT RUBY ZOOM NIGHT VISION BINOCULARS
8 x 27 with 131X light gathering power and 8X zoom with 27X telescopics!
*To order your pair today, contact your **Buddingdale's** sales rep or contact:*
Devin Grayson – script
Jim Balent – pencils
John Stanisci – inks
Buzz Setzer – colors
Albert de Guzman – letters
Jordan B. Gorfinkel – associate editor
Dennis O'Neil – editor

1 CAPTION: I can no longer remember why I thought this would be a good idea.

Above: *From Devin Grayson's script for Catwoman #56. Courtesy of Devin Grayson.*

PAGE 21, panel one

Big. Cut to Titans Island, kind of an over view, just BEFORE the fight. Which means that our original five are there, in costume, maybe in a similar formation to the one we just left them in, so that they're immediately recognizable. And our Tier Two five are there too, also in costume, and hard at work…

…Assisting a large (one could say "swarming" ::winks::) team of construction workers. They're building a base of ops under the holographic Titans Tower. Nightwing probably has a blueprint of some kind, and may be consulting with someone from the construction crew, and everyone's utilizing their powers to help. (No Lian this time).

1 CAPTION: Place: Titans Island.

Page 21, panel two

Closer in on the activity. Nightwing consults with a construction guy as behind him, Avatar and Tempest pass, both casually carrying huge, impossibly heavy piles of cement brick and conversing amongst themselves, as Damage, also carrying a huge load, follows Arsenal around excitedly pestering him while Roy just grins back at him.

2 CAPTION: Time: Thirteen hours after the Titans officially announced their reformation.

3 NIGHTWING: No, it has to be LEAD reinforcement. It's a…PRIVACY issue.

4 DONNA: …which means I'm pretty much the way WALLY remembers me, except possibly with a few NEW tricks.
5 DONNA: But what about YOU?

6 DAMAGE: What do you MEAN don't WORRY about it anymore? What'd you DO?

Page 21, panel three

Pan over slightly. Argent is in rapturous conversation with Starfire, as Jesse runs around undoing things that Flash is doing in super-speed right in front of her – they're both in multi-image blurs.

7 ARGENT: Wow, that is, like, SO cool! Did you get to KEEP the clothes you MODELED?

8 STARFIRE: Sometimes!

9 JESSE: Wouldyoustopalready!? You'vegottoWAITuntiltheydecidewherethey wantthings!

10 FLASH: Heyrelax! I'mjusttryingtohelp!

Above: *An example of full script from* The Titans #1. *Courtesy of Devin Grayson.*

why you would always try and do the right thing than it is to go, 'Okay, this person wants what they want, because they're greedy'. I'm willing to turn myself over to the characters, but it doesn't work unless they are three-dimensional enough for you to find something of yourself in them, something that you can relate to. You have to love every character and you have to understand what their weaknesses are. You have to get to know them in a pretty fundamental way.

You mentioned putting yourself and your life into the books you write. Can you elaborate on that?

I never consciously bring real life things into my work and I've never lifted a person from real life and made them into a fictional character. For me, the fictional world is already densely populated and very noisy and they are all sitting there with things to say, so there's no need to bring anybody else over. And yet, when you go back and look at something a couple of years later, the thematic content is unmistakable; you'll see how you were working through your own issues about relationships and so on. Clearly, part of my fascination with the sidekick/mentor relationship in *Batman* is down to my own ambivalence about my parents, and about trying to be worthy of and live up to these very intelligent, competent people, and trying to have a relationship with them. That's a resonant theme in the nineties, because a lot of us have two working parents who are brilliant but distant.

I never sit down with a Batman/Nightwing story and go, 'Okay, I'm gonna talk about my relationship with my Mum or my Dad', and yet I can go back a year later and go, 'Wow, look how much of that was subconsciously picking up on things that were going on in my life at the time'. I think that's to be expected, clearly the material you're mining while writing is very personal and I know Mark [Waid] has said before that if he's not invested in the story it's not going to be good. For a story to be resonant and important to you as a writer, it's personal on some level, whether it's conscious or not.

I am writing a three-part prestige format [series] for Vertigo, the title of which is *User*, that deals with role-playing games and cyber role-playing games. It's about someone having so much difficulty in her familial structure that she escapes into this fantasy world of role-playing where the archetypes are very pure, and through that she unlocks the ability to care and reconnect to what's happening in her real life. It's the most autobiographical thing I've ever written. This is the first time I've used any real material from my own life.

Do you think visually when it comes to writing?

I'm learning, but it's still a developing skill. The way most stories come to me is completely audio. I hear the voices, and the dialogue comes fully formed into my head. Sometimes what I have to do is write that down first and then go back and try to figure out what is a good visual way to represent it. Other times, like with fight scenes, I will see the whole thing in my head, and it's just a matter of getting that down onto the page. In a sense, my second pass over the script is the visual pass.

Why do you write full script?

I'm much too much of a control freak not to. The one time I didn't was with *JLA/Titans*. Since I was co-plotting with [artist] Phil Jimenez, he requested we do it plot-dialogue format, but never again. It's real hard for me to let go on that level. Although I love the interactive part, and I love when a page comes back and an artist has done something slightly different or added their own personality to what's happening, I'm only ready for that once I've let go of my full vision in the script. I can't do that until I've said everything I need to say. If I've done that well and I feel good about the script, then I'm really quite open to additions from the other people involved in the process. But if I just put out a general plot I find myself getting cranky.

In full script terms I think I'm somewhere in between Alan Moore and Neil Gaiman, and Chuck Dixon, who's more sparse. I've seen his scripts and he's definitely more trusting than I am. I'll go through a couple of pages with fairly sparse directions but then something will matter to me and I'll look up and there'll be four paragraphs about one panel. It also depends what it is. With creator-owned stuff there's obviously a need to be much more descriptive, because it's really all coming from your head. When you're working on a Batman project you can assume

---

Teen Titans

Another DC superhero team, this time featuring (at least initially) Robin, Aqualad and Kid Flash. The trio first appeared in *The Brave and the Bold* #54, and with Wonder Girl, they returned on two further occasions before débuting in their own book, *Teen Titans* (1966). The series, which began on the somewhat dubious note of wanting to help all 'teens in trouble', featured desperately inferior villains and supposedly 'hip' dialogue, penned no doubt by men with only a fleeting memory of their teenage years. It wasn't until 1980 (after two cancellations) and the creation of the *New Teen Titans* that the book finally became a bona fide hit. Featuring Robin (later Nightwing), Wonder Girl and Kid Flash, the new team also included Raven, Starfire, Cyborg and Changeling, and writer Marv Wolfman and artist George Pérez, using Chris Claremont's revamped *X-Men* as a model, fashioned solid, sweeping action stories with soap-opera style characterisation. The series flourished for many issues but never really survived Pérez's departure, and eventually went the way of its predecessor. A completely new team and book appeared in 1996, but proved short-lived. As for Devin Grayson's more recent re-launch, *The Titans*, we can but wait and see.

the artist understands certain things, and certain visuals are going to be in place that you don't have to describe. But when it's all coming out of your own head, you need to slow down and make sure the artist is really understanding your vision. Then, of course, they're welcome to add on to that, but you need to be very clear to begin with, so that everyone's starting on the same page.

You're currently one of the busiest writers around, second only to Chuck Dixon in terms of monthly output. Do you write especially quickly?

Partly I think I'm doing so much because I don't know any better, and I'm still learning to assess what my workload capacity is. I tend to write scripts in about two to three days, but the mistake I keep making is thinking if you can write a script in two days, you can write two scripts in four days, and that is not the case. You really need to allow some dead time in between, especially if you're switching projects, say going from a *Catwoman* script to a *Titans* script. If you finish the *Catwoman* script Wednesday you have to understand that on Thursday the *Titans* script is not going to get very far. I haven't quite figured out the mystery of that, but it's something to do with recharging your creative well. In a sense, though, no matter how fast the script is written, you sort of have to allow a week for each project. I often find if I've had a really good day and written fourteen pages, I can just write off the next day. At most I could finish two scripts in a week, but that's rare. Sometimes I luck out; there was one week in which I did three scripts. The ideal scenario would be to sit with *Titans* for a whole month and write four or five scripts and then move on and do *Catwoman*, but the reality of deadlines is you usually can't do it that way.

I understand music forms an important part of your writing ritual, and that you make specific soundtrack tapes for each project.

It's actually very helpful during that initial stage where I invite the characters to come and tell their story. The soundtracks usually help me concentrate on a theme, but they can also be about the characters themselves and sometimes I remake them to form an arc in a story. If the arc has a real, definite thematic content, then I need a soundtrack to support that. Sometimes when I get stuck and the day's going really badly, I'll realise I haven't done the music thing yet, and it's amazing how much it frees me up. Partly what that is, it just distracts the conscious mind when you're sitting there doing every sentence sixteen times before you move on. When you have that music going it helps you flow and go past that. You can always come back and do the 'editorial' pass later, but you need to stay with the creative waves first time through.

It matters what I'm drinking too. For the Vertigo project I found myself drinking lots of tea all day long, and in the middle of a really rocking *Titans* battle I'm pounding down the coffee or diet cola, or something. There is a particular kind of beverage ritual that happens with certain themes. You do whatever it takes, maybe even put on a different perfume if that's what's going to get you in the right head space. It's hard to say without sounding a little crazy, but you have to invite the character to come hang out with you and if that means changing the lighting in the room for a little while or changing scents or putting on a different kind of sweatshirt, if that's going to help that character feel comfortable and hang out for a while, it's worth doing.

So what does *Catwoman's* Selina Kyle smell like then?

She likes Paloma Picasso, very dark, musky, mysterious, low lights, but actually rather loud music; she's quite fond of Garbage and L7. She likes those rocker chicks. Before I start a project, I'll sit down and make a mix tape. That's actually one of my favourite parts. While I'm doing that I'm lazily meditating on the theme and stuff, and very often in the process of making that tape little dialogue snippets will come to me, or I'll see an action sequence. It's a real nice way of settling into the mood of writing the piece.

Don't you have a bowl next to your computer filled with Post-Its covered with dialogue?

Sometimes you will be working on one script and characters from somewhere else will suddenly go, 'Hey, we've got this really cool conversation', and they can't be shut up. There are certain characters that are particularly noisy, like Roy Harper from the Titans, he has no sense of decorum. I'll be right in the middle of a *Catwoman* script and he'll be, 'You know what I want to say?', and you write it down on a Post-It, so they know you've acknowledged their little tantrum. That's the only thing that makes them be quiet.

What influences your writing outside of comics?

Lots and lots of literature. I'm a huge Milan Kundera fan, and I actually sit and read Shakespeare; I think the language is gorgeous and the way he handles multiple layers of characterisation is amazing. A. S. Byatt is one of my favourite novelists these days. In music, Tori Amos — she's completely as much a writer as she is a musician. I love reading psychology and philosophy and I think that shows in my work. I'm a big fan of the Joseph Campbell stuff. My mum's a clinical psychologist so I grew up reading Jung and Freud, which is fun stuff to have in your background because it really helps when you're going to approach the archetypes. You can study Batman slyly and go, 'I can look at you as a fan and be wowed, but I can look at you from another angle and see you've got some problems'.

Does being young and female make a difference in an industry that is mainly filled with older, male writers?

The young part I'm not alone in. There's clearly a youth movement in comics right now. I'm really close friends with Jay Faerber and Brian Vaughan*, who are up-and-comers, and we hang around and make fun of the old guys. I'm starting to notice more females coming into the industry, but there was definitely a sense of loneliness and uniqueness early on, at least with the mainstream superhero writing stuff. That's been difficult, actually, because there's been pressure to make a vaguely feminist statement about it, where the truth is part of my fasci-

---

* *Faerber writes* Generation X *for Marvel and Vaughan is currently developing a new series for DC.*

nation with Batman is I am quite the tomboy. I'm completely comfortable hanging out with the guys. So to suddenly be a symbol of the female agenda... I'm not sure I'm ready for that. I do have very strong feelings about the representation of females in comics, and more importantly the way women are dealt with as people in the professional world. That it comes up so much as a question is something I still struggle with, and I'd like to turn it into something productive rather than something I feel defensive about.

What ambitions do you have in the medium?

I guess I have two main goals. The first was to get to know the characters better; I really got into comics in order to work with Batman and Nightwing in a sense, and I've been incredibly fortunate in that I've already been able to do that. And now I'm working with the Titans too, which is also really a dream come true. I've been able to cement my relationship with these fictional entities, which is ambition one. Once involved in the medium, the next goal became, 'Well, I'm enjoying this so much, I'm having fun, how do I communicate this to other people who don't know about it yet?'

Do you have any desire to write comics outside of the superhero genre?

Not necessarily. I don't really mind staying where I am as long as they let me deal with the human side of the superheroes. Their 'superheroness' to me is their

Soundtracks

When writing for comics, Devin Grayson first works up a 'soundtrack' for each particular project, one she hopes will support the 'temperament, theme and rhythm' of what she is aiming to achieve. For the curious, here is an example. *Titans*: 'Graduate' by Third Eye Blind, 'Old Before I Die' by Robbie Williams, 'Avenging Angels' by Space, 'Push It' by Garbage, 'Little Bit' by Gina G, 'Temptation' by Heaven 17, 'Never Say Goodbye' by PM Dawn, 'Sheila' by Smashing Pumpkins, 'Family' by Dar Williams, 'Come Together' by Primal Scream, 'D'you Know What I Mean?' by Oasis, 'A Different Beat' by Boyzone, 'Sunchyme' by Dario G, 'The Fear' by Pulp, 'So Much For the Afterglow' by Everclear, 'Good Day to Die' by Travis, 'Not Like' by Boss Hog, 'Feeling So Real' by Moby, 'Argue' by Matchbox 20, 'First Cool Hive' by Moby, 'Apples & Oranges' by Smashing Pumpkins, 'Kind and Generous' by Natalie Merchant, 'As Is' by Ani DiFranco, 'As Long as you Love Me' by Backstreet Boys, 'Wanted' by Refreshments and 'Glory Days' by Pulp. The selection comes fully recyclable and with no guarantee whatsoever on Devin's part that it will fit comfortably onto a ninety-minute cassette. Happy (and creative) listening.

connection with the archetypes, and I like that, but part of the thrill for me is thinking, 'What if there really were a Batman? Let's pretend for a minute that this guy is real, what would be the psychological profile of someone like that?'. I mean, these people on some level are nuts, they would have to be, and I like that about them, it makes them very interesting to write about. Catwoman's such a wonderful character because she's completely off her rocker, she's decided to run around in this cat costume embracing this very one-dimensional archetype, when in fact she's this woman with a very full and complicated and distressing life and this is how she's dealing with it. It's fascinating to play with it as if the psychology were real. With the Titans I love their relationships with each other, the superpowers are cool and all, but what's even cooler is that they've known each other most of their lives and they have these complicated relationships. As long as I'm playing with that side of it I don't care one way or another. It's wherever you can get the meat of that psychological drama. It doesn't matter to me whether they're in tights or not.

Can you see yourself in comics for the long haul or is it a stepping stone to other forms of writing?

I don't like the term stepping stone because it seems calculated, and this is really like a wonderful side road for me. I didn't see this coming and it's just been this wonderful, magical adventure where I got sidetracked in a very delightful way. But I *am* sidetracked, and I don't think I'll be in this medium forever. I definitely want to get back to the novel and play around in other writing mediums. Mainstream superhero comics do have limitations, and I like it that fresh, young voices come in. I think there is a danger of not being able to relate as well to your audience after a while and it's good to keep new blood circulating. So I won't have any feeling of abandoning, but it will be fun to pass the torch some day.

*   *   *

Check out:
Batman Animated by Paul Dini and Chip Kidd (a lush, highly illustrated companion volume to *Batman: The Animated Series*)
Understanding Comics by Scott McCloud
The Writer's Journey by Christopher Vogler

DAN JURGENS

As both writer and artist, Dan Jurgens has chronicled the life and times of a true comic book icon for many a year. One of the key Superman creators of the last decade, he has seen the character through some of the most turbulent and transitional stages of his long life. Indeed it was Jurgens who, unlike Metropolis's assorted villains, finally succeeded in killing the Man of Steel, in the highly acclaimed 'The Death of Superman' storyline. Ironically, it was this 'death' that rejuvenated the character, providing the impetus that propelled Superman into the nineties. Jurgens originally joined DC as an artist on *Warlord*, but soon began writing as well. The success of 'The Death of Superman' led him to a number of high-profile assignments, which included orchestrating DC's massive *Zero Hour* crossover and launching the successful Tangent line of comics. He was also tapped by Marvel to both write and draw a new Spider-Man title, *Sensational Spider-Man*, though ultimately the partnership lasted less than a year. Jurgens continues to plot and draw Superman's adventures, primarily in a series of prestige format specials, including *Superman: The Doomsday Wars*, which reintroduced Doomsday, the Superman-slaying monster from 'The Death of Superman', and Jurgens is also the writer of Marvel's highly regarded re-launched *Thor* title.

You started out in the industry as an artist, rather than a writer/artist. Was that where your early ambitions primarily lay?

My college training was in graphic design, but as a kid I'd had a great deal of interest in comics; I read them, *devoured* them in fact. That early passion was something I never let go of, and was ultimately realised when I met an artist named Mike Grell, who was making a personal appearance at a comics convention. Mike was a writer/artist who had created *Warlord* [for DC], and was leaving the art side of it to just write the book. He was looking for an artist to take over, saw my stuff, and about a month later I got the job. That was back in 1982, before the major conventions and certainly before publishers had anything like the portfolio review tables they have today. I had sent art samples into companies previously, but there wasn't the same zest for trying new talent that exists now and I was never serious enough to really pursue it; I never went to New York and banged on everyone's doors to show them my samples or anything like that. Part of it was I had a terrific job at the time, and was doing very well. Breaking into comics required a cut in pay, but it worked out okay in the end.

But even though I started out just drawing, I wanted to write from day one. I knew that I needed to have control over the material I was going to draw. Right from the start, that's where I knew I wanted to end up. Within a year I had co-created a new series for DC with Roy Thomas and Gerry Conway called *Sun Devils*. Gerry was the writer/editor, and after about six issues he left to do other things. But as we had plotted the issues together and I had written the dialogue, he evidently saw something there and gave me my first chance to write a whole book.

I feel strongly that combining writing and drawing is the natural way this industry should work. To me, a separate writer and separate artist should be the exception. You hear people say an artist should pencil and ink his own work, but in many respects I feel it's more important for the writer to draw his own work as well. I don't think there are any absolutes, to me it's simply a more natural way of working, a more streamlined process. I know if I was an editor I would tend to seek out writer/artists rather than separate guys for each job. I think you end up with a more cohesive product. But again, there are no hard and fast rules. If you're talking about a Mark Waid, a Kurt Busiek, a Garth Ennis or a Grant Morrison, they're all tremendously talented writers and I'm not trying to say they shouldn't be working. It's just

Place of birth:
　　Ortonville, Minnesota, USA
Date of birth:
　　27 June 1959
Home base:
　　The Twin Cities area of Minnesota
First published work:
　　Warlord #63
Education:
　　Minneapolis College of Art
　　and Design
Career highlights:
　　Booster Gold, DC versus Marvel,
　　Green Arrow, Justice League
　　America, Sensational Spider-Man,
　　Superman, Superman Vs Aliens,
　　Thor, Warlord, Zero Hour

that I find it to be a more natural process for one person to write and draw.

Was there any initial resistance to you drawing and writing?

There was not. Remember, I co-created *Sun Devils*, so when Gerry left it was natural that one of the co-creators step in. After that, the next thing I did was *Booster Gold*, which was a series I created, wrote and drew, so it wasn't like they could argue, 'Gee, you know, we think it should go to Joe Writer over here instead'. Which, if it had been an established flagship character, they certainly might have.

And yet shortly after you began pencilling one of the Superman books, you were writing it as well. How did that happen?

Around the time I was doing *Booster Gold*, Mike Carlin came over to DC from Marvel to edit the Superman books. He called me up and gave me a *Superman Annual* to draw, off a script by Jim Starlin. I had always wanted to work on Superman, and had a lot of fun doing the book. Shortly thereafter, John Byrne left the Superman books and Mike brought me in to draw one of the regular titles, with George Pérez writing. But after about three months George left, and as I had been dialoguing the book since, I think, George's second issue, I just started plotting it as well. I had obviously demonstrated enough skills as a writer/artist for Mike to trust me to take on Superman.

In later years your role on the Superman books seemed to be as the 'big event' guy. Would you agree?

My role changed over time depending on who the other creators were. I do think I was sort of the big picture guy, but I'm also known for the quieter issues I did. I loved doing the character-based stuff, whether it was the various Metropolis stories or one I did flashing back to Clark's youth, with drunken drivers as the main topic. And there was an issue I did that I was real happy with, in which Luthor has the mayor of Metropolis assassinated at the same time his daughter is born. I enjoy doing those kind of stories more, but I think that if a fair analysis is written of my tenure [on the Superman books] it'll mention both kinds. There are just some people who are detail-minded and some people who are big picture-minded, and I'm the latter. That's just the way I think. The problem is, you can sit in a meeting and say 'Here's my idea', and it can be the biggest idea going for Superman, but there's a tremendous chasm between a great idea and great execution, and more often than not where we failed was in our execution.

As one of a team of Superman creators, how did you find working with your fellow writers?

In the beginning it would be myself, [Editor] Mike Carlin, Jerry Ordway and Roger Stern, and maybe another artist or two, sitting in a room for three days cooking up a year's worth of stuff for the two, and later three, Superman books. Then the groups would get bigger, assistant editors would get plugged in and we would have all the pencillers there, as well as inkers. Then we added the fourth book and pretty soon, instead of several guys painting the direction of the Superman books, it turned into a roomful of twenty-five or so people painting the direction of a franchise. And after 'The Death of Superman' [storyline] there was much more of a corporate involvement as well. So instead of it being a creative effort, it became an effort of consensus, which I don't think necessarily leads to a good, cohesive story. In a process like that, you are only as strong as the weakest link in the chain. Our greatest failing was that among the four or five writers we couldn't even agree on what exactly Superman's character was. We certainly didn't agree on who Lois was, and I know damn well we didn't on who Jimmy Olsen was and what he should be. So if you have five writers who don't even agree on who and what the main characters are, you aren't gonna get an even story flow between the four titles. We did lose that, and that's regrettable.

Over the last few years it was an effort to come up with a direction for the character, and that means you have a high level of compromise. And I'm not sure compromise is the best way to write a comic book. People have asked me, 'Why didn't you bail out?', and I guess it's because when it does all click, and you get that creative synchronicity going, it is a tremendous way to work and the payoff is tremendous. When you're on a roll and you get everybody plugged in, it's great. I think a large part of it is we became prisoners of our own success. After

The Death of Superman

Back in the days when 'event' storylines — epic, multi-part sagas, normally running across several different titles — weren't quite as two-a-penny as they have perhaps become, the perfect way to boost interest in (and thereby sales of) a flagging title was to drastically alter the status quo, to present a 'turning point' in the life of the central character(s). Often this meant killing a key character, and surely the granddaddy of all such comic book executions was the death of Superman. Never before had something quite so drastic been attempted, especially not with a character that was essentially an American icon. Nevertheless, it was decided (among the writers, editors and artists of the Superman titles) that the Man of Steel would die. In a storyline that ran across all the Superman titles (and *Justice League America*, as it was then) in 1992, Superman perished at the hands of a raging, berserker powerhouse known as Doomsday. Subsequent stories followed — 'Funeral for a Friend', 'World Without a Superman' and 'Reign of the Supermen' — and Superman was eventually, via a tale of cyborg Supermans, cloned Supermans and even iron-clad Supermans, revealed to be alive. But then we knew that all along, didn't we?

PLOT for 22 pages
"The Dark Wars!" Part II of III

PAGE ONE

John, we're picking up right where we left off last issue. Everyone is gathered in the arena where Thor just changed to Jake. Let's open with individual shots of the following: Odin, shocked. Balder and Sif in pretty much the same state. Zelia looking smug. Adva looking mysterious and Tokkots practically drooling. Captions will detail that some thought this day was impossible, that it would never come, etc. That Thor ran away in fear. And most of all...

PAGE TWO

Splash! Something of a down shot showing Perrikus holding up his scythe in triumph. Thor is defeated. Laying at his feet is Thor's hammer, it's handle carved in two. Energy and light are emanating from the hammer. Perrikus is boasting that he's defeated Thor...

PAGE THREE

...and now says he'll end the Odinson's life with his own hammer! Pull the camera way back here to really show the arena. Odin still in chains with Balder and Sif next to him, Zelia in the arena with Tokkots, D'Chel and Adva all surrounding her, and a crowd cheering as Perrikus bends down to pick up the hammer. Behind him we see the arena wall with a hole in it that we saw Thor crawl into last issue. His hand wraps around the top section of the shorn mallet but he can't lift it! Impossibly heavy! Balder laughs and Perrikus whirls his scythe around saying he'll slice Thor's head clean off!

PAGE FOUR

Perrikus shatters the area above the hole making an even larger hole as he yells for Thor to come out! But he peers in and sees there's nothing there! Just a pipe large enough to hold a small man, but not Thor...yet there is a hole in the pipe! Perrikus turns to Zelia...he's really pissed now! Shot of Tokkots and Zelia as Tokkots says he'll find the Thunder God and kill him! Zelia says, "No, you miscreant. We'll find the Thunder God and anyone who does so will save him for Perrikus for he's his kill!"

PAGE FIVE

Cut to Jake scrambling through a dank, smelly pipe filled with just a couple inches of water. Really gross...maybe with weird alien-esque rats crawling around. He's angry, frustrated as hell that he changed back and had to run! Never would have happened like that before...maybe it's the new paradigm or maybe because Asgard has been changed. Hated to look like a wimp running...but knows he has to protect Jake's body because Perrikus would destroy it in a second. Comes out of the pipe in a very run down part of what is now a dark, black Asgard. Lots of pipes all over the place...we're somewhat below the surface here in what is something of a waste treatment plant. Jake drops to his knees intending to change back to Thor.

PAGE SIX

Slams his fist down but nothing happens! No change! Most likely because the change occurred as a result of him losing his hammer! Now he's really frustrated...a human, a stranger in a far stranger place, up against a race of Gods. Somewhere on this page I'd love to see a big panel, with Jake very small in the shot. Huge pipes that carry sludge and sewage, with some of it leaking because of bad seals, steaming vents and crumbling bricks and mortar...it should all overwhelm him as if he doesn't have a chance. Jake knows he has to get back to the hammer if he's to have any kind of chance at all. Hears a voice yell, "What do we have here?"

PAGE SEVEN

Suddenly, about four Dark God warriors (worker class but still not slaves) come scrambling in. Grabbing Jake, they accuse him of being an escaped slave! Jake doesn't know what the heck they're talking about! Tries to fight back but one slams him in the chops with the hilt of his sword, knocking him senseless. As Jake falls one of the attackers says they'll take him Slototh.

Above: *Plot extract from* Thor *#11, by Dan Jurgens. Courtesy of Dan Jurgens/Marvel Comics. Used with permission. Thor ™ and © 1999 Marvel Characters, Inc.*

PAGE EIGHT

Cut back to the Dark Gods. Zelia, Perrikus, Tokkots, Adva and D'Chel are all in the middle of the arena wondering where Thor is. Odin and company are still there as well. Zelia says she'll find him. Close on her face. The part of her mask that completely covers her eye begins glowing and a mystical energy-type eye appears on the mask's surface. She says she is unable to detect Thor on Asgard! Perrikus rages. "Impossible! He could not have left!"

PAGE NINE

Perrikus grabs Odin's beard, pulling hard and demands that the old man tell him where Thor is! Odin doesn't know...doesn't have a clue! D'Chel says he senses that Odin is not deceiving them, that he is as clue less as they. D'Chel says there are many ways of deception...that must be a way to find Thor. Tokkots says, "And when you do, I get to run him through!" Zelia rebukes Tokkots...says Thor is still Perrikus' kill! Orders Tokkots away. Shot of him slinking away saying he'll yet earn their respect!

PAGE TEN

Cut to an area even darker, wetter, sloppier and more dank than we saw before. This is the domain of Slototh, an immense member of the Dark Gods. Slototh is their garbage man, their agent in charge of shoveling shit and clean up after them. He's charged with disposing of every manner of waste they have. He's huge, think Jabba the Hut in part. He's dressed in black rubber, a suit with clear hoses that have odd colored chemicals coursing through them. His skin is laced with festering sores and boils. All in all, a gross character. The area in question is really nothing more than a huge, huge pile of shit and garbage with a big burning pit in the middle. Human slaves, all natives of the planet the Dark Gods used to control and connected by chains, all near death, are shoveling garbage and crap into the burning pit. This pit, strangely enough, is the essence of the Dark Gods power. Several huge pipes drop from the ceiling that constantly have trash, garbage and crap coming out of them. This all piles up so it can then be shoveled, burned and turned into energy.

In any case, we open the page with Jake on his knees before Slototh as the guards around him laugh. Say they grabbed an escapee. Jake stands, barely able to believe that he's on Asgard! Nowhere in the nine worlds was there ever a place this bad! Slototh laughs and grabs Jake by the collar...says it's the price one pays for servicing the Dark Gods! He throws Jake into a large pile of crap with a shovel stuck in it and tells him to start shoveling!

PAGE ELEVEN

Jake refuses but is suddenly whipped by a guard! He drops to one knee...though Thor's spirit is willing to fight Jake's body cannot take such abuse! As he stands another guard slaps a chain around one ankle and tells Jake to get to work. Slototh laughs...says there are so many more works to be used up when these die! Zelia says there is a world called Midgard that can be mined for eternity! Close on Jake...he's got to find a way out!

PAGE TWELVE

Same scene, only an hour or two have passed. The stench and gasses are unbearable and most of the workers Jake started with are already lying dead. Hears a commotion off to one side as he hears a guard urging someone to work faster...harder! The voice says, "Silence, knave! Thou shalt not speak thus to one such as me!" Close on Jake's eyes as they open wide...that voice sounds familiar...but it cannot be, can it? Then pull pack the camera to show Jake watching as four guards wrestle with a tall, gaunt individual with long scraggly hair and a long stringy beard! Jake says, "Volstagg? Voluminous Volstagg?"

PAGE THIRTEEN

Volstagg, totally emaciated because he hasn't had any food in days looks at Jake and says, "Thou art unknown to me, mortal! Pray tell, how art thee acquainted with the visage of Volstagg the Valiant?" Jake slaps him on the shoulder and says, "I'm not sure whose appearance is more different, old friend! Your or mine!" Suddenly, one of the guards slams Volstagg right in the back of his head with a mace! Shot of a boiling mad Jake!

Above: *Also from* Thor *#11, highlighting Dan Jurgen's economical plotting style. Courtesy of Dan Jurgens/Marvel Comics. Used with permission. Thor™ and © 1999 Marvel Characters, Inc.*

'The Death of Superman' there was more and more pressure all the time to make it an 'event' rather than to make it a story. I think we could do that in the beginning because the creators involved had an interest in making sure it was a story as well.

You're credited as being the man responsible for 'The Death of Superman' storyline. Is that a fair appraisal?

I went into the meeting that preceded that storyline with two ideas: one of which was the death of Superman and one of which was to create a creature of sheer brute force to fight Superman, somebody who could beat the living tar out of him. So many of his villains at that time were the 'take control of Superman's mind' type, and we didn't have that kind of visual slugfest thing going that Marvel had for all their characters. It's a case where we fused the two ideas and it went from there. But again, those ideas would have meant nothing if we hadn't had four talented creative teams executing them well. And I think if you take 'The Death of Superman', by itself it isn't the greatest of shakes. We knew the payoff would come later with 'Funeral for a Friend', which added the depth and characterisation and feeling that 'The Death of Superman', didn't have, and then 'Reign of the Supermen', which pulled it all together. That whole story arc was a tremendous achievement, and a testimony to what the collaborative process can really do.

Were the 'electro' Superman and the red/blue Supermen your idea too?

In part. The whole power change thing came about because I wanted to change his costume. I wanted to find a way to update Superman's image, which we had done several times while I'd been working on the books, just to give him a bit of a different look. I said, 'I want to freshen up his look, so let's do something with the costume'. Karl Kesel wanted to change his powers, and while I wasn't thrilled [by that], I don't think Karl was thrilled by a different costume. But as I've said, part of the effort is compromise, and I have great respect for Karl's ability, so we fused the two ideas of a new costume and new powers. The actual electro look was one I never cared for from the outset. To me, white and blue, especially that shade of blue, just wasn't dramatic enough; it didn't work for Superman, it wasn't imperial enough. Superman should always be majestic and that costume wasn't. Plus, it was fused with the new powers.

The whole thing got sold as a big event, and frankly I think that's what killed us. Whether those ideas were good or bad, the execution was just awful. It was *not* exactly our finest hour. You can't just blame the idea, it really came down to us not having a firm agreement on what was going to happen after we walked out of the room. We were in a constant state of flux; this new power means he can't do this, and this means he can't do that. Ultimately, the new powers were ridiculous, because they meant Superman could do *anything*. Even the way he finally returned to being the regular Superman was a tremendous failure in execution.

With *Thor*, which you just write, do you do thumbnails to work out how the book should look before you begin writing the script?

Strangely enough, I don't do thumbnails or sketch out a book first. I just write it. When I'm writing for myself, I write what I call a truncated plot; in that it's shorter, briefer. What I'm basically doing at that point is describing the main story and character elements for the editor, so he knows what's going to happen. When I write for another artist I do a more detailed plot, and by the time I type it up I know what it would look like if I was going to draw it. I write it for myself in terms of what I think it will look like visually, which is kind of unfair on the artist, but it's the only way I can work. But then I say to my artists, 'make it your own and take it from there'. I type out a plot so it lists panel-by-panel what will happen on all twenty-two pages. As I type it I'll say, maybe, 'Downshot: ticker-tape parade New York City', or 'Wideshot', or 'Extreme closeup, crop the face like this'. I'm writing it for myself, what I can draw and I know what it'll look like. But the artist is still free to take it and move it around, and they always surprise me. But then, that's what the collaborative process is all about.

So no sketches, character designs, layouts, anything? Is this a conscious decision on your part?

Part of it was a reaction on my part to having once worked with [writer/artist] Keith Giffen, who, rather than write out a plot, would just send in his sketches of the pages. Keith's plot amounted to a twenty-two page book that was already all drawn out. And Keith's storytelling approach is so incredibly personal, with nine panel grids and the way he would characterise the action, it almost overwhelms another artist. And I also worked with another writer who did that same thing, but in his case couldn't draw, and did not have the storytelling sensibilities that Keith had. I found it tremendously frustrating to work from [drawn plots], because what you don't get is any of the flavour. If the story or scene is set in an exotic locale you don't have anyone typing out something like, 'We're in a rundown slum area of Mexico City. Garbage lines the streets. There are rats everywhere. There's even a dead wino laying in the corner'. The atmospherics aren't there. So, as an artist, I reacted very strongly against that process, and it's why I would never do that to someone else.

Do you come up with the high concept of each story first?

Yeah I do. I always try and have the high concept stuff decided before I move beyond that. In fact, what I tend to do is know how my story is going to end. Anytime I sit down and work on a book I almost always know what the last three or four pages are going to be, and I work backwards from that. I'll jump to the front and say, 'Okay, here's how we set it up', and then I'll jump to the middle and say, 'And here's the bridge'. That's how I tend to construct a comic book.

What do you consider to be the single most important consideration in writing a comic script?

The thing I harp on about more than anything else is my assertion that eighty per cent of writers in the business don't understand comic book storytelling. They think they're writing movies or television. This applies especially to the full script guys. I find very few of them really have the ability to address the needs of the medium, especially in terms of structuring proper pages, creating impact through the visuals, and building up tension and action in a story. It's very rare. I have drawn a couple of Archie Goodwin scripts, and Archie was the master, because although it was just the written word on the page, they were tremendously powerful in terms of pacing and structure. He understood the medium, he knew we were doing comic books. He didn't think we're doing a film on paper, and there's a big difference. Take the Vertigo titles, for example. To go way out on a limb here, most Vertigo books are visually boring. They can be tremendously well drawn, but how many times has anyone talked about a single artist in that line using the same glowing terms they reserve for the writers? This is not intended as a slam — much of the reason for this is because the entire purpose of the line is to provide a showcase for writers — but I think it really stifles artistic creativity.

So how does a writer go about addressing the needs of the comic book medium?

It comes down to recognising the differences in storytelling between comics and, say, movies, and identifying the different ways in which you build tension. Consider the car chase, one of the hallmarks of the action movie, and try translating that to the comic page. It's very difficult to do a visually interesting car chase on paper. There are exceptions, some talented artists could pull it off, but it fails ninety-nine times out of a hundred. Why? Because a car chase drawn out on paper is almost always incredibly boring. Cars are just cars; there's no way to show emotion, and there's little change from panel to panel. That's something comic book writers often fail to grasp.

Also, very few writers play with the concept of time on the page, which can be used to build dramatic tension. If you're reading a twenty-two page comic and you've got an average of five panels on a page, you have a very steady pacing. The trick is to be able to speed time up or slow time down, something Frank Miller did so well in *Batman: The Dark Knight Returns*. If you break the action down into numerous small panels you get the effect of slow motion on the page. We see the gun, we see the necklace coming off Bruce Wayne's mother's neck, we see the pearls from the necklace dropping on to the ground, rolling away. Time slows down and almost stops, building tension. I don't see that technique used very often, and when I do it's very rarely structured by the writer. In movies, when they want to build tension the music gets louder, the action gets bigger, the shots come faster and everything moves more quickly, and many writers try and duplicate that. But on a comic book page, the opposite needs to happen.

Another way to build tension is to structure a page so you have twelve panels on it: three tiers of four. You start out with the character's face very small in panel one and you zoom in slowly until in the last panel you just have a tightly

PAGE SIX

1 JAKE: This place REEKS of evil! For Asgard to have become this—

2 JAKE: —is an affront to the UNIVERSE!

PNL 2

3 JAKE: One THOR will correct just as soon as I change back!

4 SFX: WUMP WUMP

5 JAKE: Nothing's HAPPENING?!

6 JAKE: The hammer! I GOTTA get it BACK or—!

PNL 3

7 GUARD: Well, well, well. What do we have here?

8 GUARD: Sad specimen. Puniest Asgardian I've seen.

9 JAKE: ZOUNDS!

PNL 4

10 GUARD: It's the SLAVER PITS for you, tiny.

11 JAKE: NO! You can't DO this to ME!

PNL 5

12 GUARD: This mallet says I CAN.

13 SFX: WUNK

PNL 6

14 GUARD: SLOTOTH wanted us to find more workers and now we got one!

15 GUARD: Won't be happy though. This weakling won't last through the day.

16 GUARD: Plenty more on Midgard!

PAGE SEVEN

1 D'CHEL: None have seen the THUNDER GOD, Majeston Zelia.

2 ZELIA: IMPOSSIBLE! He couldn't have VANISHED!

3 ADVA: Indeed. My senses stretch across the continuum gateway. He
                 never left ASGARD.

PNL 2

4 ZELIA: Then the task of FINDING the enemy is MINE.

5 ZELIA: Let my INFINITY VISION stretch out across all Asgard in search of the
                 ODINSON.

PNL 3

6 ZELIA: No corner or shadow, no door or chamber is impervious to my sight.

7 ZELIA: And yet—

8 ZELIA: —there is NOTHING. THOR is no longer on Asgard.

PNL 4

9 PERRIKUS: It's a trick! And you'll tell me HOW, old man!

10 ODIN: I knoweth not, bestial one! Thor's whereabouts are a mystery to ODIN
                 as well!

11 PERRIKUS: FOUL LIAR!

PNL 5

12 D'CHEL: The ways of deception are my domain, Perrikus. Odin speaks the truth.

Above: *Script/dialogue extract from* Thor *#11, by Dan Jurgens. Courtesy of Dan Jurgens/Marvel Comics. Used with permission.* Thor™ *and © 1999 Marvel Characters, Inc.*

cropped close-up. This slow zoom effect can often be more dramatic than one full-page splash. Another thing that bothers me is where I see writers trying to cram too much into a panel. They'll say, 'page one, panel one: Superman swings his fist and punches Brainiac on the jaw, knocking him out through the window and he falls to the ground and hits the street'. That's eight panels. Or at least four. Not one.

Do you tend to have much collaboration with your artists?

That always depends on the artist. On *Thor*, what I try and do is get a feel for what JR [John Romita Jr] likes to draw and give him those things in the script, because you always end up with a better product. You play to people's strengths. The same thing when I pencil, I know what my inkers can do and I try to play to their strengths. Same thing with the colourist. The reality of modern comics, whether they're put out by Marvel or DC or whoever, is that this is a collaborative medium, so I collaborate as much as is possible.

Is it difficult handing over visual control, especially when you say you can see the comic in your head as you're writing it?

It can be a bit strange. When a job comes back from an artist I'm either tremendously impressed or I'm incredibly disappointed. On *Thor*, JR just takes this stuff and makes it so much his own, and he draws it in a way I could not. That book is every bit as much his as it is mine, if not more so. He elevates whatever I do and takes it to the next level, and I have a tremendous amount of respect for that. But there are other times, on other books, when that doesn't happen, and I get disappointed.

Do you believe, as some comics creators maintain, that the art is more important than the words?

I think the product is the most important thing and the product is a unity of story and art and lettering and, if it's a colour book, colour. It's like saying on a car that the engine is more important than the tyres, which is complete bullshit, because you've gotta have both to make it work. I have always found any discussion of what is more important to be a total and complete waste of time. You need a unified product or nothing works. Recently, I got a comic book by a very accomplished writer whose work I'll read any time, but I got five pages into the story and I hated the art so much I couldn't progress any further. It was a case where the story and art didn't gel, and sadly that happens a lot.

Marvel created *Sensational Spider-Man* specifically for you to write and draw, but you only lasted seven issues on the title. What happened?

I loved doing Spidey and I hope I get a chance to do it again someday. I went in with the best of intentions and I think Marvel went in with the best of intentions, but even while I was there circumstances changed radically and I ended up fighting continually with the editor. I'm not saying he was wrong, and I'm not saying

I was right, but I've never had screaming matches with an editor on the phone like I did there. It was an impossible way to work. What I wanted to do was create quintessential Spider-Man stories: the type of atmospheric Stan Lee/Steve Ditko/John Romita Spider-Man stories that really defined the hallmarks of the character. When you take Spider-Man outside of that and introduce too many other elements he's no longer truly Spider-Man. We fought a lot about that and ultimately I just knew it wasn't going to work out.

You were responsible for *Zero Hour*, which effectively redefined the continuity of events in the entire DC Universe. What was the thinking behind it?

Much of what went into *Zero Hour* was governed by the reactions we got to stuff that had been done before in *Crisis on Infinite Earths*. It was also a reaction to where we were as a company at that time. The whole idea was: here's a bunch of zero issues, all coming out in one month, that will essentially provide the reader with the reason they should pick up this book on a regular basis. The issue zeros were supposed to serve as mini-bibles, so you would know who each of these characters were. You would see the writer and artist at their best, and have the quintessential aspects of this book on display for twenty-two pages. If you liked it, you'd buy it next month. If you didn't like it, you'd know why. Editorially, it was a good way to approach the problem of how to get people to pick up more of your books, and as a story it set out to streamline some of the continuity glitches in the DC line. We weren't one hundred per cent successful,

Crisis on Infinite Earths

This twelve-issue series was essentially a 'housecleaning' exercise by DC. To explain away the modern-day existence of superheroes based on 1940s versions of Green Lantern, Hawkman and the like, DC created parallel Earths — Earth One, Earth Two and onwards — on which these heroes resided. It was later decided that this was 'confusing' to readers, and writer Marv Wolfman and a team of artists led by George Pérez set out to streamline the DC Universe. The resultant epic (in every sense of the word; the series really has to be seen to be believed in terms of the sheer numbers of characters and minute detail) introduced the Anti-Monitor, a being that was systematically wiping out the alternate Earths. Though superb in terms of both execution and content (it features the genuinely moving deaths of the original Supergirl and the Silver Age Flash), ultimately *Crisis on Infinite Earths* just paved the way for a whole new set of contradictions. And even the subsequent *Zero Hour*, in which Parallax (formerly the Hal Gordon Green Lantern) attempts to wipe out time itself and restart everything with a new Big Bang, really only underlines what a tangled web of continuity DC have woven over the years.

but it needed to be done. The big stuff is fun to do. I have a couple of ideas for big projects that I think would be tremendously successful. There's one for DC and one for Marvel, but I just don't know if I want to get back into those pits again. It's a tremendous amount of work, and exhausting.

Did you try to do on *Zero Hour* what Grant Morrison did on *DC: One Million*, where he plotted virtually every single DC book that month?

I don't think you have to micro-manage that way. What I did with the Tangent line is let people do their jobs. If you have a number of writers working with you, which I did on both Tangent and *Zero Hour*, you let them do the work, since they know their characters best. In the case of *Superman* #1,000,000, I wrote a plot and it was a good story — and I rarely say that about my own stuff — that I think would have worked well. It didn't contradict anything they had to say. They read it, bounced it, trashed it, and I quit. That's why that issue of *Superman* was written by somebody else. They didn't want a writer, they want-ed a trained chimp to sit down and type whatever they wanted. I don't work that way. I would never do that. I would never insult creators the way they did me on that project. It was one of the worst experiences I've ever had in this medium, and it's largely because of Grant trying to write everybody's book. If that's the way they wanted it they should have just told everybody to take the month off! I know a number of writers who worked on the 'One Million' books and were quite put out by it. We're dealing with talented people here, and I would never presume that I know better than they do. What I try and say on a crossover is, 'Here is a key point to hit sometime during your story. Here's another one. If you have any other questions please call me, and we'll work it out together'. But I would never dictate to people.

You've spent the majority of your career as a writer/artist working in the superhero genre. Do you ever feel the need to move beyond that?

Yeah. More and more I keep thinking about doing so. It's a path I want to walk, but I just haven't found my way there yet. I keep wanting to do more real-life stuff, or work on a Vertigo-style book. I think it comes down to courage. It requires a certain amount of nerve to give up what you enjoy doing — and what you do well — and take a creative leap. But it's also necessary to do that, and it's something I should do.

Frank Miller calls *Sin City* the purest form of his work because he writes, pencils, inks, letters and edits that book. Would you like to take on some-thing similar?

It's something I would like to play around with... someday. Every creator is dif-ferent, though. I'm sure Frank does enjoy that freedom, but I enjoy the cre-ative experience more when I'm bouncing around on projects, and by that I mean having three different books on the go at once. If I had to write, pencil, ink and letter a book I would go out of my gourd with boredom. It would feel like I was doing the same job over and over and over again, just to get one comic out. That's not for me; I'm just not detail-oriented enough to want to control each and every little aspect of what ends up on the page. I prefer being able to work on *Thor* here and by the time I get done to bounce back and go do, say, an issue of *Superman*. As we speak, I'm sitting here sketching covers for a couple of issues of *Green Lantern*. I like that I get to move around a little bit. By working that way, it keeps me a little more fresh on whatever projects I tend to be writing at the time.

So, in the future, are we going to see more of you drawing and writing your own stuff, or would you be happy drawing other people's scripts?

I'm rarely completely happy drawing other people's scripts; when I draw I like it to be from my plot. Having said that, though, I'm going to be drawing three issues of the 'No Man's Land' stuff that's happening in the Batman books right now, and I'm not writing those. But usually if I'm drawing it, I'm probably writing it. The downside of that is there are a number of writers with whom I would like to work. Ideally, I'd like to collaborate with a group of writers on a unified project, which is something of what Tangent was. With that line I said, here's the Tangent world — I sort of wrote the bible — and here's a broad outline of what characters A, B, C and D do. Each of the writers involved came back and wrote something stronger by far than what I gave them, and made it richer than I would have on my own.

Tangent

Perhaps one of the most refreshing, though not always successful, comic industry trends of recent years has been the attempt by both Marvel and DC to escape the sometimes creatively stifling constraints of their single, cohesive 'universes'. Generally, this manifests itself either as an alternate take on existing characters and situations (as in Marvel's *What If?* and DC's 'Elseworlds', wherein certain key continuity events are reinterpreted), or the creation of a whole new universe. Marvel tried and failed with their somewhat unimaginatively titled 'New Universe' books, while DC and Marvel together had more success with Amalgam, literally a fusion of characters from the two universes. More recently, DC had a stab with Tangent. For one week in 1997, DC published none of its regular titles, replacing them with Tangent books. Using existing (and trademarked) names, such as the Flash, Green Lantern and Doom Patrol, new characters were introduced, giving readers the chance to start from the ground up. Unified by an eye-catching design, and based on ideas and scenarios suggested by Dan Jurgens, the books are accessible, fresh and fun, with none of the usual excess continuity baggage. The initial nine titles were followed a year later by nine more.

Overall, I think Tangent had a lot of potential and possibilities. It showed that there are different ways to work, and I believe we are going to have to find those ways in order to keep moving forwards. I don't think it's viable, economically or otherwise, to go on doing comics the way we have been. The expectations of the audience are changing, and the way we do comics is going to have to somehow change with them. I'm not sure exactly how, but collaboration will certainly become more important.

*   *   *

Check out:
Superman: The Death of Superman
Superman: World Without a Superman
Superman: The Return of Superman
(the entire Doomsday/Death/Rebirth of Superman saga)

Superman/Doomsday: Hunter/Prey
Superman: Transformed
Superman: The Wedding and Beyond
Superman vs Aliens

DC versus Marvel: The Showdown of the Century
Zero Hour

Plus... *Crisis on Infinite Earths,* by Marv Wolfman and George Pérez

JOE KELLY

One of the comic book industry's brightest young talents, Joe Kelly began his meteoric rise to the top of the comic book pile while still a student at New York University. After a summer of fill-in work, the virtually unknown Kelly, still a year shy of graduation, scooped, in quick succession, the monthly writing assignments on first *Daredevil* and then *Deadpool*. Kelly's smart, tongue-in-cheek dialogue and witty, almost slapstick approach to storytelling swiftly found favour among fans and fellow professionals alike. Indeed, the Long Island-based writer's seemingly effortless ascension to comic book stardom appeared to be complete when the then twenty-six year-old found himself hired as writer of *X-Men*. But the job of scripting Marvel's leading franchise proved — as so many writers have discovered to their cost in the past — one fraught with problems, wrangles and creative differences, and eventually Kelly, along with writer Steven Seagle (who was concurrently scripting *Uncanny X-Men*), resigned after only thirty or so issues between them. But while the experience, says Kelly, proved to be something of an 'education', he insists it has not soured his enthusiasm for continuing to work in the comics medium.

You were at NYU studying dramatic writing when you broke into comics. How did it happen?

I was working as a graduate assistant to help pay for my tuition. I was like the video guy, I ran around pushing A/V carts. One day I was in the director's office and saw a letter on her desk with Spider-Man on it. I asked the secretary what it was about and she told me Marvel had contacted the school about doing a workshop for new writers, but she didn't know if the director was interested. In a big, self-sacrificing move I said I'd run it, which I did. Mark Powers and James Felder, who were both Marvel editors at the time, came to NYU and we did assignments in class, going over the Marvel style of writing and character development. Being a comic book fan, it was a great opportunity to show them samples of my work too, and they liked my dialogue. A couple of months later they offered me a shot at dialoguing a book, and that was *Fantastic Four 2099*, issue number five, scripting over Karl Kesel's plot.

Was that a big step, to go from studying comics in class to writing for Marvel?

I was confident it was doable, for a couple of reasons. One, I thought the class was really well run. James Felder is a very smart guy and an excellent teacher; the way he organised lessons always made sense and it was easy to grasp what he was looking for. Two, there was the training I'd had at NYU in dramatic writing. Whether you're writing a play, a screenplay or a teleplay you just make little adjustments, and I saw how to make the adjustments for comics writing. It was also a small project, it wasn't like somebody said write *Fantastic Four*. It was write this little book that nobody's really reading.

What did you learn in class from James Felder that particularly helped you?

On the simplest level, he gave me a lot of tools and free advice about what makes a good comic. How the internal conflict of a character should be externalised in every issue, how to construct stories in such a way that you didn't run out of ideas after three issues, and how to build up a cast. It was an environment of honesty and openness which, when you're new, is the best you can ask for. If you're always afraid that the guy's lying to you, that he really doesn't like your work and he's not going to tell you that you suck, you can't get any better. James was always very generous with his opinions.

Place of birth:
Long Island, New York, USA
Date of birth:
1 September, 1971
Home base:
Long Island, New York, USA
First published work:
Fantastic Four 2099 #5
Education:
New York University
Career highlights:
Daredevil, Deadpool, Marvel Fanfare, What If?, X-Men

How did that lead into a full-time job writing comics?

I still had one more year at NYU, but that summer James kept giving me fill-in work. I did a really abysmal *Daredevil* story in the last *Over the Edge*, which was this weird little dollar book. But James was great; he introduced me to other editors, and Kelly Corvese gave me a couple of *What If?* gigs. Then there were two issues of *Marvel Fanfare*. Kelly's assistant at the time was Matt Idelson, and after a month or so Matt was promoted and given the *Deadpool* assignment. He figured he'd go to the normal stable of guys to ask them for proposals, but also ask Joe Kelly, just to see what the new guy would come up with. So I banged out this seventeen-page proposal, we had a couple of conversations about it, then I got the job.

If you had to name four of the most important things that a comics writer needs to know, what would they be?

Having a clear sense of what the main source of conflict in the book is. If it's a single person book, what is the main character's conflict? If it's a group book, what's the group about? If the X-Men are about fighting for justice in a world that hates and fears them, then you have to figure out a way to amplify that and construct dramatic conflict situations for every character. Once you have that conflict identified, stories just start pouring out that all have weight. Otherwise they're just fluff pieces.

Making the story specific to the character. If you write a story and you can erase Superman out of every sentence and replace him with Daredevil, it's a shitty story because it has no real weight for that character. It might as well be Joe Blow walking down the street; who cares? To that end, you really have to do the research into what makes a story specific for a character. Some of that links back to that internal conflict thing, and some of it is just gravy. If it's a Superman story, Lois Lane is going to be in there, she's not going to be in a Daredevil story. Metropolis will be there, and so on. You learn to make the environment fit the character.

Setting up the story in terms of cast construction. The supporting cast pulls at the main character in ways that'll always put him on edge. For example, in Spider-Man, Aunt May needs Peter to go get her some medicine, but J. Jonah Jameson needs him to go out and take pictures of Spider-Man. That's a simplistic example, but he has to make tough decisions because of the people who are pulling at him, and characters always reveal themselves through the decisions and the actions that they take. So if Peter blows off Jonah to take care of Aunt May you know that she means more to him than Jonah, but there'll be consequences. So you set up a cast that's going to rotate him, spin him around and constantly give him new troubles.

Sorting out your continuity. Trying to lay in subplots and long-term gags that pay off over the course of maybe two years, to give a real sense of environment to the comic book. With *Deadpool*, I spent a lot of time thinking about who the guy was, what I thought he wanted, and what he knew about himself to be true versus what he didn't know. Then it comes down to what recurring themes we can throw up. For Deadpool, he always has problems with women. In every previous appearance he tried to kill the women he was in love with. We were like, if he's going to be the hero of the book that's going to be a little tough to play. But we decided we could probably set things up so that he's always thrown into conflict and messes things up because of his self-hatred. That's a recurring theme with Deadpool. So every time a new woman appears, you know there's going to be problems.

How do you structure your scripts?

It was nice to learn in that NYU class that there's no real format. Once I realised that, I kept it as close to a screenwriting style as I was comfortable with. What I do first is lay out a long story plan, to think of the comic book in terms of a year or a season, like a television show would be. I try and pin-point where I want my character to be by the end of that year, decide what I need to get them there, then start to fill in backwards. The story develops itself once I know the end point. Then in the middle I come up with the various set-ups, the hills and valleys, and how the subplots are going to intertwine.

Once I've got that mapped out, I expand my little outline into a two-page out-

---

Deadpool

Created by Rob Liefeld in the pages of *X-Force* (previously *The New Mutants*, an X-Men spin-off book), Deadpool is a mercenary with a mouth, a killer-for-hire with a lot of attitude and a seriously bad skin condition. Though introduced as simply a supporting character, Deadpool quickly became a fan favourite, spawning two limited series (the first written by Jeph Loeb, the second by Mark Waid) and finally an ongoing series. Wade Wilson is a former soldier-of-fortune and covert operative, who, having been diagnosed with terminal cancer, submits to a sanity-stretching process of genetic manipulation as part of the Canadian government's Weapon X programme (from the Wolverine back-story, incidentally). The process saves his life, but leaves him hideously disfigured and very hard to kill. In lesser hands, this slight, vaguely derivative character could easily have disappeared without trace, but it's a credit to everyone involved with Deadpool's various appearances (from Liefeld's dynamic visualisation to Kelly's wisecracking, roguish loose cannon) that the character has grown and thrived. Traditionally, such mercenary-type characters have a very short shelf life outside of whichever book spawned them, but Deadpool has proven to be the exception to the rule.

line and submit that to the editor, so he can tell me whether he thinks I'm on the right track. I like to have a solid outline, 'cause I like to know where I'm going. Then I go into writing the script and basically each bullet point in the outline I expand into however many pages I think it's going to take. My plotting style is sort of a combination of full script and the Marvel style. I generally indicate how I think the panels should break down. I don't just say Spider-Man has a conversation with Mary-Jane and they seem agitated, and at the end of the conversation he leaves. I put in little bits of dialogue that I think are important so the artist knows what expressions to draw. When it comes back to me I go through my plot, pull out all my dialogue and I see which bits still apply, punch it all up and put it in the characters' voices.

Do you think about the story in visual terms, working out the big hits up front?

I'm aware I'm in a visual medium, but I don't necessarily sit down and go, 'pacing-wise, there needs to be a double-page spread every issue', or 'make sure there's two or three spreads'. I don't really think like that. As long as the story points are getting across, I don't care if somebody's jumping off a cliff or off the Eiffel Tower. Whatever the artist wants to draw, I want it to be fun for them. But I'm very stingy about splashes and double-page spreads, because in two pages I can do more with a character's life than a big shot of a truck exploding is worth. So I'm always really careful, I try and make them count. There are times where I do say, 'this should be a bottom up shot for effect', or 'this is the big wide view', but part of that you have to let go. I think it's important for the artist to have as much freedom as possible, and in theory at least they have a better grip on that stuff than I do. If I feel strongly about something I'll put it in, but you could also go crazy and have one of these twenty-five page scripts for a twenty-page comic book, and that's a little too much.

How much collaboration do you tend to have with your artists?

It really depends on the artist and what they're looking for. Do they understand the script? Are they the type that wants to contribute? I always indicate in the beginning that although I put in a lot of detail it's open to their interpretation. If they think they can storytell something better, as long as they don't lose any important elements, I don't care if they do that. Sometimes they take me up on that and sometimes they don't. Sometimes the artist won't necessarily know what's an important story point if I don't tell them. I worked with one artist who didn't always get the jokes, so he just didn't draw them. It was like, 'Okay, that was a good joke, and now it's not going to be in there'.

I prefer collaboration, given the choice. I think the stuff always comes out stronger, because you're always trying to spark ideas off of each other and push one another to a new level, which is kinda nice. Sometimes it doesn't work out and you just have to keep your head down and write the best stories you can. I've had experiences with artists where they've said to the editor, 'I don't think this guy knows how to write comic books. I've been doing it for a much longer time and really we should get somebody else'.

If you're stuck for a story solution do you call your editors or other writers for help?

With *Deadpool*, Matt Idelson and I have a very good relationship. He's great at bouncing ideas back and forth and helping me break stories. Sometimes it's him who comes up with the inspiration, sometimes it's me, but it works as a partnership because there's never any proprietorship over an idea. Sometimes I call other writers and editors. Certainly I talk to James on a regular basis, and [former *Uncanny X-men* writer] Steve Seagle I always call up and say, 'I don't know why this doesn't make sense, tell me what's not working here', and he'll figure it out. And I do the same for him. As long as you have people you trust, it becomes a very easy thing, 'cause you're not embarrassed to say, 'I'm an idiot and I don't understand why this story doesn't work'. I'm lucky I have those people. I'm not a genius, and I need people who have strengths in other areas to help me out, certainly in terms of structure and story logic. My strength is character development, so when you get into the intricacies of story structure that's where sometimes I need help. Having those people around makes it all kind of click.

What were your feelings when you were offered *X-Men*, which is one of the biggest writing assignments in comics?

I was completely stunned. I had been asked, prior to that, to start thinking about *Wolverine*, and I was like 'Wow! I get to write *Wolverine*'. I really didn't understand why, and I still kinda don't. I was completely flattered and honoured and con-fused and terrified.

How did you approach writing the book? What guidelines were you given?

I hadn't read [the X-Men books] seriously for a long time, and they said they wanted to focus more on character. Scott [Lobdell, the previous writer on *Uncanny X-Men*] was really good at doing big, event stuff and crazy plots, but now they wanted to get into character-driven stories again and start a little smaller. I went back and started looking at the characters that I liked the most, picking them apart: who fitted well with who, how to make them stand out. My opinion about the X-Men was they work best when they bicker, not in a sort of annoying, constant way, but you've gotta have conflict within a team, otherwise it's one big, happy, boring family.

Because you're dealing with a big group, you have to balance out the lives of the individual characters against the direction of the group as a whole. The way Steve and I would work it was to have a major event that we would build up to; some big crazy story that we thought was also going to be very poignant for the various team-members. Once we had something we liked, we'd start working backwards, seeing how to build towards the event through subplots. Once a structure was laid in, we would take the individual characters and decide what we were going to do to them. So Storm might lose all her powers, and Jean Grey would have to become leader; you know, whatever made everybody go 'Oohh' at the table.

How did it work with *Uncanny X-Men* writer Steve Seagle and the writers of the other X-books?

Steve and I spoke constantly and agreed from the beginning that we hated crossovers, and we hated the idea that we were supposed to tell other books what to do. What we agreed is how we would approach crossover events. Essentially, the way it worked was we'd set up a situation in our books that if the writers on the other books felt like playing into, they could, and if they didn't, they could avoid it. They could maybe dedicate two panels to it, then forget about it, and that kind of suited us.

The original intent was that mine and Steve's books were gonna diverge. We were gonna work on them together up to a point and then have some kind of anniversary story, after which my book was going to be one type of book, his was going to be another. They might mirror one another, but they were not going to cross back and forth. The X-office wanted us to make them part of a tighter continuity, so we'd hammer out the overall story and then just talk constantly. We both liked different characters. He liked the older ones, I liked all the younger characters. The only ones we both wanted to swing around were Wolverine and Storm.

Steve Seagle

Or indeed Steven T. Seagle, depending on which of this very talented writer's books you're reading. Equally at home in the Vertigo weirdness of *Sandman Mystery Theater* and *House of Secrets* or the spandex-clad shenanigans of *Alpha Flight* and *Uncanny X-Men*, Seagle, like Joe Kelly, first broke into comics while still in college. Early work included the Eisner-nominated *Kafka* and Comico's mini-series *Amazon*, but when *Jaguar Stories* (also for Comico) was cancelled, Seagle was ready to call it quits. Friend and fellow comics writer James Robinson convinced Seagle to give it one more try and shortly thereafter he began co-writing (with Matt Wagner, writer/artist on *Grendel* and *Mage*) *Sandman Mystery Theater*. Not to be confused with Neil Gaiman's dream-king Sandman, this contemporary, noirish take on the old 1940s Sandman, Wesley Dodds, is dark, gritty detective fiction, and still packs a considerable punch. Seagle became sole writer of the title as of issue sixty. When *Alpha Flight* was relauched in 1997, in perhaps a surprising move, Seagle was brought on board to script the misadventures of Canada's mutant superteam, and so favourably received was his work that he promptly landed the key writing job on *Uncanny X-Men*.

Steve and I wanted to give readers a sense of, 'We care about these characters as individuals', and focus on two, maybe three at a time. Then we were told, 'We wanna have as many X-Men per issue as possible'. We literally started writing out these big charts and saying we're going to have this guy get hurt in April and this one will have a nervous breakdown in May. There was constant chatter amongst editors and writers, and you just sort of had to try and remember it all.

Previously you'd mainly worked on lone character books, whereas *X-Men* has a huge cast. How did you keep track of all the characters?

To me, keeping track of their plotlines is difficult, keeping track of their characters, is not, because I know they speak differently and they have different feelings. Whenever I start a project, one I'm going to be on for a long haul, I sit down and write these massive proposals. I look at every character and say, 'This is how I think they act, this is what I think they feel on the inside, and this is what I think they want as a medium-term goal, this is a long-term goal and this a short-term goal'. Going through that process sorts everything out in my head, so when I need to invoke what a person would do it's right there.

So we had wallcharts. On my computer, I had all sorts of flow charts and spread sheets. Steve, myself and one of the editors made this stack of colour index cards, where each colour was a different character. We maybe had 150 cards in total, and they were all different events and moments in that character's life, so you could refer to them easily. I do the big proposal first, with all the little character bios, and then when I'm doing the overall series proposal I draw little lines each month for each character, so I can see that character's going to develop in this way and this character's going to develop in that way, and when they come into conflict there'll be a fight. It's kinda like having a road map. I lay it out graphically all the time.

Many writers have complained of heavy editorial interference from the X-office. Was it this that eventually forced you and Steve to quit both books?

People do their jobs in the best way they know how and unfortunately when you're in a creative situation that also has a very rigid corporate backbone, those ideologies inevitably clash from time to time. And when you're working for a company that's also having bankruptcy problems everybody's pressure level goes up a 110 notches, because their jobs are on the line. That's the foundation of why things went bad. I honestly believe if Marvel was thriving, and it was five years ago, Steve and I would still be on those books. We never would have had the editorial interference and everybody would be happy.

So how did it all fall apart?

We'd write a story, work really hard on it, hand it in and it would get approved. Then we'd get a call from the X-office saying, 'We're not doing that story any more'. We'd already put three months of work into it, but being professionals we'd go, 'Okay, we'll try and fight for it but if they don't like it, they don't like it'. So we'd do a new story and we'd go through the same thing over and over again. There'd be a situation, say, where a character did something a little bit dark, maybe flips out and beats the heck out of somebody. The editor would come back and say, 'I kinda see what you're doing, and it's kinda cool, but I don't really like that they beat somebody up at this point'. We were happy to say, 'Okay, we'll take that out and fix it, work around it'. But more often than not they'd just go, 'No, throw the whole thing out and try again'. We were continually working from a position of never knowing where we were; what story was going forward, what story wasn't.

Then we would get these sort of vague dictates like, 'I know you just wrote half an issue but there aren't enough X-Men in it, so put more X-Men in'. A concrete example of that is *X-Men* #75, which was supposed to be just the new characters learning to work as part of a team. That's all the issue was supposed to be and everybody knew it. I was literally halfway through the script when I was told to put the other X-Men in it. I was like, 'Why?'. Their response was, 'Because it's the X-Men and you need to show them as a group, and it's already been five issues and they haven't worked together as a real big team yet'. My argument to that was, 'We haven't set up that they should work together as a team yet'. I wanted to start with this step and build to the next. Of course, it's their characters, so I put all the X-Men in it, and I think it was a weaker story for that. I crammed in every character under the sun that I could fit. Everybody that was at the mansion

---

The X-Books

Without a doubt, this is Marvel Comics' key franchise and, in the face of stiff competition from DC and Image Comics, the key X-books still consistently manage to hold the top spots in the Diamond Distributors' comics chart. Created originally by Stan Lee and Jack Kirby in 1963, *The X-Men* (the Uncanny tag appeared only occasionally for the first hundred or so issues) were teenage mutant superheroes, mistrusted and feared by society and trained in secret by their mentor, Professor X. The original team and book lasted sixty-six issues, and while not cancelled, subsequent issues featured reprint stories only. Until issue ninety-four, that is, when the series proper restarted, with the 'All New, All Different' X-Men (though technically the team débuted in *Giant Size X-Men* #1). The new team proved to be incredibly popular, spawning spin-off series (*The New Mutants*, *X-Force*, *Wolverine*, *Gambit*, *X-Factor*, to mention but a few) and mini-series (far too numerous to list here). In 1991, Marvel launched *X-Men*, featuring artwork by fan favourite Jim Lee, the first issue of which broke all industry records, selling more than five million copies. To this day, the X-books continue to attract the top writers and artists, and their popularity with fans shows no sign of letting up.

is in the story and half of the team has a pointless role. I tried to make it as cool as possible, but it was always after-the-fact coolness. That started happening regularly. You can only do that so many times before you start to go crazy.

Back in the old days, which are really only maybe five years ago, it didn't matter if you wrote a script three times, because the amount of money that was involved really made up for it. You could work only on *X-Men* and pay all your bills, but that was no longer the case when Steve and I were on the books; they weren't selling anywhere near the sort of numbers they used to. It's not just about money by any means, but when you're doing extra work it becomes about money, because you can't do other work. All of a sudden you're in a situation where I might as well quit *X-Men* and work on two books, because it will be the same amount of money as if I worked on one issue of *X-Men*.

We tried all sorts of ways to iron out the communication process but nothing ever really worked, and we just kept getting frustrated. Then the anniversary story [which ran across *Uncanny X-Men* #360 and *X-Men* #80] really got butchered, that 'All New, All Deadly' story was not what we wanted. Once again, we tried to make it as good as possible but that Cerebro* thing was not our idea; we wanted those new X-Men to be actual people, to be real characters, and we were told to make them holograms. We had no creative freedom.

When did you and Steve decide that enough was enough?

The final straw was when it was time to do the 'Hunt for Xavier' story. We hammered that out and again it wasn't what they wanted, and we had problems. By the time we'd come up with something we could all agree on it was time to do the next big crossover story, which was this Magneto arc, and we were basically called up and told that the main office was gonna write the overall story for us and we were just going to execute it in the books. There are situations in which that works fine: soap operas and television series do it all the time. Except, that's how it has to be from the start. To go from, 'Hey, we want you guys to lend your voices to these books and make them different and unique', to 'We're gonna write the stories for you', you know you can't go any lower. We had to quit. It became a self-respect issue. This was a fight that we knew we couldn't win, because who do you argue with?

One of the comments we kept getting was, 'What's this thing about editorial interference? They're not interfering, they're doing their job'. I understand that point of view, and that Marvel owns these characters, so at the end of the day they can do whatever they want, but there's a difference between collaborative editing and interference. It's a line that may be fine and entirely subjective, but it was a line we felt was crossed.

Style-wise, you seem to go more for pithy, tongue-in-cheek dialogue and character interaction than big fights. Do you agree?

Definitely. Not that it's just talking, but certainly to the degree that the characters and the characterisation hold more interest for me than the fighting. There

---

* *The X-Men's mutant-locating computer, which gained sentience and temporarily took the place of its creator, Professor X.*

is a lot of talking, I guess, certainly in a book like *Deadpool*. I want to make sure that the characters come through, because that's where I believe you hook the reader. The big fights and stuff like that, that's where I talk about it being the artist's job; I want him to make it look really cool and exciting. My job is to make sure the soap opera elements are in there, like this person's in love with this person and this one's frustrated. I just hope it doesn't come off as talking all the time, because that would be boring. Whatever the next project is I end up working on, I'm trying not to do something that's too dialogue heavy. There's always gonna be dense characterisation, but I don't wanna do another *Deadpool* because I don't want people to think that Joe's whole gig is just wisecracking people in red costumes. That was the joke for a while, that was all I did. I would like to do something a little serious and make sure there's some variety to it.

What about your future, do you see it being in comic books?

I would like to be doing this for as long as possible. I love comics, I love the medium, I love the characters and I love the idea you can do things in comics that would cost a gazillion dollars to do in a film and you would never be allowed to do on television. The process of having to go to a store, buy a book, flip through it and take the time to read it, connects you to somebody in a way that television maybe doesn't. When you're a kid and you have a comic book and it's rolled up in your back pocket and you run into your room so you can read it, it's a magical experience.

Are there any characters you'd like to write?

I grew up on Spider-Man and I would love the opportunity to do him. Batman's another favourite. Some of the horror characters, maybe. I like *The Phantom Stranger* and *The Spectre*, these weird books I inherited from my uncle. I like Green Lantern a lot, Moon Knight, Werewolf by Night. They're all characters that for one reason or another appeal to an odd sensibility. Some of them I've really thought out and some of them I haven't. Micronauts would be another one. And, of course, Superman. Superman is a perfect example of the type of thing I'm looking for. It's a book that has a nice history to it, it's got some import to it and it's a cool book. You could do some interesting stuff with that. I wanna do a book I'm gonna be proud of, 'cause after you've worked on something like *X-Men*, as much as it's a nightmare, it brings a certain level of prestige, and it's kinda difficult to take a step backwards. I'd like to put out a creator-owned book. It may suck, it may be a real piece of crap, but at least I can say with pride that this is something I really believe in.

What about the thing that you were studying when you got into comics, screenwriting?

I'd still love to do that. It's funny, the types of movies I'm interested in writing don't really have anything to do with comic books. They're either comedies or they're really serious heavy dramas or stories about families and tragedies in families, stuff like that. So I actually don't know if writing comic books is gonna help or hurt in the screenwriting. If the opportunity comes I would absolutely love to write a script, or be a script doctor. That would be kind of an ideal job. I would like to see it happen. In a three-month period Steve Seagle got a movie sold, a TV pilot sold and an animated series sold. It was great. Every once in a while we'll sit down and collaborate on something or I help him punch up the kids' show. Right now we are collaborating on a screenplay.

*   *   *

Check out:

Deadpool: The Circle Chase by Fabian Nicieza and Joe Maduriera
Deadpool: Sins of the Past by Mark Waid, Ian Churchill and Lee Weeks
(The original two *Deadpool* limited series)

JEPH LOEB

Hollywood screenwriter and producer Jeph Loeb, whose film credits include *Commando* and *Teen Wolf*, is perhaps best known in the comics business for his collaborations with artist Tim Sale — notably on the award-winning maxi-series *Batman: The Long Halloween* and the similarly acclaimed *Superman For All Seasons*. Loeb's terse, economic writing style and use of strong internal narrative, coupled with Sale's rich, expressionistic visuals, produced two deeply atmospheric and personal tales that have cemented the pair's reputation. Loeb and Sale first worked together on DC Comics's *Challengers of the Unknown*, and their creative partnership is one of several Loeb has forged down the years. Preferring a collaborative approach to comics, Loeb's career has been characterised by close working relationships with just a handful of artists, including former Image Comics founder Rob Liefeld. Loeb's association with Liefeld continued and expanded to include a two-year stint as co-publisher for Awesome Comics, Liefeld's new company, for which he created *The Coven* with artist Ian Churchill. While never having totally forsaken his screenwriting career, Loeb has nevertheless managed to maintain a prolific comics output, plotting — at one time or another — the adventures of *Captain America, The Avengers, X-Force, Cable* and *X-Man*.

You're a screenwriter and film producer by profession, with more than forty scripts to your credit. How did you come to be writing comics?

A friend of mine, Stan Brooks, produced a one-hour television special called, I think, *Happy Birthday, Superman — You're 50*, and through this he became friends with [President and Editor-in-Chief of DC Comics] Jenette Kahn. Stan knew of my love for comics — I have every comic book published by Marvel and DC since about 1964 — and suggested I get in touch with her. Jenette said, 'You should write a movie for us', so I took her at her word and pitched this *Flash* movie. When the deal fell through, Jenette called me and said, 'If you're not going to write a movie for us, would you like to write a comic book?'. It was like it was Christmas morning! And that's the short version of how I came to write *Challengers of the Unknown*.

Why *Challengers of the Unknown*? Was that a book you particularly wanted to write?

Not exactly. Jenette turned me over to Dick Giordano, who asked me what I wanted to do. Of course, I said I wanted to write Superman, it just never occurred to me that there was only one writer. I thought of it like television, where there was a team of people. I didn't even want to write Superman on a regular basis, I just wanted to do one issue. Well, Dick said, 'No, there are people who do that'. Well, how about Batman? 'No'. So eventually we turn to this list of characters that are currently in the closet. I must have gone through about fifteen names before I got to *Challengers of the Unknown*, which I didn't really know, and he said, 'Yeah, you could do something with that, why don't you write a proposal?'.

Were there any earlier attempts at writing comics?

Around 1972, my stepfather was working at Brandeis University, where Elliot Maggin was a student. Elliot had written [a *Green Arrow* story titled] 'What Can One Man Do?', which a lot of people consider one of the best DC ever produced. My stepfather came home one night and said, 'Do you know a guy by the name of Elliot Maggin, and would you like to meet him?'. Elliot came to the house and brought me a copy of the [*Green Arrow*] book signed by Neal [Adams, the artist], upon which I sat down and wrote a Superman story — Elliot was writing

Place of birth:
  Stamford, Connecticut, USA
Date of birth:
  29 January 1958
Home base:
  Sherman Oaks, California, USA
First published work:
  Challengers of the Unknown #1
  (1991 mini-series)
Education:
  Columbia University, NYC
Career highlights:
  The Avengers, Batman: Legends of the Dark Knight (Halloween specials), *Batman: The Long Halloween, Cable, Captain America, Challengers of the Unknown, The Coven, Superman For All Seasons, X-Force, X-Man*

Superman at the time — called 'Why Must There be a Superman?'. [In my story] the Guardians of the Galaxy approach Superman and ask him why he does what he does, and if he understands he is affecting the outcome of human history. It eventually turned into — and I have to cop to this — the end of *Amazing Spider-Man* #100. I sent it to Elliot and he wrote me this long letter that basically said you can steal from movies, you can steal from books, you can steal from plays, but you *can't* steal from other comics. Don't do it ever again.

Flash forward twenty years and Elliot is living in California, I'm living in California. We go to lunch one day and there's a comic book store nearby. Inside, Elliot is looking though a rack of comics and picks up one [containing a story he wrote] called 'Must There be a Superman?'. He says, 'You know, this was always one of my favourite stories', and I look at him and say, 'Yeah, it was always one of mine, because I wrote it'. It was like someone had dropped an anvil on his head [when I explained]. For the rest of the day he just kept apologising. Ultimately, Elliot's is a different story, because mine was *Amazing Spider-Man* #100. But I always found it odd that Elliot never mentioned it. So that was really the first comic I ever wrote. Elliot continues to apologise, most recently in the foreword to *Kingdom Come*.

If you were so interested in comics, why didn't you try and pursue that as a career rather than screenwriting?

I would have to say the practical nature of it. In my mind, you just couldn't make a living being a comic book writer. Also, there was a kind of magical quality to comics. One of the problems with being a movie screenwriter and producer is I understand the process of making a film down to the coffee on the set. It becomes a struggle to go to a movie and not be constantly aware of how it was made, so much so that you aren't able to get into the movie itself. I think on some level I didn't *want* to know how comics were made.

When you began writing *Challengers of the Unknown*, did you find the process different from writing a screenplay?

People asked me at the very beginning what the difference was, and I would say 'budget'. You can blow up the Earth in a comic book in one page, or even a panel, and in a movie you can't without it costing millions. That was very attractive. I do think my film-making career made a big difference in terms of the way I approached it. I tend to write comics as little movies. I have a visual style in my head and I work best with people who understand that visual style. I always tell artists from the very beginning that I see my plot — I don't write full script — as a blueprint, and if they can find a way of drawing it that's more interesting to them, they should.

I'm surprised that you don't write full script, considering your background in screenwriting. Why is that?

I believe the artist should have the opportunity and the ability to be able to draw what he wants. I do write little snippets of dialogue with the plot, so the artist knows whether the face should be sad or happy or something like that. But very often the pages will come back to me and I'll think I wanted this to be about something completely different, but I can use the same images and change the dialogue. More often than not that happens with Tim [Sale], because his faces are so expressive. And because I've done the majority of my work with Tim, I tend to go in that direction. When I first started writing comics, I would take a credit card, a yellow legal pad and make twenty-four boxes running down the long side of the pad over two pages, and then I would literally put stuff in the boxes. I can't draw, so they were generally the shape of the panel with maybe a stick figure. But it at least gave me a rhythm of what was going to be a double page spread and what was going to be a full page, and how many panels I'd need on the page.

What did you bring to comics from scripting movies?

I was taught by Paul Schrader [the writer of *Taxi Driver* and *Raging Bull*] that fifty things happen in a movie. Not fifty scenes, fifty *things*. So, you number one-to-fifty on your pad and you write bullets of what's happening in the story: John meets Mary, Mary loses her leg, John goes off to war, that kind of thing. And those can be one act, one scene or they can be a whole group of scenes. By the time you get to the end of the story you've written out a whole plot. I adopted that for comics, and I number pages one through twenty-two and on one line I write very short bursts: Batman enters, Joker recoils. Batman smiles, Joker gets punched in the face. That then translates to a paragraph, and that paragraph can sometimes be panel one. Sometimes it can be, 'okay folks, before we start, what we want to do is tell a story that's extremely noir, so all of these characters are going to be poking in and out of shadows'. Then, depending on whom I'm working with, there might be a note: 'Tim, let's discuss this further. I don't want to see anyone's face, I want it back-lit. When Batman enters it should be the scariest thing in the world'. Sometimes those paragraphs are two or three lines and sometimes they can be half a page, but generally a plot for me tends to be eight-to-ten pages in total.

Stylistically, your comics are very sparse in terms of dialogue. Was that a conscious decision from the very beginning?

For me, this is a visual medium. The joke I've heard is: the time it takes to read a comic book is the time that it takes for a person to take a crap, and the time it takes to read a Jeph Loeb comic book is the time it takes to pee! I tend to write fairly sparsely. When people say to me, 'I read your comic book, it took me like eight seconds', I kinda say to them, 'Well, you're not reading it the way I intended you to read it. I would rather you slow down and look at the pictures'. It's sort of like when I watch people walking around an art museum. With some it's like a race, they go from painting to painting to painting. What you could do is stop in front of a Monet and feel the emotion of what's going on, or look at the technique, and you could be there for the rest of the day. And I think comics, when they're well done, and animation likewise, work this way. If you just stop and watch the 'movie', comics take a very long time to read.

PAGE FIVE

Panel one

Shot of Arkham Asylum as the snow starts to fall on Christmas Eve.

Panel two

GORDON and BATMAN walk down the hallway, past doors marked for "Jonathan Crane" -- and others..."Pamela Isley"..."Jervis Tetch"... Gordon asks Batman if it...concerns him that ever since Batman's arrival they've had a rise in the "peculiar" cases here at Arkham. Nearly double.

Panel three

They turn the corner, we see a long row of doors -- as if the number of...disturbed cases goes on forever...

Gordon, backpedaling, tries to point out, awkwardly -- not that there is a *direct* correlation between your appearance and the appearance of so many disturbed... What I mean is, do you give it any thought?

Panel four

They stop outside the cell door of JULIAN DAY. There, Batman responds "No." But internal narration tells us..."*I know what Gordon is implying. That my appearance on the Gotham scene has somehow <u>attracted</u> these men and women to my city.* "

Above: *Jeph Loeb's script for page five of* Batman: The Long Halloween *part three, 'Christmas'.* Courtesy of Jeph Loeb.

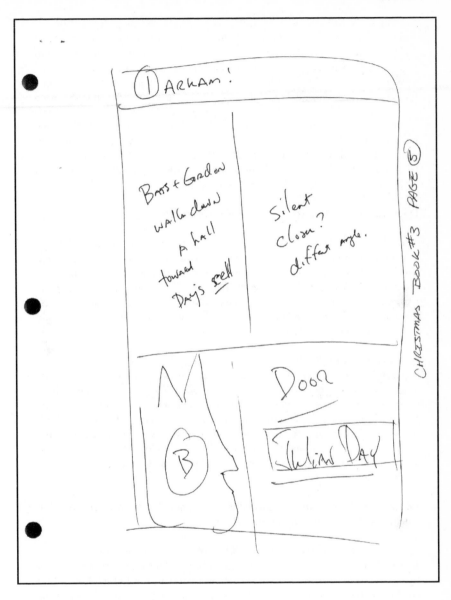

Above: *Loeb's rough of the same page for artist Tim Sale. Courtesy of Jeph Loeb.*

I'm not a big believer in cluttering [artwork] up with lots of word balloons. *Superman For All Seasons* was the most dialogue and narrative intensive thing I had ever done, and that's after writing comics for about ten years. I don't believe in writing captions that describe what's happening in panels, which was something I was regularly asked to do when I worked in the X-Men group, and it always bothered me. I never understood the point. I was much more drawn to the internal narrative of, say, Batman, where you could have Batman fighting some guy and in the internal narrative box you could say, 'It's on nights like this I remember my father'. You had two stories going on at once: the visual story and the narrative story, and the dialogue was there to assist the visual story. That sort of became my style: how can I do this in as few words as possible and how can I make the words not repeat what's going on in the image?

Does that again stem from writing for the screen?

The thing I think I've brought to my [comics] writing is realistic dialogue. A lot of people working [in the field] grew up with comics and have only ever written comics, so the tendency is to write what's called comic book dialogue; the 'leaping lizards' of it all. I tend to write dialogue the way I would if an actor had to read these lines. Of course, that doesn't mean I don't love the clichés of the medium; there's nothing better than Captain America raising his shield and yelling, 'Avengers assemble!'.

Also, I tend to cast the roles when describing my characters. I'm not interested in getting a caricature, but I know if I say 'Michelle Pfeiffer', I'm not going to get a big fat woman. It doesn't necessarily mean that the character's going to look anything like Michelle Pfeiffer, but at least the artist knows what I have in mind. I'm very drawn to the civilian side of the characters, that's why a lot of my writing, particularly in the Batman and Superman books, deals with Bruce and Clark. I think it's important that the reader be able to identify with the hero as a mortal, while at the same time seeing that they're larger than life and they can do these amazing things.

Challengers of the Unknown marked your first collaboration with artist Tim Sale. How did the two of you meet?

I was asked who I wanted to draw [*Challengers of the Unknown*], and I said I want somebody who can draw guys that look different. There were three people I really wanted to work with — Jim Lee, Whilce Portacio and Rob Liefeld — and all of them were under contract at Marvel. We kept going to the San Diego Comic Convention trying to find guys who could do this, and it was probably four years later that we found Tim. My editor brought me these large, oversized graphic novels called *Thieves' World*, and the thing I loved about [Tim's artwork] was he drew really ugly people. I said, 'This is the guy'.

How did you approach working with an artist the first time?

I assumed the process was very much like working with a screenwriting partner:

he writes ten pages, gives them to me, I then rewrite them and send them back, and you sort of chase each other through the script until you're done. That includes throwing out scenes and re-doing stuff. So when Tim turned in the first pages I phoned him up and said, 'No, this isn't what I want. You have to re-draw them'. We took about a year, and Tim drew probably forty pages for a twenty-two page story before we turned anything in to DC. I think they thought, 'This book isn't scheduled, so when these guys get around to finishing it we'll publish it someday'. It was what we like to refer to as a critical success, and at the time I thought — I'm out, I'm going to go back to being a screenwriter. I'd had a new experience, got to write a few pages of Superman in a cameo and a couple of other guest-stars and that was it. I was never gonna do comics again.

Which, of course, wasn't the case. Once you've written your plot, do you send it to your editor first or the artist drawing it?

I always turn my plots in to the artist first, for his comments. Some editors like that, some don't, and I tend to gravitate towards those who do. Archie Goodwin was the kind of person who not only liked me doing that, he encouraged it. I don't do it that way because I think I know better than the editor, I do it because it's very important to me that I don't send in something that's essentially only a first draft. By the time the artist makes comments and I rewrite it, it's about a third draft that the editor gets to see. All of this is happening in a very short

Archie Goodwin

Generally, and rightly, regarded as one of the nicest people in comics, the other thing professionals (and fans) all agree on was that Archie Goodwin knew his stuff. Whether as writer or editor, Goodwin's thirty plus years in the business were well spent, crafting a vast number of excellent titles and grooming the next generation of comic book superstars. Goodwin cut his creative teeth at Warren, on titles such as *Blazing Combat* and *Vampirella*, before moving on to DC and Marvel. His run on Batman in *Detective Comics* and its back-up strip, *Manhunter* (with artist Walt Simonson), are fine examples of Goodwin's economical and character-driven style. Other notable credits include a long run on the *Star Wars* newspaper strip and the adaptation of Ridley Scott's *Alien*. But it is perhaps his role as editor, Group Editor on Marvel's Epic line and a brief time as Editor-in-Chief at Marvel, that defined Goodwin's comics career. At both Marvel and DC, his level, amiable demeanour and the sheer depth of knowledge he was happy to pass on, won him countless friends and admirers. When he died in March 1998 after a long and typically stoic struggle against illness, the comics world was palpably the lesser for it.

amount of time. Then the artist starts drawing, and I go in and script.

When I script [a comic] it looks like a movie script. I keep the description I had in the plot, so that when the editor reads it he's following what I had in mind and what's been drawn. Then I write the dialogue. But again, I don't write the dialogue the way everybody else does, which is more like a play format, where the characters names run down the left side with a number next to it, and the numbers refer to the balloons. I indent to the middle of the page, so my scripts look like a movie script. I only chose to do that because all of my writing programs are formatted for movies, and it was easier to stick with that. No one's ever asked me to do it in a different style.

You've worked with the same few artists — Tim Sale, Ian Churchill, Steve Skroce, Rob Liefeld — over and over again. Was this by preference or accident?

I work very closely with a lot of the same people because they become my partner. I could never work in an environment — and I've bumped into it a couple of times with editors — where I can't talk to the penciller daily. It was certainly the way we ran Awesome Comics. I'm so aware that an artist lives by himself, doesn't have any feedback and rarely gets much from his editor other than, 'Great. When are the next pages coming?'. I get it from my movie background, the same way a director at the end of every shot will say, 'That's terrific people, let's go again', or 'That was really amazing, let's move on'. That's not blowing smoke, it's part of the collaborative process. So, I spend a lot of time talking to my artist, because I want to make sure that they're interested in drawing what I'm writing. Again, part of that is from working with Archie Goodwin, who encouraged that sort of thing.

I have bumped into editors who have said, just write a great script, we'll take it and get an artist for it. That to me is like writing a script for a movie and never being able to talk to the director or the actors. Some people say that means I'm a control freak, but I just believe in keeping everybody part of the team, and that includes the colourist and the letterer. I think everyone should know what everyone else has in mind. That's part of the reason why I enjoyed being the publisher at Awesome Comics, being able to put those elements together and talk to everybody about them.

Have you ever had any bad experiences with artists?

At some point in a comic I will slow it down to a conversation and have what's called in the movies 'talking heads', and when that happens it really needs to be done for pacing. I had one experience where I was working with an artist who looked at the page — there were eight or nine panels of talking heads — and decided instead to draw a full page panel of two characters standing next to each other. I tried to explain to him that there was no way for the reader to understand that the dialogue was going to go A to B to C to D, and so on, cutting back and forth, if there were two people standing next to each other. The balloons were going to be all over the place, and I was going to wind up covering up his artwork. That was the last time I worked with that person.

You credited Mark Waid as influencing the genesis of _Batman: The Long Halloween_. Was this another example of the collaborative process at work?

I would never set out to write a screenplay without first talking to friends who are in the business, if for no other reason than so they can say, 'You know that someone _else_ has told this story, don't you?'. I was speaking with Mark about something and he asked me what I was working on. I told him the idea and how it was set in 'Year One'*. What he said was very provocative: 'If you're going to work in Year One, you might want to consider thinking about Harvey Dent before he was Two-Face, because no one's really dealt with that'. It's covered in Frank Miller's _Batman: Year One_, of course, but after that no one really went back there.

There isn't really any project I've set out on without getting two or three people's reaction to it and input. Then it's up to me, my editor and the artist to figure out how it goes from that point on. Also, if I read a comic and I dig it, even if I don't dig the person's work, I'll call them on the phone and strike up a conversation, because I don't think we do enough of that in our industry. I'll say, 'I read your book and thought it was great'. There's an old saying that goes something like, 'When you cast your bread upon the water it comes back cake'. What tends to happen is when I write something good, a lot of people call me.

You worked on the X-Men group of titles for a while. How did you find that experience?

It took some getting used to, but I responded to it favourably in a lot of ways, and I have to say that was mainly because of Scott Lobdell. Very early on Scott and I became friends and I was really amazed, and still am, at his ability to tell a story. I would call him and say this is what I want to accomplish, and he would say, 'Wouldn't it be really interesting if during that story Domino was blind', and this small thing that I had never considered would change the way the whole story was told. Another time I would say, 'I'm thinking about doing a story with Cable and Gambit and I want them to go to Paris together and have to stop some master criminal', and Scott — and it was almost an editorial kind of thing — would say, 'That's interesting, what do you think of doing that story with Iceman instead?'.

Now when we would do something like 'The Age of Apocalypse', and I was simply told by editorial this is what you're going to do, the idea was to tell the best story possible. Sometimes that was frustrating, but we all wanted to tell really fun stories. Towards the end it became a competition, and it was very difficult to work because there were some people who felt like they weren't getting to tell their story. I never really got caught up in it. Fortunately, it was at the end of a three-year period and I knew at that point it was time to move on.

---

* _A vaguely generic term that has come to mean any story set in a hero's formative years, Frank Miller's_ Batman: Year One _being the prime example._

Batman: The Long Halloween stretched over a period of thirteen months. Was the plot locked in from the start or did it evolve while you were writing it?

I found the original proposal recently, and it was really interesting to me because there was no Holiday character. It was Calendar Man through the whole thing, until DC asked me not to use him because it would establish a different continuity. That's pretty important given how the story revolved around this new character. And the mystery, there was no mystery initially, it was just Calendar Man out there killing people.

Long Halloween changed as I was telling it. [Originally,] Harvey got the acid thrown in his face in book six, and in the final execution [that happened] in book eleven. That was five months later, and it really changed the structure of what was going on. By the fourth or fifth issue it became very obvious that the response was growing about the mystery, and that changed the April's Fools story to one that focused entirely on the mystery. That's one of the joys of being able to work on something where you get reaction to it and are far enough ahead that you can actually change it.

In *Superman For All Seasons*, it was originally intended that the second book was going to open with about a ten-page montage of Superman fighting Brainiac, Metallo and all these other supervillains, to show how he had grown in the hearts and minds of [the citizens of] Metropolis. DC called and said they were not sure at the point the story takes place that Superman had met

Scott Lobdell

As becomes clear over the course of this book, working in the X-Men office on one (or indeed more) of Marvel's most prestigious titles, can be both blessing and curse. But one thing is certain, it's a career-making move. It certainly was for Scott Lobdell, who came from almost nowhere (most notably a run on *Alpha Flight*, made notorious by issue #106 in which Northstar 'came out', a first for comics) to script both *Uncanny X-Men* and *X-Men*, quickly establishing himself as a fan favourite, essentially because he took the stories back to the earlier, soap opera-ish feel of the Chris Claremont era. Lobdell became one of the most prolific X-writers (after Claremont), and co-created (with artist Chris Bachalo) *Generation X*, which filled the 'students-in-training' void left when *The New Mutants* grew up into *X-Force*. Lobdell was largely responsible for the top-selling 'Age of Apocalypse' storyline (in which, for four issues, all the key X-books changed their titles, charting an alternate future). As ever, things fell apart, and Lobdell left the X-books and ultimately Marvel, finding a warm welcome (as so many others had) at Image Comics.

any of these people yet. That's the continuity demon, and what it forced me to do was tell a story about this nuclear missile coming into Metropolis and have Superman pick up this submarine. In the end, I liked that much better and it's certainly more in the tone of what I was doing. So that book also changed along the way.

Also on *Superman For All Seasons*, I never intended to have anyone narrate the books. It's such a strong element of the story you would think I must have had it in mind from the very beginning, but it was never my intention, it was always going to be a third person narrative. It wasn't until I got all the artwork for issue one that I realised how big the pages were. I started thinking the readers are going to finish this in about eight seconds, I'd better put something on the page here. But what I didn't want was long, laborious descriptions, as I used to do when I was writing in the X-office. Then I started thinking about Pa Kent, and how the story really revolved around him, and it just clicked; he became the narrator of the first book. After that I thought, 'I want to do different voices throughout the whole thing'. And we were well into issue two when that decision was made.

You're no longer as involved with Rob Liefeld and Awesome Comics as you once were. What happened?

The book I primarily look after is *The Coven*, with Ian Churchill, which I write, though I'm also very involved in the production and the other elements of it. [Awesome] is certainly different than it was. I hope someday it's going to come suddenly roaring back, because that's the world Rob lives in. Rob and I talk every day about the company, but it's not the priority that it had been over the last two years. My life changed when Awesome took off, and I decided at that point if I could do one project a year at DC, I would otherwise devote myself exclusively to Awesome. The same with my screenwriting. There was stuff I had committed to that I needed to go back and look at, but other than that I pretty much stopped being a screenwriter. But that's turned on its ear again, and I've stoked up that stove and I'm back to where I was two years ago, where my primary source of income is as a screenwriter. I still write comics mostly out of love.

Has writing comics affected the way you write movie scripts now, or even what you write about?

What I've found is, I've written a lot of action/adventure stuff, so the two have always intermingled with each other. A lot of people say to me of my screenwriting, 'Wow — I can really see how comic books have affected what you do'. I'm not quite sure that's a compliment all the time, meaning it goes back to that comic book dialogue versus real dialogue. But what has happened in a very strange way is *Superman For All Seasons* was the most personal thing I had written. It was personal because of my love for the character, but also because I had to flex my writing muscles in a different way. I had to create a voice for Pa Kent, for Lois, for Lex and for Lana, making each of them describe how they saw Superman. It was two women, a father and a villain, and those are very different voices acting as the storyteller.

What I really found during that process was — and I have to give a lot of credit to Tim — after the sort of intense darkness of *Long Halloween*, Tim wanted to tell a story that was far more gentle and much lighter. Not in terms of a lighter tale, but in terms of brightness. He used to say to me we're going to go from the dark into the light. We finished the first issue and it's very emotional, it's about a father having to say goodbye to his son, and being a father it's something I think about a great deal, even though my son is only ten. And what really took me by surprise was the number of people that the story touched, and I don't think that had ever happened to me writing comics. That changed the whole focus of the way I wanted to write comics. I suddenly realised I wanted to tell stories that were more emotionally driven, and emotionally driven in a way that was very personal to me.

I'm now back to writing movies, and I'm finding that the things I want to write about are much more emotional and much more personal. I had always liked to tell stories that I thought people would enjoy, but I don't know how much of me was in them, in the writing. Some of that may be because for seventeen years I wrote with a screenwriting partner. When I went off to run Awesome Comics I had to separate from him, and he has now gone on to a successful writing career of his own. That split enabled me to sit down and say, 'Okay, what would you write if there was no one else influencing you?'. What I'm finding is, I'm choosing to tell stories that are far less biff-bam-boom and more about family and its dynamics, and love and how people interact with one another. It's a very early

Awesome Entertainment

Rising from the ashes of Extreme Studios and Maximum Press, Awesome Entertainment was Rob Liefeld's *après*-Image comics publishing venture, forged in the wake of a falling out with his former partners and some messy litigation. One of the founders of Image Comics, Liefeld struck out on his own, forming a partnership with Jeph Loeb, who served as Publisher and general talent recruiter. In short order, Awesome managed to draw in such artists as Ian Churchill, Jeff Matsuda, Ed McGuinness and Steve Skroce (all from high-profile assignments at Marvel), retain the services of Alan Moore (already writing *Supreme* for Liefeld at Extreme) and be taken to court by Marvel over plans to publish *Fighting American* (citing major similarities between this character and Captain America). Financially backed by a multi-media company with a proven track record in elevating small companies into large ones, the future looked bright. Ultimately, though, Awesome stuttered and almost ground to a halt, with only Loeb and Churchill's *The Coven* sustaining the imprint. Liefeld, though, is nothing if not a survivor, and sold a screenplay for the comics-based project called *The Mark* to Universal for a tidy sum, ensuring that in some shape or form, he will return.

stage in the process, and I don't know how people are going to react to it. But ask me a year from now and I can give you a sense of whether or not I'm writing *Gigantor the Space Age Robot*, or something more like *City of Angels*, which is about the human condition.

*   *   *

Check out:
Askani'son (with Scott Lobdell and Gene Ha)
Batman: Haunted Knight (collects the three Halloween-themed *Batman: Legends of the Dark Knight Specials*)
Batman: The Long Halloween
Superman For All Seasons
Wolverine/Gambit

TODD MCFARLANE

From an office over the garage of his house in Phoenix, Arizona, the same office that he's worked out of for more than a dozen years, Todd McFarlane presides over a multimedia empire that encompasses comic books, movies, music videos, computer games, an animated television series and a toy company — an empire built essentially on the back of just one character, Spawn. Born in Calgary, Canada in 1961, McFarlane began his comic book career as a freelance artist working on various titles for DC and Marvel, including *Infinity Inc*, *GI Joe* and *Batman: Year Two*, before finding fan fame and fortune as the regular artist on first *The Incredible Hulk* and then *The Amazing Spider-Man*. McFarlane's energetic, dynamic visual take on the webspinning superhero was an immediate success, culminating in the launch of an all-new comic titled simply *Spider-Man* in 1990, which he both wrote and drew. Despite its success, the first issue selling in excess of three million copies, McFarlane increasingly found himself at odds with the Marvel way of working and barely eighteen months into his run, he and a coterie of fellow artists split from the publisher, co-founding a rival company, Image Comics. Then came *Spawn*, and the rest is comic book history.

Were you a big comics fan as a child?

Not really. If we'd be going on like a ten-hour drive, say, Dad would load up the family, buy a couple of comic books and throw them in the back seat. But no, other than casual reading I didn't really collect comics until I was seventeen. I remember the day: I had a couple of bucks in my pocket — comics were only about thirty cents back then — I walked to the store and bought six. That was it, the floodgates opened, I became a fanatic. I collected everything, started working in comic book shops, and just fell in love with the medium.

Was your interest in comics purely an artistic one?

I was the proverbial best artist in my class — I'd always been drawing — and I was looking for a focus. When you buy every comic book there's inevitably a couple of bad ones in the batch, and the bad ones were very inspiring to me. Those were the ones where I'd go, 'Christ, if this guy can do this, then so can I'. I went off to college on a baseball scholarship, but once I got there I ended up getting a degree in graphics because my dad's in the printing business and I was intent on following him into that trade. The comic book stuff I did at night, from about eleven o'clock till about one o'clock in the morning. I sent off around 700 samples before I finally got someone to bite on one of them.

So when did baseball's loss become the comic book industry's gain?

The day the baseball people told me to go away. Then, about two or three weeks before I graduated, I got my first professional work, so I never had to go and look for a real job out in the real world. I literally went straight from college into comic books. The first job was ten pages of back-up story in some obscure book, so you could say they started me in the mailroom and I just worked my way up.

You were drawing The Incredible Hulk and then The Amazing Spider-Man. What was it that made you want to write yourself?

It wasn't because I thought I was a writer, and it wasn't even because I thought I had anything big to say, it was because I didn't feel like drawing three issues in a row of Doofusman, or whoever the bad guy might be. The only way I was gonna be able to control what I got to draw was if I was in control of what was

Place of birth:
Calgary, Alberta, Canada
Date of birth:
16 March 1961
Home base:
Phoenix, Arizona, USA
First published work:
Spider-Man #1 (as writer)
Education:
Eastern Washington
University
Career highlights:
*The Amazing Spider-Man,
Batman: Year Two, The
Incredible Hulk, Infinity Inc,
Spawn, Spider-Man*

being written. I was drawing what the writers wanted to see instead of what I, the artist, wanted to see. It's very easy for a writer who's never drawn anything in his entire life to sit there and say what we need now is this scene in New York City, and we need all eight million people out in Times Square and then we need, like, two million attacking alien ships and within the alien ships there's 57,000 little mini space aliens and each one of them is running around with five cases of Coca Cola. They can write that in thirty seconds, but it takes two fucking days to draw. I wanted to turn around to the writer and go, 'You draw this! If you had to draw this once, you would *never* put it into a story again'.

The great thing about writing your own stuff is, if you're bad at doing shadows you never do a story at night. If you're not good at drawing fat people, then you make sure you're always hanging around the skinny farm. And if you like doing horses, then make sure your character has a horse or you meet The Lone Ranger. If I'm bad at drawing spaceships, why would I write a story about spaceships? Once you write, you can play to the strengths of what you do artistically.

You credit Jim Salicrup, your editor on *The Amazing Spider-Man* at Marvel, for giving you the opportunity to write.

He was the best editor I ever had. Jim is either a very smart man for giving me the amount of latitude he did, or he's the stupidest guy around for having the amount of confidence in me that he did. Maybe he sat there and said, 'Todd McFarlane is a hot guy, he sells books and he has a reason behind everything. I don't agree with everything, but every time I ask him why he does something he gives me a half-hour dissertation. And this kid, you've just got to leave him alone and give him a lot of leash and he won't disappoint'. Now you can't do that for every creative person, but Jim was smart enough to know I wasn't just some kid who's doing his second monthly issue. And he told me, 'You wanna draw, fine, you wanna ink your own stuff, ink it, but you better be pretty damn good, and you better learn fast. You wanna write your own stuff, fine, I'll give you some writing, but you better learn how to write very quick. I'll give you the opportunity, but you better succeed, otherwise I'm going to have to come back to you and say, "Todd, you're not capable of doing it"'. So the pressure was on me first and foremost.

Did you run up against much resistance to artists writing?

A little bit, but the tough thing was trying to divide Todd McFarlane into two. At that point Todd McFarlane the artist was winning all the awards and was one of the top guys, as compared to Todd McFarlane the writer who had never written one sentence. No one could seem to differentiate between those two people. There was a great expectation that Todd McFarlane, this artist that they liked at that time, and who at that point had five or six years of honing his artistic abilities, was going to basically be the equal in writing. Except he didn't get the five years to grow into writing; he actually had five minutes to grow into it. It was always odd that people would go, 'Todd's a hell of an artist, but his writing sucks'. I think if you take most writers and look at their first stories, they'll probably not hold up as their high water mark either. Five years later, they actually are a better writer than when they first started. So it was always gonna be catch up for me. In two or maybe three years I'd be a horrible writer, an average writer or a good writer, but people wanted me to be the equal of my artistic ability on my first writing assignment.

In the letter columns of those early *Spider-Mans*, you were very conscious of your flaws and wanted people to accept you as you went along.

If you look at the letters page in *Spawn*, a lot of times I still address the same concerns to some degree. But back then it was frustrating to people because they liked the artwork so much, they wanted the writing to match it. But the only way they were going to get the artwork was if I was also writing it. So, they had to have a little bit of patience and go through the growing pains of some of the stuff with me. By the time I got to issue number eight [of *Spider-Man*], I did this story about some child killing thing that to me was out of the norm for what you'd expect from a Spider-Man book. It was still awkward, but at least [the writing] had advanced from issue one. That was all I was looking for.

Did you find the actual writing process difficult?

Sure. Sometimes it comes a little bit easier, but then I can honestly say I still find the drawing to be difficult. I don't consider myself a guy whose skills are so natural I can just close my eyes and do it. I've had to work at everything I've succeeded at or failed at because it is labour intensive for me, all of it. As time goes by, some things become easier, like conceptually putting stuff together and coming up with ideas. That's because you start to get into formulas and ideas click, and you've got a broader résumé in your brain of what it is you're trying to accomplish. Sometimes I look at some of the stuff I wrote in *Spawn* and I don't recollect writing it. Sometimes I go, 'That was pretty good', and the frustration is, I don't remember doing it, so I don't know what I was going through that got me to write that.

Do you spend more time working on the visuals than the words?

As an artist, I make the building blocks from the images first. Some of it is, what kind of mood do I want? What kind of atmosphere? If you take a look at even the very first *Spider-Man* stuff you'll see all of them took place mostly at night and all of them dealt with monsters. And to some extent there's an extension of that in what I've done since in the world of *Spawn*, and even the toy company I own. It's still a lot of monster stuff. I just wanted to get to that place, which I guess is why I was always so enamoured with Batman, because Batman ran around at night and lurked in the shadows. I don't think it's an accident that Spawn is, on some levels, kind of close to Batman, because Batman was always a more enthralling character to me than Superman.

Can you describe the way you normally construct a story?

Given that I started with the images, then what I would do is work out the three big spots: a beginning, a middle and an end. Everything inbetween I sorta fudged it. There were a lot of occasions — and I know it would be appalling to a writer to have seen what I did — where, out of a twenty-two page story, I would literally draw about seven pages and then I'd figure out what I wanted to do. I'd throw the seven pages on the ground and sometimes I would like rearrange them and go, 'this would make a cooler story if this happened first and then this happened'. And then I'd draw more pages.

There were times where to some extent I had all twenty-two pages done, and I would literally lay the twenty-two pages on the floor in the order I thought I wanted, and then start to rearrange them. I'd go, 'That page actually looks better over here, and this scene looks better over there'. Just like an editor on a film, right. Then I'd look at all the permutations and start to put a story in my brain about how this scene could butt up to this scene and what would the dialogue be. Then I'd just kinda grab all the pages up and I'd go, 'Okay, I need to start writing the story right here'.

I remember people coming into my office while I was doing this and being shocked. They were like, 'You'd better not let a legitimate writer see what you're doing. You're making it up as you go'. Yeah, pretty much. But I could say that about a lot of things; me, I just kinda fly by the seat of my pen. What it did was it

Speculation

The comics industry was booming in the early nineties. A huge wave of collector/fan-driven interest and speculation (comics were viewed not simply as collectable in terms of their stories, but also in terms of their rareness, desirability and resale value) had raised sales to levels previously only attained in the forties and early fifties. One of the key factors in determining a comic's value was the name (normally, though not exclusively, that of the artist) attached to it. A 'hot' artist and an element of collectability (anything from a variant and not widely available cover to bizarre printing errors... as in an early issue of *Spider-Man* wherein the normally green Lizard turned blue) meant big bucks, and collectors would often buy multiple copies of certain issues, keeping them untouched, unread and bagged in protective plastic sleeves for resale at a later date. When the first issue of Todd McFarlane's *Spider-Man* appeared, at the height of this collectors' boom, it was almost guaranteed to do big numbers. Not only was McFarlane a bona fide 'hot' artist after his run on *The Amazing Spider-Man*, but shrewd marketing on Marvel's part (including the requisite number of variant covers) resulted in sales of more than five million copies.

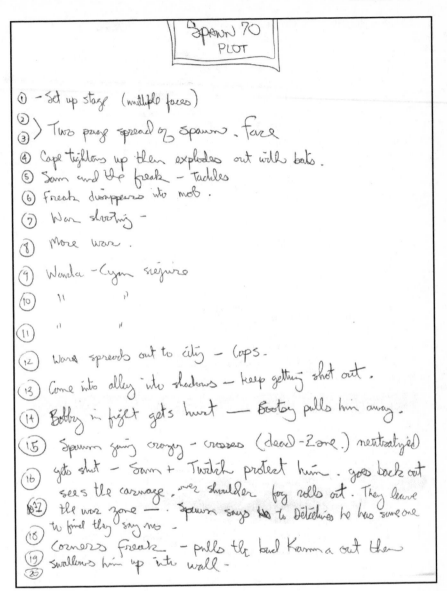

SPAWN 70 PLOT

① - Set up stage (multiple faces)
②
③) Two page spread of Spawn. Face
④ Cape tightens up then explodes out with bats.
⑤ Sam and the freak - Tackles
⑥ Freak disappears into mob.
⑦ War shooting -
⑧ More war.
⑨ Wanda - Cyan siejuro
⑩ " "
⑪ " "
⑫ War spreads out to city - Cops.
⑬ Come into alley into shadows - keep getting shot out.
⑭ Bobby in fight gets hurt - Bootsy pulls him away.
⑮ Spawn going crazy - crosses (dead-zone.) neutralized
⑯ gets shot - Sam + Twitch protect him. goes back out
   sees the carnage, over shoulder fog rolls out. They leave
⑰ the war zone — Spawn says No to Detectives he has someone
⑱ to find they say no -
⑲ Corners freak - pulls the bad Kamma out then
⑳ swallows him up into wall -

Above: *Todd McFarlane's handwritten plot breakdown for* Spawn *#70. Courtesy of Todd McFarlane.*
Spawn ™ *and* © *1999 Todd McFarlane Productions, Inc.*

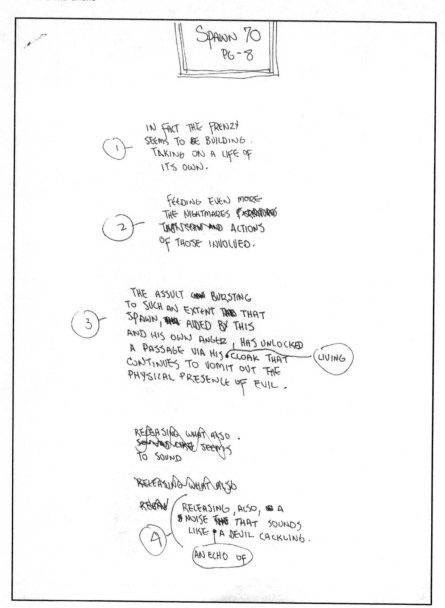

Above: *Dialogue, numbered for speech balloon/caption placement (see opposite), by Todd McFarlane.*
Courtesy of Todd McFarlane. Spawn ™ and © 1999 Todd McFarlane Productions, Inc.

Above: *The same page from* Spawn *#70 with corresponding mark-ups and notes. Script by Todd McFarlane, pencil artwork by Greg Capullo. Courtesy of Todd McFarlane. Spawn ™ and © 1999 Todd McFarlane Productions, Inc.*

never got me locked into any kind of formula, good or bad, and that worked as well as it could for a guy like me.

So you'd never write out a full script or a plot before you started drawing?

You're writing for yourself, right; I don't have to write a plot for myself. What I would do is tell the story over the phone to my editor and then sit down and just make some notes. The only thing I really do, and still do to this day when I'm working with [*Spawn* artist] Greg Capullo, is take a piece of paper, number it from one to twenty-two down the spine, then I put about four, five words next to each number. I go, what's the story? Sometimes the story is literally page one: Spawn in alley. Page two: Spawn still in alley. Page three: Cogliostro comes into alley. Page four: more Cog. Page five: more Cog. Page six: cut to Sam and Twitch. Page seven: Sam and Twitch. Eight, nine and ten: fight, fight, fight. Literally it's that simplistic.

Then what ends up happening is when I'm drawing [the page] I'll actually put in all the detail and choreograph it. Or when I get on the phone with Greg we talk the story out and he usually just tapes the conversation. I go, 'We got three pages of fight; here's the reason they're fighting and here's the end result — I need one of the guys to end up next to a bucket and the bucket needs to have marshmallows in it'. But as to how he gets them from the beginning of the fight to the marshmallows... well, Greg Capullo's a very skilled artist and I don't need to tell him how to beat people up. That's where the artistic interpretation comes in, and you actually start to assert yourself stylistically.

When you were writing and drawing *Spider-Man* and later *Spawn*, would you sketch out little thumbnails or go straight into the art?

The first couple of years I was in the business I did thumbnails. But at some point you have to have confidence in your drawing. I thought that doing thumbnails and then transferring those thumbnails [to the page], you always seemed to lose a little bit in the translation. Some people's thumbnails are really cool, there's lots of energy and motion because the strokes are made very quickly. But then, when they lightbox* it and you see them, it's become stale and very staged.

What I would do is literally scribble out little drawings with a blue pencil. They were so loose that when I was writing *Spider-Man* and I had to give the pages to the letterer so he could put the word balloons in, I'd literally have to put arrows to the blobs and note, 'This blob is Mary-Jane, this blob is Peter'. Then, when I got it back, I would go straight into the inking. People would go, 'You start inking from the scribble drawing?'. Well, yeah, I had built up enough confidence in my inking. What's the difference between taking an ink pen and starting to draw and taking a pencil? The only answer I ever got from artists was, 'What if you make a mistake?'. Well, if you make a mistake with a pencil, you erase it. If you make a mistake with ink you just get whiteout. There. Done. I fixed it as fast with whiteout as I could with an eraser.

---

* *The artist blows up the thumbnails or roughs to full page size and traces them down onto the artboard, thereby limiting extraneous linework.*

At that point I was writing, pencilling and inking. That's three full-time jobs. So I had to basically figure out a way to be very economical with how I spent my time. So, in the writing process I figured out how to cut corners 'cause I was drawing for myself. In the artistic roughing out I figured out how to cut corners. Even in the inking I figured out how to cut corners. Because you were in control of the whole package you were able to massage it and get through the monthly grind.

You only stayed on *Spider-Man* for a year or so. What happened?

There were a lot of little things that wore me out over my time at Marvel. Number one was editors asking me to redraw panels. Why? Because they didn't think it would pass the Comics Code. Had anybody shown it to the Code? *No.* So they were asking me to make changes based upon assumptions, rather than fact, which was always a waste of my time. Since I left Marvel, I've made it a rule never to correct anyone's work in mid-flow. Instead, I will have a discussion about it after the fact, and we'll decide whether we should do it in the future. I'd get arbitrary calls about things like: you can't put a foot out of a panel, you can't overlap panels, you can't do this, you can't do that. I had a conference call one time with five editors and they were debating whether I should redraw something because [Marvel Editor-in-Chief] Jim Shooter might not like it. Not 'Jim had seen it and doesn't like it', but 'Jim might not like it'. My response was, show it to him and if he doesn't like it, then I'll fix it. It became such a hassle and I just got tired; I didn't need that kind of bullshit in my life any more. My wife was having our first child and I think I finished the last two pages of *Spider-Man* the day before and the day after she was born. That was it, I just took five, six months off. I was going to quit anyway.

And this led to the formation of Image Comics?

Somewhere along the line I started making some phone calls, and Rob Liefeld was going to jump boat, Erik Larsen also, so there were always going to be three of us. And then we started thinking, well, since there's three, let's see if we can make it four, five and the final count was seven. Jim Lee was a very key player in all this, because Rob Liefeld and Todd McFarlane were like these loose cannons, so hey, let the psychos go. But Jim Lee was the golden boy, he was the guy who had just started the new *X-Men* book and it had sold a ton of copies. It was a big statement.

We all gathered in a hotel in New York and went up together to Marvel to tell them we were quitting and here were our reasons. Marvel has a distorted version of what happened; they claim we came in there demanding the copyright to *Spider-Man* and *X-Men* and silly stuff like that. We made no demands. They asked us what it would take for us to stay and we said nothing, we're not here to negotiate. The exact same day we walked across the street to DC, and we quit DC, even though none of us were even working there. But we wanted to tell them, 'Listen, here's what just went down at Marvel, and you guys should maybe pay attention to this'. None of us ever stood up and said that we had more relevant stories to tell, we never said we were astute businessmen and we never said we were going to revolutionise the comic book industry. We just said that we were sick and tired of where we stood.

Did it all go to plan, right from the word go?

When we left, we all skinned our knees to some degree in terms of the amount of bad business decisions we made, or by not being focused on our projects, or by not trying to put together stories that made some kind of overall sense; finding a vision or a voice for what it was we wanted to do. I think all of us were floundering a bit at the beginning, and though we did find a little bit of a niche for a time, we then lost it to some degree: Erik Larsen is still doing *Savage Dragon*, and I'm still involved in *Spawn*, so neither of us have lost our original baby. Jim has *Wildcats*, but that's no longer truly his. Marc Silvestri is still doing well, but he's not doing [his original book] *Cyberforce*. We went off in different directions for different reasons, and have had varying degrees of success, depending upon your arbitrary definition of success. There was no big gameplan, really. To have that you needed to be all working in unison, and I didn't want to tell Jim Lee what to do, all I wanted was the freedom to tell Todd McFarlane what to do. We all wanted to do our own thing; whether we all agreed with it or not wasn't relevant.

How exactly does Image Comics work?

Essentially, Image Comics as a whole was kind of like a clearing house, in that

Image Comics

It was 1991, and for perhaps the first time in its history, the mighty halls of Marvel were rocked by a major mass-exodus of talent, notably seven artists all at the height of their fame. The list read like a who's who of comicdom's movers and shakers: Erik Larsen, Jim Lee, Rob Liefeld, Todd McFarlane, Whilce Portacio, Marc Silvestri and Jim Valentino. All seven had been headlining top-flight books for Marvel, and between them had sold millions (indeed, Lee and McFarlane had, between them, racked up sales of eight million plus copies of their respective *X-Men* and *Spider-Man* launch issues). Having left Marvel, McFarlane, Lee and the others formed Image Comics, an independent publisher with real clout and, certainly for a year or two, a major portion of the comic book market share. Image, though, was merely the central linchpin, around which several other, smaller studios revolved. McFarlane created Todd McFarlane Productions, Lee Wildstorm, Silvestri Top Cow, and so on; each responsible for their own titles, rights and characters. Several other creator-owned titles, including James Robinson's *Leave it to Chance*, Matt Wagner's *Mage* and Kurt Busiek's *Astro City*, have subsequently been published under the Image umbrella.

each one of us started up our own little entities. Some of the guys started up studios immediately and others, like me, we just work out of our house and do our own book. I didn't want to have five, six, seven, eight books right off the bat. What we did, as a company, was set ten, maybe twenty generic rules, like: nobody should say fuck in their comic books; you have to make sure you have solicitations on the first week of every month; we'll all get our cheques eighty days after the books come out; everybody has to pay their own FedEx bills and so on. So there were some rules, and I think we talked about pricing to start with, and then that was it, it was up to each one of us to market ourselves, to create our own characters, to hire our own talent and to exploit (or not) our characters outside of the comic book community.

To some extent those rules still apply, and when we bring on board new people, other than again some very basic rules, all the onus is still on the guy doing the book. Image Comics will cast its eye over the project, will help you with solicitations and with accounting, then the rest of it is your problem. So all the onus is on the creative person, in that the more they sell the better they do. Some people have had bad experiences with Image Comics because they didn't take advantage of how it's set up to be taken advantage of. The deal we offer is ten times better than any deal that's out there right now. You give us a flat fee and everything is yours. We don't want any rights to your trademarks, copyrights, and if you do succeed with your book we don't get any ancillary rights. We just get a little flat fee for putting that 'I' in the corner. Thank you.

Let's talk about Spawn. He's much more a horror superhero than a conventional one. How did you come up with the character?

Spawn was a character I created in about 1978, just after I started collecting comic books. In fact, about a year after I bought those first six. Visually, that Spawn was pretty damn close to what he is today. He was always sitting in my back drawer, some place in my portfolio. Having total freedom, I thought, I wanna do a dark, cool character. I wanted to burn him. That was a conscious decision 'cause I wanted him to be a black man. But if you burn him you can kinda trick the public into thinking that they're not looking at a minority. See, I'd lived with the real Al Simmons — which is what Spawn's called — when I was in college, and I thought we were kinda the exact same person other than the colour pigmentation of our skin.

I'd always wanted to do a scene in *Spider-Man* where you have a black man mugging a white Wall Street stockbroker and Spider-Man comes and saves the day. Then the white guy goes, 'Those fucking...', and he uses some derogatory term about the black man, and Spider-Man nails the stockbroker against the wall and says, 'What colour do you think I am underneath this mask?'. And the stockbroker, like, shits his pants, 'cause of course nobody knows who Spider-Man is. Why is it that we always make the assumption that he is a good, pure, white guy? How do we know he isn't Asian or Hispanic, other than he didn't have a heavy accent? Because that's how our society sort of ticks. We just make these broad assumptions.

I wanted Spawn to have a bigger appeal, so I figured if I burnt him he would just become Spawn. Now he's been around so long in the burnt form I don't think people think about who he was or what he was. He was a man and now he's just Spawn, right. They don't really define him by what he was before. So stripping the man of his identity automatically gets you into who he is and not hung up on any of the social or economical kind of stereotypes that each culture has. *Spawn* can be whatever it wants to be to whatever culture. Because he has no face, he can be anybody.

Dramatically different from, say, Superman then?

To me Superman was the most boring character that there was. There was nothing I could do with that guy. He spins planets and he's completely impervious to anything. It's like, big deal. That's why Batman was always cooler. Batman could actually get shot and die. I wanted to create a guy that had the potential to be Superman, 'cause he has all this energy, but if he uses it, then he is basically wasting his power and eventually he'll die. So I wanted to give him the option to be a superman if he needed to. For the most part, though, Spawn was still Daredevil or Batman, he was just a guy who basically used his natural God-given talents.

I put another layer in there which was the costume. That ended up being alive, so when he couldn't solve the problem with a baseball bat or brass knuckles or a gun — unlike Batman, Spawn's not averse to using a gun — then the costume comes to his defence. And if the costume can't do it, then eventually he has to make use of his powers. But that's kind of a last resort, because he doesn't want to be a hero and he's aware that if he does [use his powers], then potentially it's gonna kill him. The other thing was the way Superman always knew how to be a hero from the very first day. I don't believe that anybody, if you gave them the power of Superman tomorrow, would be a hero the next day. They would just be very strong.

Did you have the whole story mapped out from the beginning or has it evolved organically over time?

As you live it you start to make your mistakes, and you start to see what works and what doesn't work, then you start to build what the story is. So even in comic book form, I've only just begun to get into some of the stuff that's cool to me, that actually defines what Spawn is. Then, in the sequel to the *Spawn* movie, if they use my script, you're going to see more of that; because I'll go straight to the meat and potatoes stuff of who Spawn is and what he's about.

How much of Todd McFarlane is in Spawn?

He laments for his wife a lot, and the most important thing in my life is my wife. His wife is named Wanda, my wife is named Wanda. His buddy is named Terry Fitzgerald, my good pal and right-hand man in my company is named Terry Fitzgerald. Al Simmons was kind of a blue-collar worker, given that he was a government assassin, and I consider myself to be a blue-collar kinda guy, even to this day. I try not to lose sight of where I came from. Spawn's got a bit of a bad attitude, and I would definitely say I also do in certain circumstances. Spawn's kind of put in this situation where big ideas and big, overpowering things are trying to dictate his life, and he's trying to fight against it. So the bad attitude comes from him not accepting that just because somebody gave him superpowers he has to do what the guy wants him to do with them, even if the guy's called Satan. He wants no part of it. To me, the attitude isn't 'cause I think I'm gonna be fighting heaven and hell some day, but I do think I'll be fighting — and have fought — the government and corporate American entities; big, faceless bodies that none of us know who the hell's at the top of, but that try to dictate what we do on a day-to-day basis. Like me, Spawn doesn't fight if you don't push him, and he only pushes when he gets pushed.

There's definitely a marked political subtext in *Spawn*, in addition to the racial issue. You have him living among the homeless, and in one story you dealt with the issue of child abuse.

We also had a Klan issue. The homeless thing, well, here you have a man that has no home, that's disfigured. If we saw Spawn walking on the street we would be appalled by him. If he was walking down the sidewalk we would cross the street to make sure we didn't get near him. And we are supposed to be a

---

Spawn

Few comics have generated such massive acclaim, popularity and sales in as short a time as Todd McFarlane's *Spawn*. Right now there are: two regular *Spawn* comics — *Spawn*, a consistent bestseller, eighty plus issues and still going strong, and *Spawn: The Dark Ages*, which replaced *Curse of the Spawn*; a *Spawn* movie (which did well at the box-office and on video) and a planned sequel; an animated HBO series (also available on video); a computer game, *Spawn: The Eternal*; and a massively successful toy line. All this from a character that only débuted in 1992. Al Simmons is a covert government operative killed by his bosses and sent to Hell, where he is offered a no-win deal by arch-demon Malebolgia and returned to Earth as a Hellspawn, a general in the army of the damned. While the concept behind *Spawn* may be straightforward, the execution is never less than stunning, with McFarlane's or Greg Capullo's dark and moody artwork complementing stories and scripts that drip with horror, angst and torment. Spawn has, quite simply, become an industry, but McFarlane has maintained such rigorous and concerted quality controls over the end product that it remains as fresh and exciting as ever.

SPAWN 69
PG - 4 AND 5

⑤ GOD ONLY KNOWS WHAT KIND OF UNHOLY POWER IS NOW RUNNING ~~OUT~~ UNCHECKED.

① FOR A MOMENT BOTH DETECTIVES DRAW IN ALL THAT THEY SEE. COGLIOSTRO HAD WARNED THEM THEY WERE ABOUT TO ENTER A SOME KIND OF BIZZARE WAR THAT WOULD ~~EXTEND~~ ~~AND PRESENT SOM~~ ~~THOSE~~ EXTEND BEYOND JUST THE NORMAL PERAMITERS OF A TURF WAR.

④ CONTINUED

BUT THAT'S NOT WHAT STOPS SAM DEAD IN HE

THE HEADLESS VISAGE CRUCIFIED BEFORE THEM SIGNALS ALL THAT COGLIOSTRO FORTOLD

HE'S ~~A~~ SEEMED ALMOST INVULNERABLE AND THE THOUGHT THAT SOMETHING MIGHT BE ~~AS~~ LOOSE THAT CAN ~~DOING~~ MUTILATE TO SUCH A DEGREE ~~AS WHAT PUTS THE~~ ~~FEAR OF GOD~~ THAT SCARES THE DETECTIVES.

② CRUCIFIED AND HEADLESS THE LIMP VISAGE OF SPAWN SERVES NOTICE ~~THAT TO INDIVIDUALS THAT~~ TO ~~ALL~~ THE SIDE OF THE UNSEEN ENEMY.

③ BUT THAT'S NOT WHAT STOPS SAM AND HIS PARTNER DEAD IN THEIR TRACKS.

④ WHAT CHILLS THEM IS BOTH HAVE ~~THEY'VE PRESUMABLY~~ SEEN THE INCREDIBLE STRENGTH AND ~~REGULAR~~ RECUPERATIVE POWERS OF ~~SPAWN~~ OF SPAWN DURING PAST ENCOUNTERS

Above: *Dialogue, numbered for speech balloon/caption placement (for* Spawn *#69), by Todd McFarlane. Courtesy of Todd McFarlane. Spawn* ™ *and © 1999 Todd McFarlane Productions, Inc.*

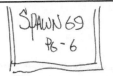

SPAWN 69
PG - 6

(7) SPARE ME YOUR ~~NICE~~ INNOCENCE ACT. I'VE KNOWN FOR A LONG TIME OF YOUR PRESENCE HERE ON EARTH. BOOTSY? ISN'T ~~IT~~ THAT THE NAME YOU GO BY NOW? WELL, I APPLAUD YOUR BEING ABLE TO MERGE SO EFFORTLESSLY WITH THE ~~HUMAN~~ HUMANS, BUT YOU ~~HAVE~~ HAD TO KNOW I'D BE AWARE OF YOUR SERVALENCE DUTY.

ELSEWHERE

~~BY~~ WHILE ELSEWHERE ON THE FRINGE OF TERRITORY THAT IS TWO LEVELS REMOVED FROM THE HEART OF 'RAT CITY' ~~ANOTHER~~

(1) ~~CONFRONTATION~~ A CONFRONTATION OF ANOTHER SORT IS ABOUT TO BE JOINED.

~~HEAVEN ISN'T YOU~~

(2) INVOLVING REPRESENTATIVES OF TWO ETERNAL CLANS. HEAVEN AND HELL.

(8) HEAVEN CAN'T BE THAT FOOLISH? CAN IT?

(3) IRONIC ISN'T IT?

~~(N)~~ ~~BOTH OF US WANDER~~ SO NEAR THE ACTION. ~~SO CLOSE~~ TO BATTLE, YET NEITHER OF US ~~CAPABLE~~

(4) THAT WE'VE GOT A WAR RIGHT UNDER OUR NOSE AND NEITHER ONE OF US IS CAPABLE OF DOING ANYTHING ABOUT IT. ~~IT~~ MAKES ME WONDER WHO IS REALLY IN CONTROL OF HUMAN DESTINY.

(5) ~~SEE I'VE BEEN NEUTRALIZE~~

BOTH OUR MASTERS SEEM TO ~~BE~~ BE GAINING NOTHING OUT OF THIS SKIRMISH.

~~YOU~~

~~YOU'VE~~
(9) IT'S NOT. BUT I STILL MUST ADHERE TO MY ORDERS. ~~NEEDLESS~~.

(6) WHAT ARE YOU ~~CRABB~~ BLUBBERING ABOUT, OLD MAN?

Above: *More from* Spawn *#69. Script by Todd McFarlane. Courtesy of Todd McFarlane.* Spawn ™ *and* © 1999 Todd McFarlane Productions, Inc.

compassionate people! But the homeless, who are the dregs of the world, the losers, they're the only ones who are willing to take this guy in. I was just trying to put a little bit of a twist on the 'Don't judge a book by its cover' thing, because everything isn't what it professes to be. You can sit there and go, 'Yeah, those homeless, why don't they get jobs?', but at least they gave this guy a little bit of warmth, comfort and compassion. They socialise with Spawn, where we would take him and put him in an institution.

So are these political issues that you're particularly keen to bring to your readers' attention?

They're issues that I think are important, that shouldn't be ignored. But, given that you are doing them in the realm of fantasy and superhero comic books, I don't think it's proper to be heavy-handed with them. So, that Spawn is black has never been a big issue. That Spawn is homeless has never been a big issue. That Spawn basically believes in the family unit has never been a big issue. I've never written a dissertation or story specifically on any of those things.

The child abuse issue I did bring to the attention of people, but the end result was Spawn sorta trying to play God and ending up exacerbating the situation. By lecturing the Dad and tattooing him with 'I beat my kids', he thought that he could embarrass him into being a decent guy. Instead, it triggered the Dad into becoming even more hostile and led not only to his death, but also turned the juvenile into a murderer. Spawn thought he was doing good, but because he just walked away he had no idea what happened until I did a follow-up to that story where the two kids show up in New York. Spawn's like, 'What the hell are you doing here?', and the older kid goes, 'Didn't you hear? We killed our Dad and went to a foster home, and then we ran away 'cause we wanted to be cool like you, 'cause you just fucking took our Dad and gave him shit and so we're giving everybody shit'. Spawn doesn't want to have anything to do with them, because ultimately they're like miniature mirrors of what he is. He was the one that created them to some degree, so he has to live with the fallout of his actions*.

To me there are more interesting ways to deal with a subject than just doing an action story. As I get older, those are more compelling to me than having the bad guy of the day come in and kick the crap out of the good guy and the good guy do something that saves the day. I've seen that a million times. I can write that story in my sleep. My mom can write that story.

Early on in the *Spawn* run you collaborated with several big-name writers, including Neil Gaiman, Alan Moore and Frank Miller. Did you give them much freedom in terms of story direction?

I gave each one of them as much freedom as they wanted. The first phone conversation with all of them was, 'I want you to do an issue. You can do whatever the fuck you want, what do I care?'. That was my hook. And some of them said, 'Cool, I'm

---

* *The original story appeared in* Spawn #29 *and the follow-up in* Spawn #58.

in'. And some of them said, 'Cool, I'm in, but let me ask you a few questions'.

The reason you got into writing in the first place was to draw what you wanted to draw, so how was it working with writers again?

Not as satisfying as when I do my own stuff because again I had to go and do stories they were interested in, but not necessarily that I was interested in. The difference was it was a position I put myself in, so it's tough to get mad at yourself. I didn't have to do it, and I knew it wasn't going to last forever.

Do you think you have matured as a writer?

I'm writing the screenplay for the next *Spawn* movie, and it's going to be very serious and a lot more sophisticated than the first, in terms of it's not special effects driven. It's going to be a *Silence of the Lambs* type thing, and a couple of the ideas I'm looking to put into Hollywood are also along those lines. To me, that will decide whether I've made the next step, not where I am now in terms of the comic book writing. It's whether I can actually start to put together real stories, with real people, ones that actually don't come across as stiff. Depending on what happens in the next year with these screenplays, I'll be able to make a better judgement on whether I've actually been able to make the jump into what I consider to be pretty decent writing. It's like drawing, just 'cause you've got an image in your head doesn't mean that it comes out of the pencil. You have to fight for it. Sometimes the exact same thing is true with writing. I've got to get to the point where I can actually pull out what it is that's in my head.

What's left for you to achieve in the comics field?

I want to get into publishing material that's closer to what the original intent of graphic novels was. I want to do anti-comics comics, because [superhero] comics are so stereotypical. It's like, if your idea could actually work in *Superman* then fuck it, it's the wrong idea. If it couldn't work in *Superman*, then I want to hear about it. We're doing a *Crow* comic, but I don't want the Crow to be fighting the villain of the day and I don't want the hero to be good looking and I don't want the colours to be nice. I want it to look like a novel, something I could ship to Europe, and the Europeans would look at it and go, 'Cool, this isn't American comic books'.

With all your many responsibilities, how much actual writing are you able to do?

On *Spawn* I'm doing the plotting. I go over ideas and make sure the book's going in the right direction. If it doesn't, or I'm not completely satisfied with the writing, I'll either get somebody else or I'll just jump back on it again. But there's things I have to do with the toy company and the movies and the Hollywood stuff and with directing another music video. I create a lot of stuff, it's just not all in comic book form any more.

Do you miss it?

Do I miss the simple life? Sure. My life is a lot more complicated and has more aggravations, though there's more rewards too. Unfortunately, to stand up for your beliefs you have to take control of all aspects of your life. It was nice to be able to draw for ten hours and call it a day. Now I have to draw for five and be a businessman for five.

*   *   *

Check out:

Spawn: Creation
Spawn: Evolution
Spawn: Revelation
Spawn: Escalation
Spawn: Confrontation
Spawn: Retribution
Spawn: Transformation
Spawn: Abduction
Spawn: Sanction
Spawn: Damnation
Spawn: Corruption
(collects *Spawn* #1–58)

Batman: Year Two (with Mike Barr and Alan Davis)
The Incredible Hulk: Ground Zero (written by Peter David)
Spider-Man: Torment (collects issues #1-5 of *Spider-Man*)
Spider-Man vs Venom

FRANK MILLER

The publication in 1986 of Frank Miller's *Batman: The Dark Knight Returns* was a watershed in the acceptance of comics as a mainstream art form. Suddenly comics were no longer considered solely in the realm of children, but rather a legitimate, adult concern worthy of serious critical evaluation and respect. Miller first gained widespread recognition as the artist on Marvel Comics' *Daredevil*, and within a year was writing the book as well. During his tenure on the title, he was responsible for the creation, death and even rebirth of the immensely popular character, Elektra. Miller left Marvel to write and draw *Ronin*, a sprawling, ambitious tale of a masterless samurai and his mortal enemy, a shape-shifting demon, who are both transported from feudal Japan to a dystopian New York of the future. Complex, evocative and beautifully rendered, it set the tone for Miller's land-mark work, *Batman: The Dark Knight Returns*; a cautionary, sociopoliti-cal satire which delved deep into the heart and soul of ageing, embit-tered crimefighter Batman and his millionaire *alter ego* Bruce Wayne. Miller relocated to Hollywood for a time, seeing his screenplays for *RoboCop 2* and *RoboCop 3* produced, before returning to comics. Since then, almost everything he's touched has turned to gold, from his gritty crime noir series, *Sin City*, to the epic re-telling of the battle of Thermopylae in *300*.

When did your interest in comic books begin?

Probably before I was able to read. When I was very, very young, my father — who at the time was a travelling salesman — would return from New York with a pile of comic books for me. Back then it was *Superboy* and *Legion of Superheroes*, and before that things like *Dennis the Menace*. I was born in 1957, so it was pretty much the classic DC stuff from the sixties until I was seven, eight years old and the Marvel stuff started coming out. Back then, they seemed absolutely revolution-ary and I rapidly became a Marvel Comics nut. It was initially the artists that inspired me, but with the Marvel material I became much more focused on the characters; Spider-Man was captivating to me. I went through a period of many years barely aware of the real world, I was so absorbed by the monthly adventures of Spider-Man and the Fantastic Four.

In the introductions to the tenth anniversary edition of *The Dark Knight Returns* and the *Batman: Year One* compilation you mention the revelation of seeing a Batman comic for the first time.

It was really quite a moment. I remember it so vividly, and my memory of childhood is often quite vague. The best way to describe it is feeling like I fell into the comic book. The pictures just seemed to explode before my eyes, and even though I'm sure if you showed me the same comic now it would seem very innocent, the use of perspective and blacks made me feel I was peering into a much darker, more frightening, more heroic world. I had other interests which collided with my interest in comics; primarily detective novels as I got a little bit older. The real classics: Chandler and Hammett, Charles Willeford and Jim Thompson. But there's a lot that's going on now that I'm catching up with or thoroughly enjoying. Carl Hiaasen for instance, his book on Disney [*Team Rodent*] is the most hilarious, vindictive piece of writing you'll read all year. The angrier he gets, the funnier he gets.

When did you consider a career in comics?

My mother said I was seven years old when I declared to her I was going to be a comic book artist, and by then I was already taking sheets of typing paper and drawing my own. There was an art teacher in high school who was very encouraging; [though] he thought comic books didn't have much of a future.

Place of birth:
Olney, Maryland, USA
Date of birth:
27 January 1957
Home base:
Charlottesville, Virginia, USA
First published work:
Daredevil #168 (as writer)
Education:
Union 32 High School
Career highlights:
Batman: The Dark Knight Returns,
Batman: Year One, The Big Guy and
Rusty the Boy Robot, Daredevil,
Elektra: Assassin, Elektra Lives Again,
Give Me Liberty, Hard Boiled, Ronin,
Sin City, 300

I also had a writing teacher who was a great influence on me, and tried to talk me out of going to art school. I ended up following neither, by not [studying] at all after high school and instead pursuing comics. As my life progressed, I found I was really unemployable as anything else. I didn't make a very good truck driver and I was a terrible janitor. I really had to do this or end up being a street person. Aged twelve or thirteen, my interest as a would-be artist started moving away from superheroes. As I got more serious in my ambition, by virtue of just getting taller, I switched my focus much more to crime stories. That's how I wound up moving to New York when I was nineteen, with an armful of detective and crime comics, hoping that [someone] would publish them.

Did you want to be simply an artist at that stage?

The intention was ultimately to write and draw comic books. From the beginning, the separation of the two disciplines was, to my mind, patently silly, especially having witnessed Will Eisner's work. But I had gotten smart enough to realise I needed to think a little more tactically. Since I could draw, simple logic told me it would be easier to sell myself as an artist than as a writer. Asking someone to read a manuscript is a much bigger demand than asking them to look at some drawings, and since the factory system was in place, and one usually did one or the other, I decided to sell myself as a professional artist. My first job was a *Twilight Zone* story for Gold Key comics. Three pages; it only took me a *month* to pencil! At the time, Gold Key was a very good place for novices. They had lots of short story work available, and didn't have the most extraordinarily high standards, so it was a wonderful entry point. Once I had made a sale, though, I was then a professional and could approach people like DC Comics. I did various short pieces for DC and a five-page Hulk spin-off, *Doc Samson*, for Marvel. Then I got to do two issues of *Peter Parker: The Spectacular Spider-Man*, guest-starring Daredevil. With all the arrogance of childhood, I immediately volunteered for the job of taking over on *Daredevil*, and after the editor stopped laughing she started pushing for me.

You worked on issues 158 to 167 of *Daredevil* as the pencil artist, with Roger McKenzie writing. How did you end up writing the book yourself?

I was never a good collaborator, in that I would dominate which way the story would go. I tended to draw [the script] the way I wanted it, and I tended to dislike whatever the writer did. So we were often at loggerheads, and I didn't handle it all that diplomatically. After a while I plainly wanted the writer job and eventually took it. The writer and I got into a big fight and the editor just picked one of us.

Was it a struggle to get people to accept you as both artist and writer?

I never got that from the readers, though I was once stopped by one comic book writer in the hall at Marvel who declared to me, 'Artists draw, writers write — what do you think you're doing?'. It was virtually unheard of at the time for one person to do the whole package.

How did you approach the task of writing?

It was professionally necessary to first submit a plot. Sometimes that would be done verbally, and back then it was often very primitive; name the bad guy, say how it's going to end up, and [indicate] where the big fight's gonna happen. At first I approached the task with tremendous prejudice. I wanted to prove I was a writer, not just someone who wrote his own stuff, and I would study what I thought was really good writing and imitate it stylistically. It wasn't until I had a few jobs under my belt that I started to find my own way of doing it. The story always has to dominate. If you don't have a story you really don't have anything. The art then flows from the story, and is as much the story as the words are. The pictures themselves are an act of writing, because they're conveying the bulk of the information, and then the words become the soundtrack. I really don't think art and story are separate things.

What writers did you look to for inspiration?

It was mostly Will Eisner and Stan Lee. Those were the two biggest influences. I learned an awful lot from studying Stan's writing, in particular how to make things work. One of the techniques he developed was, ironically, a way of making artwork work. Like when an artist would leave something out or go on a tear with a magnificent, visually virtuous combat scene with very little story content. Stan was a master of introducing false subtext to keep you engaged in a narrative, even though it was utterly bogus at times. But what served me best on *Daredevil* was the

Will Eisner

Without a doubt, Will Eisner was a man ahead of his time. Back in the forties and fifties, he was a writer/artist (or indeed, cartoonist) who continually pushed the bounds of the medium he loved, exploring new avenues of graphic storytelling and creativity. In an era where artists and writers signed away their work for a slender pay cheque, Eisner dug in and fought for creator rights, holding tight to the copyright for his most famous creation, *The Spirit*. Born in Manhattan in 1917, Eisner's first work appeared in *Wow, What a Magazine* when he was just nineteen. But it was the move to Quality Comics that led to the creation of *The Spirit*. Published mainly as seven-page newspaper inserts between 1940 and 1952, *The Spirit* was a whimsically hard boiled slice of pulp fiction, centred around a (more or less) masked crimefighter, and peopled with voluptuous women, icy gangsters and one of the best rogue's galleries in comics. While Eisner has only returned to comics work in the last twenty years or so (after a long stint working for the US Department of Defence) with graphic novels such as the award-winning *A Contract With God*, his influence on several generations of writers and artists is unparalleled.

Eisner influence. My very first professional writing job was *Daredevil* #168, and I ripped off an Eisner story cold. I created Elektra in imitation of Eisner's Sand Saref from *The Spirit*, and even kept the structure and some of the settings from the story.

Did anyone notice?

Denny O'Neil, the editor. Though I essentially bragged to people about it. It's very hard to explain the mentality of the time, but there was no real sense of intellectual property [in comics]. Doctor Octopus was simply a character that someone pulled off a shelf and got to use. It wasn't anything that anyone 'created'. And while my pastiche of Eisner was well-intentioned, I'm kind of amazed I felt no embarrassment while I did it.

Was there an editor who encouraged your writing back then?

Yes. In particular Jo Duffy, who was then at Marvel. She not only [had a hand in getting me] the job on *Daredevil*, but she was also a natural born teacher who helped me a great deal along the way. Also, I have to mention Jim Shooter. He was, at the time, a volcano of energy and determination to make Marvel produce better comics, and he and I had enough chemistry to be able to work together. We also had many fights, but that can also be part of a great creative relationship.

What did they teach you specifically?

With Jo Duffy it was the fundamentals of simple good writing; having a story that was coherent, that had a focus, and went from one point to the next organically. With Shooter it was more the definition in his mind of what Marvel Comics was, and what heroics were. One time he told me that nothing in a Marvel comic should ever be repulsive, that at the ugliest they should be glamorous. And he had certain attitudes to the challenges a hero had to face. In a way it was a simpler, comic book version of everything Joseph Campbell spent a lifetime writing. Those were useful tools for me, because they were the [type of] comics I was doing. Often it's very good training to work within a set of strictures early in one's career, because then you can play the rebel and constantly be [banging] against the walls. If the structure [is sound] enough, something coherent will come out of it. That's what makes it such a leap to go straight into creating your own material, unless you're doing a naked imitation of what is already being published.

How long was it before people began to take you seriously as a writer?

There are times when I think they never have, and other times I'm amazed at the reaction my stuff got as early as it did. I was just an artist who wrote for a number of years and then one day it reached the point where an editor would call me up and ask me if I would write a job.

How do you see yourself now?

Cartoonist. The two flow together so much in my mind. Sometimes I am simply

Above: *An example of Frank Miller's page breakdown for* Sin City. *Courtesy of Frank Miller.* Sin City ™ *and © 1999 Frank Miller, Inc.*

a writer. When I'm working with artists such as Dave Gibbons, Geof Darrow or Bill Sienkiewicz, then the visuals are entirely their job and I get to enjoy what they're going to do and play against it, which is great fun. But most of the time I am doing both myself and I don't know which name I put on my hat.

In those early days, did Marvel ever throw your stories back at you?

There was amazingly little of that. It was very early on that I was essentially given my own way, though there would be occasional comments on where I was taking the series. Jim Shooter and I had a very long discussion about whether or not I could actually have my character Elektra die in the story. But when I told him why and how, he agreed and approved it.

Didn't you receive a death threat after you killed off Elektra?

That was a spooky night. I walked home from Marvel with literally a sack of mail that had come in on that issue [*Daredevil* #181], many times what I had received before. I spent a really strange, disturbing and lonely evening reading the mail, and in it there was one direct death threat and several other letters that made threatening noises. Unfortunately, the practice at Marvel at the time was to take the letters out of their envelopes before they went to whoever did the letter column, so there was no way to prove the death threat had actually been mailed. It said something along the lines of, 'You bastard, you killed the woman I loved. I'm going to do the same to you'.

Elektra

Frank Miller has often acknowledged his debt to Will Eisner's Sand Saref in the creation of Elektra, the lost love of Matt Murdock (aka Daredevil), who returns as a lethal assassin to plague and torment him. Indeed, Sand Saref was the Spirit's old girlfriend, who came back as a villain for the Spirit to bring to justice. The pursuit even ends at the docks, as in *Daredevil* #168. Regardless of this, Elektra remains one of the most popular *femme fatales* ever to stalk the comic book page, and her sudden, savage death in *Daredevil* #181 at the hands of fellow assassin Bullseye stunned readers with its raw power. It was a bold move, as Elektra had driven and fuelled Miller's run up to that point, but in fact her saga was far from over. Apart from her resurrection in Miller's later issues of *Daredevil*, several graphic novels and limited series followed. *Elektra: Assassin* (by Miller and Bill Sienkiewicz) features a tale from Elektra's past and *Elektra Lives Again* (Miller, with colour by Lynn Varley) features an essentially alternate take on the character. When Marvel brought back Elektra as a derivative 'bad girl' for a recent and short-lived series, Miller was not best pleased.

How does it make you feel, to know that people obviously take your work so seriously?

Mixed reactions. I love the depth of involvement, but it's unfortunate that the occasional loon who comes along stands out so much, because I've got a wonderful relationship with my readers. I really enjoy the appearances I make, where I get to chat with them. They're very, very involved, very intense readers. That's a writer's dream, and nothing to complain about. It shows they're dedicated to their end of the job too.

You left *Daredevil* and Marvel to do *Ronin* for DC Comics. Did you have a falling out with Marvel?

Taking *Ronin* over to DC demonstrated a kind of falling out, but it was also my effort to change the rules in the industry. I was able to get better terms at DC, who had just barely introduced the first royalties [to be paid by] a major [comics] publisher. Marvel quickly followed suit, but the actual amount of royalties paid was extremely low, and when I negotiated with DC I saw several advantages. One was they would give me total freedom, which I knew at that point I would never get from Marvel. Another was I would be able to arrange a contract wherein I would get a better royalty. And I was also after ownership. Back then I was a flavour of the month, and it seemed like the logical time to start playing the big guys against each other. It was the only way the artists were gonna win.

Was this a defining point for you, creatively?

It was a period I'll never forget, because it was the first time I really felt that the handcuffs had come off, and [*Ronin*] was going to be whatever I made it. At the time I was sharing studio space with Howard Chaykin* and Walter Simonson. It was also around then that I met Lynn Varley, who was working there as well. The collision of those three influences introduced me to a world of graphic art I hadn't seen before. Overnight I was exposed to everything from Jean Giraud to Goseki Kojima. And devouring all these influences they just spilled right out of my guts into *Ronin*. I was trying to do everything a comic book could do in one series. So it was wildly ambitious and utterly undisciplined.

Was it a case of the visuals coming before the story?

With *Ronin* the powerful starting point was the Japanese comic *Lone Wolf and Cub* and what I'd learned on *Daredevil*, where I'd had to study a great deal about martial arts. In *Daredevil*, we're dealing with a character who's chief characteristic is that he can't see. So he needs every advantage he can get. That led into Elektra and the ninja stuff. The more research I did, the more I wanted to do a samurai story. So yes, I guess all the early instincts were visual; *Lone Wolf and Cub* and the work of Moebius. Looking at *Ronin*, it's not real hard to see the influence of those two forces on it. Essentially I did what any artist does in his first project, which is find all the stuff he wants to draw and put it in.

---

* *Writer/artist on such titles as* American Flagg, The Shadow *(1986 mini-series) and* Big Black Kiss.

Above: *Drawn on tracing paper using marker pens, Miller's amazing roughs for 300. Courtesy of Frank Miller, Inc. 300 ™ and © 1999 Frank Miller.*

Above: *A further example of Miller's roughs for* 300. *Courtesy of Frank Miller.* 300 ™ *and © 1999 Frank Miller, Inc.*

That said, I worked very, very hard on the story. Decadent New York, samurai, hi-tech stuff — that's quite a hodgepodge of material, and I [needed] to pull it all together. It was 300 pages, an enormous piece of work. I wrote and rewrote things many times, but it was not entirely scripted by any means when I started. Early on, I had a notion of the underlying point of the story. Freud wrote a brief section on the role of fantasy art in the life of the fantasy artist, and essentially what he described was someone who is deprived of money, power and the love of women, and who therefore fantasises these things. But because the fantasy creates such a steady stream of pleasure they then achieve them in reality. So, in other words, a fantasy artist is something of a successful neurotic. That was an underlying theme I wanted to play to in this story; that the character that fantasises for Ronin became him.

Did you have the story plotted out from the very beginning or was it a constantly evolving process?

One lesson I learned early, and have tried never to break, is: always know your ending. If you don't, you're a ship in the doldrums. I usually start with a kernel of an idea; a something I want to try, a character I want to portray. For the first *Sin City* it was, 'Conan in a trenchcoat'. Days can pass before I think about it [again], and then an idea flashes, and usually the second thing that comes up is the ending. After that, the beginning, and by then the theme has thoroughly emerged and I start setting landmarks for myself across the story. Not this happens on this page, but this happens down the road, this pivots the story in these directions. There's often a sketch or two of what somebody's going to look like, but nothing more than that. Even before they have a name they have a face. I was well into working on *Sin City* before Marv ever had a name, because I was trying to come up with something more vainglorious, something more heroic. And then I thought, 'No, just go normal, all the good names are used up anyway'. Mainly, though, it's a matter of setting up those landmarks, and once that's done, that's when I get really careful and start working things out in much greater detail. There's [a lot of] note taking and writing that goes on before I draw anything beyond the little character sketches to get me focused. By the time I've started laying out the first issue, I've got the ending and all the pivotal moments of the story in my head and on a sheet of paper taped to my wall.

How do you approach the actual process of writing itself?

If I'm drawing it myself it never gets on the computer because I'm scribbling notes and lines of dialogue as I'm doing a layout. I longhand it, I letter it and by then it's essentially been through three drafts, so there's no reason for a formal script. It's one of the reasons I letter my own material, I don't have to type the damn thing up.

How about when you're working with another artist?

I tend to put things together longhand, because I physically enjoy that process more. Then I sit down at the computer and, depending on who I'm working with, I'll either type up a whole script, complete with panel descriptions, or I'll

PAGE NINE

1 - MEDIUM ANGLE - MARTHA's in a rage, helpless, glaring into
the HOLOGRAM that shows RED MIST drifting across a SPACESCAPE
that features distant JUGGERNAUT. BEHIND MARTHA stand COOGAN--
and the two VENUS DROIDS. One VENUS has her hand to her mouth
as she clears her throat.
                    MARTHA
          CLOWNS! Pack of ASSHOLES! If I
          could've TALKED to them--TOLD them
          that VENUS is DEAD--
                    VENUS
          Ahem.

2 - CLOSER ANGLE - MARTHA whirls, horrified, ready to take on
the VENUSES. VENUSES are placid, smiling. COOGAN intercedes
with fatherly charm.
                    MARTHA
          Tricked. Been tricked. Damn it. You
          even tricked WASSERSTEIN.
                    (2)
          You really DO rule the whole damn
          WORLD, don't you, you lunatic
          PROGRAM?
                    VENUS
          Of COURSE I do, Martha.
                    COOGAN
          Take it EASY, baby. We've got us a
          BIG MISSION on our hands, here. We
          need all the help we can GET.
                    (2)
          And you won't be finding any better
          CREW MEMBERS than THESE two. Not
          ANYWHERE.

3 - CLOSE ON MARTHA - her face lighting with a self-deprecating
smile. A little embarrassed.
                    we MARTHA
          I'll bet you COULDN'T. SORRY, all.
          SILLY for me to hold onto old
          GRUDGES. With a MISSION as IMPORTANT
          as THIS one, I oughtta let BYGONES
          be BYGONES.
                    (2)
          Say--am I the only one here who's
          HUNGRY enough to eat a HORSE?

4 - SAME ANGLE - sudden CONFUSION from Martha. Her mouth is
loose in anger. Her eyes are those of a drunk.
                    MARTHA
          No. No. What am I SAYING? What am I
          THINKING? I HATE you. What. What've
          you DONE to me?

Above: *An extract from Miller's more formal script for* Martha Washington Saves the World #2.
Courtesy of Frank Miller. Martha Washington ™ *and* © 1999 Dave Gibbons and Frank Miller, Inc.

simply write up a scenario. With Bill Sienkiewicz or Geof Darrow I'll write a scenario. They prefer to work that way, and they're such mavericks that every time I've written full scripts I've had to rewrite them anyway. On *Elektra: Assassin* I had written a full script and when I saw the artwork I realised it was a completely different comic to what I [had envisaged]. It's the end product that has to work, and ultimately [*Elektra: Assassin*] was much better for Bill doing what he did. With *Hard Boiled*, when the pages came in I simply threw the script away and spent three or four horrible days looking over this magnificent artwork with no idea what to do with it, until I realised the book had become a comedy. Dave Gibbons and I work very formally, in that I send him stuff with brief panel descriptions — I'm not trying to compose the drawings for him because he does that so well himself — with all the captions, word balloons and sound effects in place. But I don't make them do what's in my head; I want to see what's in their heads. Since I don't collaborate with other artists that often, I get to work with the best and I wouldn't want to handcuff any of them.

After the success of *Dark Knight,* Hollywood came calling. Writing a comic seems very similar to writing a film script. How do the two disciplines compare?

The resemblance is simple, in that they both involve telling a story in pictures and the screenplay format looks, physically, something like a comic book script. But the differences are vast. A screenplay, by it's very nature, is a blueprint for a motion picture which employs sound, constant movement and, more often than not, real living people. So you lose all the advantages of cartooning, meaning the reader does not feel the joy that comes with seeing a good drawing, and the characters themselves are less the creation of a single person. Also, movies are strict about length; they have to be very linear and very short. There really isn't room for that many scenes in a movie and it requires a very disciplined, focused kind of story. I learnt this the hard way, because I originally approached writing screenplays almost like writing a novel, and what I came up with would have been unproduceable. Even with the movies I have had produced, I feel they weren't linear enough or coherent enough to stand up.

Did you enjoy the experience ultimately?

Yes. It was maddening, but it was also glamorous and fun and exciting and paid wonderfully. I wrote a total of three other scripts, two adapted from my own material (*Sin City* and *Elektra*) which basically I have put on the shelf until I decide I really want to get serious about movie-making someday. I'm a bit of a prima donna, and I want to have a lot more control than I would if I was writing part time.

***Sin City* is perhaps the purest example of Frank Miller out there, harking back to those crime comics you were producing in your late teens. Was this a reaction to the Hollywood experience?**

It was my goal for quite a long time to reach the point where I would work this way. Ever since Eisner's *A Contract With God* came out, I made up my mind that I wanted to live the life of a novelist, have my stuff come out in book form and also maintain total control over it. I worked as a factory hand for a very long time and I wanted to take the gamble and have the power. *Sin City*, even though it wasn't the first creator-owned thing I did, in many ways was the most daunting. I was doing the whole thing, and on the face of it [the subject matter] isn't as 'fantastic' as most of what sells in comic books. There certainly weren't crime comic books around then. I knew I was taking a chance, but I also knew I had to do it. Having spent several years working in Hollywood and having had so many bosses for so long, I really felt like I wanted to work simply to satisfy myself.

Dark Knight Returns came out over a decade ago, and is still the book with which you are most often associated. Did you know how successful it would be?

No. As a matter of fact I was afraid that the title, Dark Knight '*Returns*', might be used against me to refer to what the distributors would do to it. You never know coming into things what the reaction is going to be, and all I knew was I was madly in love with the project, to the extent where I invented a new format for it. I thought perfect bound really suited the story well, but I was gambling like always. I'm not as fond of the format now, partly because it's been used to death, but at the time I thought it was a good move to put a more dignified face on the project.

Sin City

Sin City stunningly combines Frank Miller's dark, stylised artwork and stripped-down dialogue with his love of hard boiled, violent pulp fiction. Basin City is a hotbed of crime and vice, an urban combat zone ruled by hoods, thugs and hookers, with the cops often presented merely as peripheral observers. Presented in stark, solid black and white line with the occasional spot colour, *Sin City* first appeared in instalments in *Dark Horse Presents*, an anthology title published by Dark Horse Comics. Featuring Marv, a truly monstrous and violent man who, strangely, is the most sympathetic character in the series, *Sin City* pulls absolutely no punches, and underlines Miller's attitude to depictions of sex and violence in comic book form. A collected edition of *Sin City* was followed by several further limited series, including *A Dame to Kill For* and *That Yellow Bastard*, one-shots (notably the acclaimed *Silent Night*) and an original graphic novel, *Family Values*. While Miller constantly varies his cast of brutal sociopaths, maverick cops and lethal, rollerblading ninja hookers, linking story threads weave in and out of each tale, forming an intricate whole. For a truly 'right between the eyes' comics experience, this really can't be beat.

Above: *Miller's roughs for* 300. *Courtesy of Frank Miller.* 300 ™ *and* © 1999 Frank Miller, Inc.

Above: *Miller's roughs for 300. Courtesy of Frank Miller. 300 ™ and © 1999 Frank Miller, Inc.*

Does Dark Knight Returns ever feel like a bit of an albatross around your neck?

I'm very proud of it and very happy I did it. I was able to build an entire new phase of my career on *Dark Knight Returns* and it certainly established my name more than anything else I'd done before. It was a creative bridge for me that made things like *Sin City* possible. It shook people up a lot and in a way it misled people. *Dark Knight* and *Watchmen* were treated as a revival of the superhero, but I once remarked to Alan Moore that it was more like he had done the autopsy and I had done the brass band funeral.

You once said that superheroes had lost their magic. Do you still believe that to be the case?

I think that for the present the idea has run its course. I just really don't see any rejuvenation going on. Mostly what I see is sometimes very artfully crafted nostalgia, and that has its place as well. But I don't see superheroes being a place for new ideas. I like to compare the comics industry to the music industry, were the music industry to produce nothing but Elvis impersonators. Room needs to be made for new variations and ideas. I think it would be healthy for a larger portion of the industry to dispense with the tights and the traditions of the superhero and tell stories without them. That said, I love the romance and the sweep of adventure stories. I just don't think it has to be caused by a radioactive spider, or that people need to be able to fly to have a good time adventure.

You've constantly striven to push the boundaries of the medium. Where else do you want to take comics?

Virtually anywhere I can. I'm finding every time I turn around and try to make something else work, it does. *300* was another stage for me where new vistas just opened up. I guess I'm like a kid in a candystore. The possibilities are endless and sometimes it's a bit maddening that so many people are playing in such a tiny little sandbox. I want to see more and more avenues explored. I love the larger-than-life opportunities in comics, I love the fact I can create a whole cloth of characters as hideous as Marv and across pages make them real to the reader. I'd basically like to see the whole thing open up and let people see what a flexible, wonderful form this is.

There is some promise on the horizon, in that the field is loaded with talent. But it remains trapped by bad habits, limited ways of thinking and our stoic cowardliness in relation to the rest of the world. Essentially, it's up to the writers and artists to fix things, because the publishers don't know what they're doing. There are a substantial, if not enormous, number of people like me who are the pretty boys of the field, who can start a project and find a publisher on the strength of our names. These are the people in a position to change things, make it easier for other people who don't have the advantage of the name to come in and do more inventive comics.

Do you see it as your responsibility to try and push the limit of what's acceptable in comics?

I suppose there's a part of me that likes to provoke, that likes to point out the absurdity of prohibitions against things like male nudity and such, and I certainly aim for a strong visceral impact in my work. But I don't sit down and consciously say today I'm going to violate this taboo or that taboo. It flows from the story. Writing fantasy stories involves digging deep into the guts and pulling out images that are iconic and strong, and making scenes that are powerful and resonant. In the course of doing that, of course you provoke. That cuts to the heart of the whole reason I despise things like the Comics Code. I don't believe that comics should be part of a homogenised media world. I think our roots are closer to literature and that we will always be a bit of an outlaw fringe that disturbs and does not attract the vast majority of people, but attracts some people fiercely. If you look at comics when they were at their best, and arguably you can say that would be the EC* run, those were also the ones that people complained about the most.

Do you think comics should be even more political and rooted in real life?

It always struck me as odd, considering the strength of editorial cartoons in newspapers, that comic books were so meticulously apolitical, or even worse politically correct. The opportunities for satire and outright sarcasm are endless, especially when you're dealing with iconic figures like Superman and Batman. It's fun having people like Ted Koppel talking about them. So yeah, I'd like to see comics get more political. I'd also like to see them get less political. One of the most refreshing moments I've had in recent years was the first time I saw and read an issue of *Bone*†, which is as far afield from what I do as you could ask for, but I just adored it. Here was this unusual imagination and superior talent working on something that he devotedly loved. So all I'm saying is I want to see walls come down. I don't want to start evangelising about some one direction we should pursue. I've got my direction, I want everybody else to have their own.

*   *   *

Check out:

Sin City (collects the original story from *Dark Horse Presents* #51-62 and the fifth anniversary special)
Sin City: A Dame to Kill For
Sin City: The Big Fat Kill
Sin City: Booze, Broads and Bullets
Sin City: Family Values
Sin City: That Yellow Bastard

Batman: The Dark Knight Returns
Batman: Year One
Daredevil: Born Again
(collects *Daredevil* #227–233)

Daredevil: Gang War
(collects *Daredevil* #169–172, #180)
Daredevil: The Man Without Fear
Daredevil: Marked for Death
(collects *Daredevil* #159–161, #163–164)

Elektra: Assassin
Elektra Lives Again
The Elektra Saga
Give me Liberty
Hard Boiled
Martha Washington Goes to War
Ronin
300

---

* *EC's output of graphic horror and fantasy comics such as* Tales from the Crypt *and* Weird Science *provoked a moral backlash in the fifties, leading to the establishment of the Comics Code Authority.*

† *Writer/artist Jeff Smith's whimsical and endearing fantasy tale of three cousins, of indeterminate species.*

GRANT MORRISON

In Grant Morrison's comics universe, no limit is put on the power of the imagination. Although he's been working in comics for more than a decade, the Scottish-born writer has consistently amazed and dazzled readers with his fantastical ideas and intellectually dynamic, often psychedelic approach to storytelling. From his earliest work on Marvel UK's *Zoids* strip, through his tenure on *2000 AD* — in particular his award-winning superhero strip *Zenith* — to his bestselling recreation of the DC superteam book, *JLA*, Morrison's creative genius remains unsurpassed. Picked up by DC on the strength of *Zenith* and given the forgotten superhero title *Animal Man* to revamp, Morrison rapidly brought his anarchic, often philosophical visions to American mainstream comics. Author of the bestselling Batman deconstruction, *Arkham Asylum*, Morrison has found an outlet for his imaginings in comics like *Doom Patrol*, *Spawn*, *Skrull Kill Krew* and *Swamp Thing* — and graphic novels such as *Kill Your Boyfriend* and *The Mystery Play*. Indeed, whatever the format, Morrison continually delves into the possibilities offered up by alternate dimensions, quantum physics and the evolution of science, whether filling-in on *The Flash*, spearheading the *DC: One Million* crossover, or creating the three-volume, multi-dimensional mindtrip that is *The Invisibles*.

It's obvious from your work on *JLA* that you have a deep affection for superhero comics. When did this begin?

The first thing I remember very clearly is a British black and white *Marvelman* comic. It must have been from 1963, because I was definitely three and I must have been able to read — I learned to read before I went to school. It was about Baron Münchausen, so it was quite appropriate; the whole thing was about lying and making a living out of it. Somehow it remained a primal influence, but I don't really remember getting into comics until a little bit later. They were always around. My mum read a couple, but it was mostly my uncle who'd leave them about. It was a bohemian household and comics were just there. I remember seeing Jack Kirby's *Fantastic Four* and Ditko's *Spider-Man* — they scared the shit out of me — and I kinda liked the Superman ones and Justice League.

But I never really got into comics until I was twelve, and I got some given to me in hospital. I started collecting them, I guess, because I associated them with getting better. I was given three comics and they formed the basis of my collection. They were a *Superboy* comic, an issue of *Action Comics* and a copy of *The Flash*, which was the one I liked the most. When I looked back later it turned out all those stories I really loved were written by the one guy, who turned out to be a really big influence. His name was John Broome, and he was pretty much comics' answer to the Beat Generation; a young guy who grew dope and wrote these fantastic bizarre *Flash* stories from Paris and Hong Kong; he was constantly on the move. I thought, 'This guy's cool'. I'm proud it's his comics that are the ones I always remember. They were really weird, psychedelic transformation kind of stuff.

Did you always want to write comics?

From the age of five I stated my intention to become a writer. At eight, I wrote a little science fiction book for my mum called *The People of the Asteroids*. So, yeah, I always wanted to write. I just never considered writing comics. I did them when I was twelve, my own Justice League comics, so I was interested in them, but all I really wanted to do was write, and comics was just one outlet. I had given up on them by the mid-seventies and it wasn't until 1980 when *Warrior* came out and I saw Alan Moore was getting away with doing sensible, forward-looking work in the comics field that I decided I might as well write for comics.

Place of birth:
Glasgow, Scotland
Date of birth:
31 January 1960
Home base:
Glasgow
First published work:
Near Myth #2 (*Time is a Four Letter Word*)
Education:
Allan Glen School for Boys, Glasgow
Career highlights:
Animal Man, Batman: Arkham Asylum, Doom Patrol, The Flash, The Invisibles, JLA, Judge Dredd, Kill Your Boyfriend, The Mystery Play, Zenith

What was it about Moore and *Warrior* that inspired you?

Alan will hate me saying this, but it was *my* sort of stuff [he was writing]. I remember reading *V for Vendetta* and there was this one thing V says: 'I'm the black sheep of the family, I'm the bogeyman of the twentieth century', and I thought, this is what I want to read, it's like *The Prisoner*, it's like the stuff I'm into, the whole anarchy thing. And I enjoyed [Alan's] *Marvelman*. Especially as at the same time I was doing this strip called *Captain Clyde* for a local newspaper. It was kind of about a superhero in the real world, but here was Alan doing it a lot better than I was.

Were you interested in both drawing and writing back then?

Oh yeah. I drew that newspaper strip. I was pretty good, and if I had kept going, I would have been really good. This came around the same time as I was working for *Near Myth*. I was about seventeen, still at school, and I heard this bunch of guys from Edinburgh were starting up a comic. They were trying to create what were called 'ground level' comics, which basically entailed mainstream artists drawing tits and bums. It was pretty pathetic sex fantasy stuff in retrospect, but at least it was guys you knew from drawing Superman and Batman doing interesting new work. Anyway, this British comic started up in an attempt to emulate that. It had Bryan Talbot doing *Luther Arkwright* in there, among others. I met them at a comic convention, showed them some samples and they said we'll give you £10 a page. About a year later the comic was published and I had some stuff in it, a story called *Time is a Four Letter Word*. At the same time I answered an advert from DC Thomson* in Dundee, who were looking for writers. *Star Wars* had just come out and they were looking for people to write science fiction. I sent in some stuff and got work from them. The magazine was called *Starblazer*, and I wrote and drew the first one I did. Then, after that, I just wrote them because it took so long.

Was the experience of working for DC Thomson a particularly formative one?

Through them sending things back that were wrong I learned how to tell a story, how to make people interested in your characters and to want to turn the page. That's profound stuff, because with so many comics you don't want to turn the page after the first one. It all comes down to the main character. If you don't have a strong character your story is in trouble. I learned to start with the character, that he or she should be really strong, memorable. Your character should look like nothing else out there, or, if they do, it should be someone we instantly recognise. The character in my first space opera was basically Clint Eastwood's Man With No Name in space, so you had this instant visual recognition. Based on that I created other things; what his origin might have been and so on, and suddenly he became a fully-fledged character who turned out to be a major god-like force at the end of the universe. Which is strangely like the stuff I always do now, but back then was purely because I was trying to solve a problem. Then, who's his friend? His friend's a little kid and the little kid's got a back story and

---

* *More generally known for their quintessentially British kids' humour titles such as the long-running (sixty years plus)* Beano *and* Dandy.

the little kid's going to grow up and be the Emperor of the Galaxy and suddenly you're interested. If you look at all the successful characters, they come equipped with a distinctive look, and there's things that they do that no one else does. They tend to have a great headquarters or base of operations, and gadgets, all kinds of things that only they have. You look at *Batman, Captain Scarlet, The X-Files*, their characters are so well defined. The main thing then is to come up with a really good character and hopefully it will write itself.

That first strip I did was called 'Star Barons', or something, it was a cowboy story in space. They liked it. Then I sent in one which was a bit more avant-garde, about a pacifist doctor who's forced into this war situation and has to make all these moral choices. I got this letter back saying, 'More space combat', and I thought, 'Okay, now I know what they want. If I want to do a pacifist doctor story, do it elsewhere'. I was lucky, I had two outlets from the start. One for the avant-garde stuff, where I could just blow out any shit from my head onto paper, and one for really mainstream commercial work.

So even from an early age there was this duality of mainstream and weirdness going on in your head?

It took me a long time to synthesise it. I remember real long talks with [artist] Brendan McCarthy about this, because I love [the gentle, observational humour of] Alan Bennett, but at the same time I love William Burroughs and all that complete out-there shit, and how do you combine the two? I remember Brendan told me the story that kind of did it for me in my head. He said to think about Aleister Crowley, he was so far out-there with all this magic stuff and wrote these wonderful books which probed the limits of human understanding, but he ended up in this little Hastings boarding house with no money, eating boiled eggs. And Brendan said, 'think of Aleister Crowley eating boiled eggs — it's Alan Bennett'. So there you were, you could do an Alan Bennett story about a guy with telepathy and that kind of united it for me. *The Invisibles* was my real effort to combine those two strands. It tips either way every now and again, but I think it kind of gets it. It's easy to tell a simple story, and I always love it when I get one that works, but if I do a lot of them I start to miss the other stuff and vice versa, so it has to be a blending of the two.

Do you ever go back and look at any of your really early work, such as *Zenith* or *Zoids*?

I've recently re-read *Zenith* for the first time and was like, 'How did I do this? I was really good here. I could do this stuff in three words where now it takes me forty'. It was so spare, but all the characters came across. It takes me a lot longer now — why? What I'll do every so often is I'll go back and read the early stuff because there's loads of things you forget. When you come in without knowing the rules you can do good stuff, if, that is, you've got the temperament for it. It's like with a band, when you listen to their early stuff it's the best, because they didn't know what they were doing. It's just pure creativity, pure enthusiasm. Then you learn the ropes and you get good, and you can do it technically better, but not necessarily creatively better. So there are things you forget, and it's always good to go back and try and pick out little techniques that you once had. In the case of *Zoids*, the freaky thing I realised was that even there I was telling essentially the same story as in *The Invisibles*. I go through the old work to find hints of the future, and I realise I knew stuff that was about to happen, and things occurred because I wrote about them. That became a theme in *The Invisbles*.

What things specifically?

When they asked me to do a monthly *Zoids* strip I thought, how can I possibly extend this story? It's basically big toys fighting each other. Then I thought, so what if they are toys? And I thought, who could control toys on that scale, so the people involved don't even know it's toys they're fighting? I'd been reading a book about the fifth dimension, and I thought that if you lived in the fifth dimension you'd be able to look at the universe from outside of all space and all time. You could move through it to any point in spacetime and your body would be seen as a cross-section of three-dimensional parts. So I thought, I'll put these cross-section creatures in *Zoids*. They were actually the toy masters and our universe was the game they were playing. It was just this idea in my head, and then *Zoids* was cancelled and I forgot all about it. Then *Animal Man*, without my even thinking about it, also became about something from outside, which in this case was me. I was outside of his universe, and yet fucking about with it.

Zoids

Falling into the 'before they were famous' category, *Zoids* features some of Grant Morrison's earliest work, and began his long-standing collaboration with artist Steve Yeowell (continued on *Zenith*, *Sebastian O* and *The Invisibles*). Published by Marvel UK, originally as a two-page strip in their *Secret Wars* reprint title, *Zoids* was, in common with the concurrent *Transformers* title, based on a 'giant robot' toy line. Originally written by Ian Rimmer and drawn by Kev Hopgood, *Zoids* developed its own following and survived the folding of *Secret Wars*, reappearing in the relaunched *Spider-Man* comic (swiftly retitled *Spider-Man and Zoids*) with an increased page count and the new team of Morrison and Yeowell. The strip is a fine example of what can be done with an essentially lame concept if the parent toy company isn't breathing down the creators'/editor's neck. *Zoids* developed a life of its own, and Morrison — unwittingly or otherwise — road tested some of the larger themes he would later bring to play in *The Invisibles*. By the time the strip was brought to a (reasonably unforced) conclusion, Morrison and Yeowell had already been snapped up by *2000 AD*, and thereby put on the fast track to America.

Then it happened. Things from outside this universe came and fucked around with *me*, and told me what they were doing, or so it seemed. Since I've been doing *The Invisibles* I've tracked down every alien abduction book to see if there's anything in them I can find that's similar to my experience, and Philip K. Dick had the same thing happen to him. So I find these things in the comics start to appear in life, and I realise they can maybe work that way, that comics can be used magically.

Are you saying you had a contact experience?

I met these entities from the fifth dimension, or something like it. I went to Kathmandu with a friend, just to get away, take some drugs, listen to some ambient records and look at the Himalayas. On the last day something happened. Maybe it was a drug effect, but the results lead me to believe it wasn't just that. I was taking hash, so I was pretty stoned, but in my defence I will say I know the difference between hallucinations and this. I've taken every drug, so I know the full range of effects you get. Anyway, these things came into the room. They looked like those big blobs you get in rave videos, silvery things with no shape. They were kind of coming out the walls and the furniture and then going back in. Basically, it turned out *I* was one of these things and they told me you've managed to get yourself into a state where you can remember the truth, and we're here to make sure you remember it. You've been trapped here, you're all trapped here and you're all one of us.

I was taken to this place that seemed to be made of pure information. The way I describe it is the way dolphins swim in the sea and they have complete freedom, complete three-dimensional movement within the medium in which they swim. These beings lived in liquid information, and they swam about in it. It was outside space and it was outside time, and you could look at spacetime as an object. I could see the dinosaurs, but right next to the dinosaurs, separated by just a little valley, was Shakespeare writing a play, and separated by another little crinkle there's World War Two and around here there's like some kid dying in Vietnam and round here there was the first amoeba. But it was all the same object, just separated by the folds and crinkles, and that was time.

You *saw* this?

I'm using sense, but I'm translating. These things were saying, 'Do you remember what you are?', and suddenly I'm thinking, 'Of course, how could I forget, this is the most obvious thing in my life'. And they said, 'you got trapped, because what we do is we play and everything that happens to you comes from our creativity'. I was surrounded by raw information, swimming through pure data. It was like being in the internet but extending to whatever is outside the four dimensions we've got in this universe. They told me I'd got stuck in their game and when I asked them what they meant, they told me to imagine you were playing chess and got so involved in the game that you forget you're sitting at the table moving the pieces, instead you think it's your mind. Suddenly, the way you move around the chessboard becomes the rules of your life, and if that piece were to be taken, you'd feel you were dying. Of course, you wouldn't be, you'd just be put back in the box, ready to play another game. They said, 'This is how it works, we'll show you how the game is played, and if you remember nothing else, please try and remember this'. Then I'm lying on the bed in Kathmandu and I'm back to being this game piece. I met them four or five times in the months after and it was really weird, filled with synchronicities and bizarre happenings. That's the gist of what they told me and I thought, 'That's *The Invisibles*, that's what it's all about, that's what my work has always been about'.

Are you sure it wasn't the drugs?

That's a legitimate question, but I know it's not. I've taken a lot of drugs and what happens now is the magic does me, I don't do the magic. I've talked to other magicians and they say that's what happens when you pass a certain threshold. I can trust it because it's visibly working [in my life]. It's the best technology I've ever discovered. *The Invisibles* was just a way for me to make sense of it all via fiction.

So you believe in magic?

I've done magic to get John Lennon to appear by using the method you saw in the first issue of *The Invisibles* — that was real. If you treat Lennon like a god, then it works the same way you would summon any other god. You put on some Beatles albums, get a guitar in, and go and play 'Tomorrow Never Knows' and you summon Lennon. And surprise, up comes Lennon, this huge head. Try it. It's not to do with drugs. Drugs might be involved sometimes, sometimes they're not. What they do is relax you enough to be able to accept these things, to allow those boundaries to fuzz a bit.

Is it true that you believe the comic itself, *The Invisibles*, is magic?

Before *The Invisibles* I'd always been interested in magic. Something like *Kid Eternity* was about magic, and *Zenith* mentions chaos magic, that kind of stuff. But they weren't a magical thing in themselves. All it was, I was interested in magic and I was throwing references in. Then I started to think about the potential of the comics to actually *do* magic. That was where the idea for *The Invisibles* came from. I thought I'd do a comic that's not just about magic and anarchy, but will actually create them and make them happen. *The Invisibles* radiates magic. Initially, I didn't realise this, and I blithely put myself into the book. I figured, King Mob, he's cool, I'll make myself more like him. I'll shave my head and then all the girls who read the comic will like me. So I'm doing all this stuff to King Mob. I wrote the storyline in the first book where he gets captured and thinks his face is being eaten away. Two months later a bug eats through my cheek. It ate right through and I just kept writing.

Then I put King Mob through his shamanistic experience, where everything that he is gets torn apart. Shortly afterwards, everything collapsed in my life; my girl-friend left me and I end up in hospital dying of a bacterial infection, two days to

(6)

The white knight sits on the square it has just captured in foreground - some other chess pieces are on the board around us (Mark Millar is a chess expert, Chris. Call him if you want to lay this out like a real game. He may be able to do a computer schematic with his 'Junior Chess Champion Sissy of the School' software). Satan fills the background, looming over the board like a great blind god. His hand comes down, huge to reach for a black pawn.

SATAN: THE SIMPLEST GAMES CAN BE THE MOST <u>ADDICTIVE</u>.
SATAN: DON'T YOU THINK ?
SATAN: SOMETIMES I BECOME SO DEEPLY INVOLVED THAT I FORGET I'M PLAYING AT <u>ALL</u>.

Frame 2 Close up on Satan's fingers as he lifts the black pawn up in front of his blind eyes.

SATAN: IMAGINE BECOMING SO WRAPPED UP IN THE GAME THAT YOU EXPERIENCE EXISTENTIAL <u>DREAD</u> AND LOSS OF IDENTITY WHEN A PIECE IS REMOVED FROM THE BOARD.

Frame 3 Jack fairly close up, eyes narrowed as he listens.
JACK FROST: WHAT ?
JACK FROST: I DON'T THINK I'VE GOT THAT GOOD AN IMAGINATION, EY.

Frame 4 Overhead shot. Satan gestures to the empty chair. Jack moves forward.

SATAN: YOU'RE FAR FROM HOME, ENGLISH BOY.
SATAN: SIT DOWN.
SATAN: YOU'VE BEEN FOUND TRESPASSING ON A HIGHLY CLASSIFIED MILITARY BASE. YOU'RE WORKING, I BELIEVE, WITH A GROUP OF DANGEROUS AND UNSTABLE REVOLUTIONARY ACTIVISTS WHO HAVE ALREADY BEEN RESPONSIBLE FOR THE DEATHS OF <u>HUNDREDS</u> OF PEOPLE...

Frame 5 Side shot of the table as Jack sits down opposite Satan. The two confront one another across the chessboard. Satan leans forward, chin on fists. Jack leans back in his seat, surly, arms folded across his chest.

SATAN: PLACES LIKE THIS PLACE ARE NOT <u>KIND</u> TO THE UNINVITED. SECRETS MUST BE MAINTAINED.
SATAN: PEOPLE LIKE YOU JUST...<u>VANISH</u> AND, IN THE END, NO-ONE REMEMBERS WHO THEY <u>WERE</u> OR WHY IT

Above: *An extract from the chess scene in* The Invisibles *Volume Two #19. Courtesy of Grant Morrison.*

live. I really thought that was it. And all the stories I'd been writing beforehand were about invasion from beyond by insectile, bacterial beings. Something in my body knew I was writing about it. Or else it's voodoo, whatever you choose to believe. Then I thought, 'Wait a minute, what if King Mob has a good time?'. So I took him to America and gave him Ragged Robin as a girlfriend. I did it deliberately. I got the Brian Bolland cover and I said, 'I want to meet that girl' and I did a magic thing on it. Within months I met a girl who looked exactly like Ragged Robin.

I get letters and photographs from a shamanistic transvestite, a Brazilian transvestite that's living down in Brighton and does magic. Now I know people exactly like The Invisibles; they're real, and they have all started to come out. I communicate with them, I go and meet them. My life has become the comic, it's become fiction, it's become fantasy, and the more fantastic I make it, the better it seems to work. These are big, mad claims to make, but this is the way it's working. I decided to make *JLA* magical as well, in a completely different way, but to essentially the same end. *JLA* is full of mythological references and folk tale stuff, but nobody needs to know about it. If you do know about it, it will enrich your reading, but if you don't know about it you'll still get a rollicking good laugh. I finally figured out what my agenda is with *The Invisibles*, and with the superhero stuff as well. Within a year we'll see man's first contact with a fictional reality, seriously. That's what the magic's all about. Fiction and reality are going to become interchangeable. It will happen very slowly, but the first thing I'm gonna try and do is change places with King Mob.

The Invisibles

It's very hard to sum up *The Invisibles*, certainly in around 200 words, but the series represents something of a creative gelling of many of the weird and wonderful ideas that have, often subliminally, characterised Grant Morrison's previous work. At its very broadest, *The Invisibles* centres around a loose-knit, worldwide group of radical subversives led by the ultra-cool King Mob, battling a race of other-dimensional creatures that crave eternal control and total, unthinking obedience. If this all sounds very 1960s, that's probably because it is — Morrison being a big fan of *The Prisoner* and other cult television series of the period — but in and around this framework, he loads in paranoid fantasies, deceptions, conspiracy theories, high science, time travel and many of his ideas about magic and the crossover nature of fiction and reality. It's a huge melting pot of ideas and altered states of consciousness, the sheer amount of which in any given issue can often leave the reader reeling. But with patience and persistence, *The Invisibles* — split into three series or 'books', the final one tellingly counting down from issue twelve to one as it approaches the new millennium — is a thoroughly enjoyable, not to mention mind-blowing, experience.

You're going to be *in* the comic?

I'll be in the comic and he'll come out the comic. It's a technology; one of the things we can do with the comics universe is go into it. I've already done it in *Animal Man*, but I went in as myself. I realise now you can go into any comic or any piece of fiction wearing a Fiction Suit. This is pioneering stuff, we are now astronauts entering fiction as a dimension. I can go into the comics world wearing a Superman body and walk around and tell them stuff like what's going to happen on page sixteen if I want. I thought, what if you treated that reality as being its own real autonomous world? In the same way that those hyperbeings could get me out, can I get anyone out of there?

Let's talk about the mechanics of writing. Do you think visually when you're scripting or does the story come first?

Because I've got a background as an artist I tend to think visually. I've usually got a vague idea to start with, and then I get a bit of paper and draw twenty-two or twenty-four little pages on it. I'll just start drawing and get some big images and work the story around those. From the sketches I get the little dialogue things, and make notes. I type that up, describe what I've drawn and polish the dialogue up. Usually, it only takes about four days to do an issue.

Do you have to finish one comic before beginning the next?

The writing is ongoing. I'm doing it all day, every day, and that's what it takes to get the necessary amount of stuff done. *JLA* finishes and then melts into the next issue of *The Invisibles*. Anyone who's reading both will see the parallels, it's quite clear. The Hand of Glory pops up in *The Invisibles* at the same time as the Philosopher's Stone in *JLA*; they're both essentially the same object. And there's lots of other little links. Mason Lang in *The Invisibles* is Bruce Wayne really. Prometheus in *JLA* is actually King Mob, and so on. It's interesting to work this way, as it makes it a lot easier to write. It just flows from one to the other.

How do you feel about the process of collaborating with artists?

As far as artists go, I've always had real trouble getting the top echelon. The people I've worked with have tended to be pretty good, but there have been some that haven't worked out. On *The Invisibles* they've been pretty good, especially the second book with Phil Jimenez and Chris Weston. I like collaboration, but sometimes it fails. When it works, it's amazing. Obviously, I would like to work with only the greatest artists of all time but it never seems to happen like that. It's partly because I can't be bothered to talk to artists a lot of the time. When I'm trying to avoid the fact that I've been writing all day and I'm out doing something else, drinking or having a good time, I don't particularly want to socialise with artists. I like to meet them at conventions and hang around talking and stuff, but that's probably why I don't get the good artists, because other guys are willing to chat them up, be on the phone to

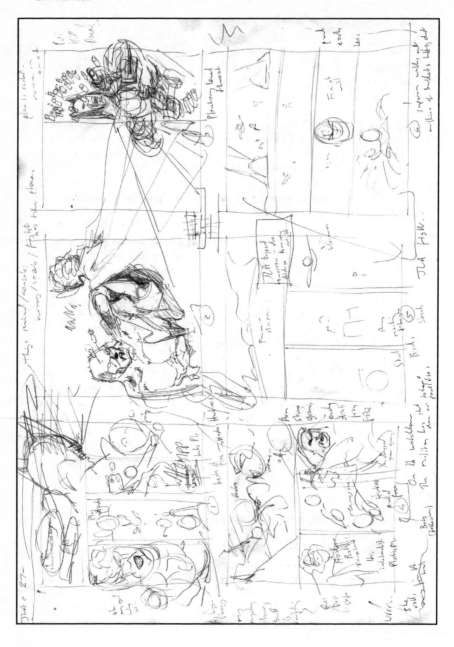

Above: *Grant Morrison's thumbnail sketches for* JLA *#26. Courtesy of Grant Morrison.*

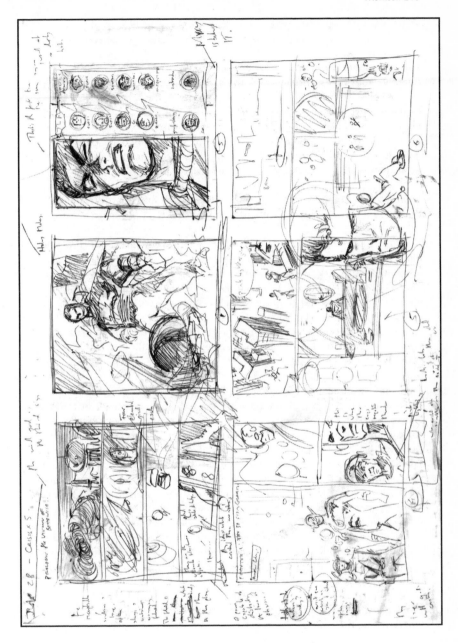

Above: *More Morrison thumbnails, from the first part of* 'Crisis Times Five'. *Courtesy of Grant Morrison.*

them, telling them they're great. I love what Chris Weston did on *The Invisibles*, but I never called him once and so Chris thought I hated him.

You've collaborated with fellow comics writer, and Scot, Mark Millar frequently. Does he essentially think the same way you do?

I couldn't survive without Mark because he's the only one who knows what it's like to do this kind of stuff. I can't talk to friends, girlfriends. As much as people can see you working, nobody believes that writing's work, so the fact that Mark's there and the fact that we think alike means that we can actually collaborate. You need another writer to talk you down or stop you going crazy.

Your work is steeped in techno jargon and way-out scientific theories. Were you interested in science and physics at school?

No, I hated it. I was good at English but that was it. As I got older I thought, 'Why didn't I like it?'. Because it was badly taught, I suppose. Now I read the stuff myself and try to make sense of maths and physics. I still don't really know that much. I can use it poetically, I can translate it and make it work in a comic, but it's not real science. I still go blank when I see columns of figures and graphs.

Conspiracy theories, which are integral to *The Invisibles* and are present in your work as far back as *Zenith*, is another recurring theme. Is this something you have strong views about?

I don't believe in the type of conspiracies Fox Mulder believes in, but like you say, I've had them in my work from way back. I know where that comes from: my Dad and Mum were CND activists and I lived in a world where the men in black would come to the door and say, 'If you keep this up, we're going to make you disappear'. I've seen that happen. I went with my Dad and broke into nuclear bases up in Edinburgh. Seriously, it's like James Bond and *The Prisoner*. So based on those experiences, the idea of a hidden world manipulated by people we don't get to see was obviously very strong for me, and it became one that I go back to from time to time. There's a general somewhere under Nevada who'll be able to explain *everything* to us. We have to believe there's something bigger, something we don't know about. So when I was doing *The Invisibles* it became about the myth of the conspiracies, which is why I'm giving you every possible explanation for everything, so that it eats itself alive. It spins out like a fractal; you'll never know the truth and that's fine, because it's a myth.

What do you think about the current state of the comics industry and where it's going?

It's a mess, but Mark Millar and I are absolutely convinced we're about to hit a boom and so everybody's laughing at us. The main boom will come in 2005, but it's building already, just through the cyclical nature of the comics business. Also, there's the fact that we're entering a recession. As soon as you enter a world recession, anyone who's in the entertainment business is ideally placed, because when people are depressed, worried about money, what they want is to be entertained. So the most popular stuff is going to be bright, aspirational, adventurous superhero stuff, and that's what we're doing. I think it's going to get massive.

Mark and I think really seriously about what we do and how to market it. We're looking at what's going to be successful in two years, not what's going to be successful in six months. You work it out by seeing how comics have functioned in the past. We've got a sixty-year history to consider and the trends tend to repeat themselves. All you have to do is go back and see the huge cycles, which you get around every twelve to fifteen years. The first one began with the creation of the superheroes in the late thirties, and that took us into the fifties, when nobody was interested any more and the superheroes started to die. Then, suddenly, once the space programme was underway, superheroes were revamped as astronauts or Kennedy-type figures. You had the Flash, a police scientist who could run at the speed of light, the Atom, a scientist who could shrink; everyone was a scientist or a pioneer. The heroes worked because they were embodying the spirit of a forward-looking Utopian America. That in turn lasted for fifteen years and peaked in the mid-sixties. By that time the bright ideal was becoming a thing of parody, and Batman for example was starting to look ridiculous. The kids still believed in it, but if you were an adult watching the television show, it was just comedy. Then the decline started in earnest, and though nobody really noticed it at the time, you can see it with hindsight.

Around 1974 or 1975 you get to the first glimmerings of what you might call the Dark Ages. Writers like Don McGregor appear, who show heroes getting badly hurt in everyday situations. McGregor did one story where the Black Panther was fighting in a supermarket, and because this old woman sees him as a black man she starts laying into him, even though he's the good guy. She splits his head open with a tin of catfood. Nothing like that had ever been seen in a comic before. It was real blood and the description was of terrible pain. This trend towards realism reached full flower with *Dark Knight Returns* and *Watchmen*, and suddenly you've got superheroes in the real world; in pain, sexually tormented and fucked up. That was hugely successful for the eighties, because self-made men were important. As that progressed it became parody as well; big, muscled men with chains and guns, no stories, scenes of rape in alleyways in every issue. It reached its limit.

Then you get people like me and Mark Waid who come in and go back to the opposite extreme again. We know the only way to follow up that dark thing is to make the heroes heroes again. It's obvious. And it's gigantic, because it got to the point where every hero's a psycho. There was nothing aspirational to read, so why bother? The minute we brought back superheroes again — in costumes, not unshaven, not wearing trenchcoats, not carrying double-barrelled shotguns — they were huge. The next thing that's going to come in is 'Superhero Sitcom'. The young writers now grew up in the eighties, so they like that realistic stuff. You can see the first glimmers of it in the stuff Devin Grayson's writing, or the guy who does *Chase*, Dan Johnson. Their stuff's all about relationships and superheroes being real and sitting round drinking coffee. It's not in vogue yet, and only features in little comics that nobody's keen on, but when this current superhero wave starts to wear itself down, comics will be a lot more down-to-earth. It'll be like *Friends*, but with super-powers. There'll still be fights, but they won't be the big widescreen variety.

What about creativity in today's comics?

This medium is as diverse as any other. You couldn't say that ten years ago, but now there are comics about everything. It's just that people don't know about them. Comics have got so shy and embarrassed about themselves, they've reached adolescence after being in childhood for so long and are now stuck with specs taped up with elastoplast. What they have to do is get a girlfriend, get out and start being cool. The guys who run the industry now are frightened to go out, face the world and say we are sexy, and the stuff we are doing is fun and readable. Some of it's really artistic; you've got art spiegelman's *Maus*, for instance, that's as good as any novel or theatre production. But we've also got some trash, just like every other entertainment medium, but the guys behind it are geeks, and they look at me like I'm gonna beat 'em up. Comics have shrunk back into comics shops which now look like porn shops and people are frightened to go in there. In the old days, when *Superman* was selling six million copies a month, you could buy them anywhere, in any shop, and one of the things they've got to do is get them back in the hands of children and out of the hands of weird thirty-five year-old men, who are just collecting them. It could be done, because we've got characters that everyone knows. The Superman/Batman cartoon show is on every day in America, and is watched by two million people. Clearly those characters have got an audience, so why isn't the comic selling at least a million copies?

Do you think the industry still perceives you as this 'Vertigo guy' who writes all the weird shit?

In your bleakest moments you think, 'Fuck, nobody takes me seriously'. I'm seen as leaping from one thing to another, never quite sure what I'm going to be doing next. They thought Aleister Crowley was a charlatan, they thought Andy Warhol was a charlatan, and that's what happened to me. If you do a lot of different stuff and you're not consistently 'something', then you must be faking. Am I a charlatan? Maybe. That's certainly something people have said of me. Back in the eighties, when I was doing *Zenith*, the persona I had then was Morrissey; he slags everybody off, he's really clever; all that Oscar Wilde stuff. So I started saying cruel things about everybody else in comics. No one had ever done that before and it made me famous, but it was a horrible way to get famous. It just seemed funny but I was upsetting a lot of people, and it became a persona I had to escape from because everybody hated me. In the early nineties I shaved my head, wore a target T-shirt and started working out. I told the press that I'd taken steroids, lost my mind and was now a violent kung fu artist. And they believed me! Then, recently, I came back as like the elder statesman of comics, who'd been away. The way it's going now is 'mad guru'. If you want fame and people to know you and your stuff, they need to think of it as an extension of you; so if they meet you it's like meeting your character. So you create personas, make stuff up, make yourself into something that people would want to be. The whole *Invisibles* period has been me saying I'm James Bond, a superspy; I jet around the world and go out with these glamorous women. It just becomes real to people, but that's just a persona. The next one'll be different again.

What sort of fans do you attract?

Smart, odd people. My fans are the Midwich cuckoos of the world who don't really fit in, but suddenly read something and go, 'This guy thinks around corners the way I do'. It's the same way I was when I discovered Burroughs: 'Fuck, yeah, this makes sense'. That's what it's about, you send a signal or a little telegraph out to the world. It starts off with me in my room and then people send me stuff back. If I'm working on something like *The Invisibles* they send me a big novel and it's amazing, it's like *The Invisbles* but from a different direction. I love it. It's like me getting the Sex Pistols album, like me seeing *If....*, and then wanting to translate that energy into my work. Hopefully that's what *The Invisibles* does for people.

What have you left to achieve with the comics medium?

I've been doing comics for so long now, I kind of bump against the ceiling. Where do I go? I've done the biggest characters, I've done my personal experimental projects. I need another resting, I need to get into other areas; do stuff for books, the telly, for papers. I need to have the same voice, but in an even

---

Maus

art spiegelman (no, that isn't a typo, he spells his name with all lowercase letters) is a very unorthodox comics creator, one whose work — particularly *Maus* — doesn't fall into one neat category. spiegelman certainly comes from the 'underground' school of comics, with much of his work published by companies such as Fantagraphics and Kitchen Sink, but *Maus* (begun in *Raw* magazine) is so completely different it's hard to even call it that. *Maus* revisits the horrors of the Nazi occupation during World War Two, focusing particularly on their ethnic cleansing programmes, and casts the Jews as mice and the Nazis as cats. The metaphor is clear, but *Maus* has another layer, in that the experiences are being recounted by spiegelman's father, Vladek, and the relationship between father and son is fractious to say the least. What develops, therefore, is on the one hand a horrific tale of Nazi atrocities, but counterpointed against it are the author's attempts to reconcile his conflicting feelings about his father. *Maus* pulls no punches, either in its depiction of the death-camps or its frank, autobiographical introspection. Harrowing, involving, multilayered, *Maus* truly demonstrates how much can be achieved within the comics medium.

wider context, just to stop me getting bored. I love comics, I always want to do them, so I'll keep at least one thing going and around that I'll do little projects. I won't be stopping comics but I'll be definitely shifting emphasis onto other kinds of stuff. Everything here is sustained by imagination. If I stopped thinking this stuff tomorrow, this would go away in six months, it's magic. It's how to live in the world using the resources. You can twist probabilities, you can make things happen. There's work involved. I couldn't do magic from this and then not write. The trade off is that I write, and then the magic makes it go mental.

*   *   *

Check out:

The Invisibles: Say You Want a Revolution
(collects issues #1-9 of Volume One)
The Invisibles: Bloody Hell in America
The Invisibles: Counting to None
(collects issues #1–13 of Volume Two)

JLA: New World Order
JLA: American Dreams
JLA: Rock of Ages
JLA: Strength in Numbers
(collects issues #1–23)

Animal Man
Batman: Arkham Asylum
Batman: Gothic
Doom Patrol: Crawling from the Wreckage
Kill Your Boyfriend
The Mystery Play
Zenith (vols #1-5)

SAY YOU WANT A REVOLUTION

In 1996, in something of a bold but ultimately very successful move, DC re-launched the Justice League of America as *JLA* with writer Grant Morrison at the helm, controlling the destinies of seven of the company's key characters, including both Superman and Batman. Well established as a comics industry maverick and no respecter of established traditions, many suspected that Morrison's take on *JLA* would be radical, to say the least, but he surprised everyone by revealing a hitherto untapped vein of mainstream reverence. While the surrounding stories were replete with Morrison's trademark cutting-edge high-science and mysticism, the characters themselves were iconic with a capital 'I', representing an ideal to which the reader could aspire. Far from the vigilante/anti-hero that been popularised in the preceding decade, Morrison set out to turn back the clock to a simpler time, when heroes were heroes. The success of *JLA* propelled Morrison into a fill-in run (for Mark Waid) on *The Flash* and the massive *DC: One Million* crossover story, a superhero epic that spanned every DC Universe title for one month, all of which Morrison plotted.

Although your run on *JLA* has been an enormous success, in retrospect you were something of a wildcard choice given your previous superhero work and 'Vertigo writer' reputation.

Oh yeah, but I got lucky. The previous incarnation of Justice League was not selling at all and was filled with characters that no one had heard of. The guys writing it were good but they were working with really hopeless material. I had told DC I wanted to do some more superheroes and I made a list of the ones I liked. They said, 'Everything's taken here, but by chance Justice League's come up, is there anything you can do with the book, because it's dead?'. I told them I could do Justice League but that we had to have all the top characters in it. They said they thought it wouldn't sell, and I said, 'Let me do this, and I promise you it will sell'. Throughout writing the first eight issues of *JLA* I was constantly told it was going to be a disaster.

Where there any specific parameters as to what characters you could and couldn't use?

I was told you can't have Batman, and you can maybe have Superman for one issue, but otherwise don't touch these characters, make up some of your own. I said it won't work. People want the big characters. It was such a struggle and is still a constant struggle, no matter how much success you have. Once the figures came in they couldn't say anything. The comic was a hit and so I kept pushing the envelope. I kept making it more extreme, more widescreen and more epic and it got more and more successful. They thought the *DC: One Million* series was going to be a dog, but it was gigantic. Every time I say, 'Why don't you try this?', it's 'Oh, we can't try that, it'll get us into trouble'. But there's no arguing with success.

Your stories, especially the six-part 'Rock of Ages' in JLA, are resoundingly epic, but they're more ideas and action than straightforward superhero storytelling. Was that intentional?

The story is the least important thing to me. The way I look at it is comic book superhero stories are pretty simple. There's one guy who's got one set of powers and he's got to fight another guy who's got another set of powers, or else he's got to deal with a natural disaster or something. But instead of seeing that as a limitation, I looked at it as if you're a blues musician and you've just got three chords: C, G and D. That's it. But if you add two minor chords you've got every Beatles song. So you go in there and you start to really improvise, add in those minor chords. If, say, Superman has got to come in and this baddie beats him up a bit, then Superman rallies and comes back, then what I have to do is disguise that enough so the readers don't realise they've been reading the same story all their life. That's where the creativity comes in. The bad guy comes in and the good guys kick his arse, that's essentially every issue of *JLA*, but you fill it with ideas that will set people's heads off in a different direction by making them think about scientific or philosophical stuff, or just the idea of what a superhero could really do with their powers. If you were the Flash, what could you do? That's become something of a trademark of my superhero stuff. I work out what that hero's power does and play with that. If you could run fast and were up against a guy who was made of ice, what is the potential for interesting visuals and tricks that you can play? That's the way I've worked it, by doing clever little improvisations on a basic structure.

Did you set out to achieve anything specific within the context of the superhero medium?

What I'm doing now are the sort of comics I read when I grew up; those really mind-boggling, psychedelic *Flash* issues. There was something about them that stuck in my head the way fairy stories used to; they had that real primal code. My aspiration for this current phase of the work I'm doing is to restore that edge to superheroes, so you can put in all these fantasy elements but make it for real. If a superhorse comes up and looks in your win-dow with blazing eyes and a storm behind it, you're going to shit yourself. It wasn't the concepts that were stupid, it was the way they were done, they looked old fashioned. You can take the same concept and bring it back. A superhorse can either be done stupidly or it can be done in a way that readers will never forget having seen. It's a way of re-thinking things for each generation, seeing how to freshen those concepts up and take them a little bit further.

When I read those *Flash* comics as a kid they would have little bits that said, 'Flash Fact: Flash can run so fast he can skip across the surface of water like a stone'. It was all about science, so I just thought I'd put science back into comics. But the science I'm getting in there is the weird, quantum science, the science that's around now. They were writing about the science of the sixties, but now we're in an era where we've got science fiction in our homes. DC's always been about science — I'm just making it weird science. All the stories I tend to do in *JLA* tend to be based on some little quirk I've discovered in *New Scientist* or some book on hyperspace. Those are elements of what I'm trying to do.

How did the *DC: One Million* crossover come about?

It was one of those things that came out of a conversation with Mark [Millar]. We were just sitting around talking, about how they've done the zero issues, and what's the most ludicrous thing you could think of in the other direction. Issue one million was the answer. I suggested it as a crossover and it just grew out of the idea of what would be these titles' millionth issues, and what year it would all take place in?

Did you have to sit down and think about every DC character for that story?

Oh yeah, that was the biggest work I've ever done, because basically I plotted everything that month, every single comic except for *Hitman*. With that I just said, 'Garth, take the piss', that was my plot. The rest of it was quite detailed. The Batman stuff, the Superman stuff was really detailed. I plotted something like sixty-four comics that month and wrote five of them. It was big. That took a few months. I was working non-stop.

You took lesser known characters such as Resurrection Man and made them pivotal to the whole crossover. What was the thinking behind that?

Resurrection Man was an obvious choice, because if he can't die he's one of the people who might conceivably still be alive in the far future. So obviously he's gonna be some kind of linchpin. I was looking through all the stuff that was being published, and I thought about how, with the way *JLA* was going, everybody had me pegged as like this retro writer. People who are doing that stuff now are mistakenly thinking it's retro, and they're going back and doing sixties-style stories. All I'm taking is the attitude and the energy of that era, and the creativity, and adapting it for today. So one of the things I really wanted to do with *DC: One Million,* and what I've been doing in later *JLAs*, is to show I like *all* the stuff. I threw in eighties stuff like the Rocketmen and I thought I'd try and do something with nineties characters. I've not really been particularly interested in them before, but every character is good if you take a new look at them. I wanted to throw in stuff that DC was publishing now, so that's why Resurrection Man's pivotal and Cronos has got quite a big role, even though it's in the background. I wanted to put them in as a commitment to the fact I wasn't just interested in the past.

Where else do you want to take the superhero genre?

I came into *JLA* at a time when most comics were about guys in trenchcoats. So I thought, let's make superheroes colourful again, let's make them somebody to look up to instead of look down on. Hence the first *JLA* cover was sort of an upshot and Justice League in the eighties was a downshot of disgruntled people looking up at you. I wanted to keep pushing the boundaries of the genre until we'd got superhorses and supermonkeys, and that got me as far as the *DC: One Million* series, which had both of those in it. I've expanded the parameters enough so that stuff that seemed stupid is starting to look interesting, because you find a new way of thinking about it. But I'm now seeing every hack in the world copy that style. All you do is use the word 'vast' or 'calculate' or 'quantum' or 'hyper' as often as you can. I'm seeing that happen and I'm thinking I've got to make the next jump. So for me now it's what's after this? How do I push this again so I'm not doing what the rest are doing?

So where will the future lead the superhero?

I think the real interesting work's going to come when we get past the year 2000 mark and there's no longer the need to recycle old stuff. Because suddenly we'll have one hundred years ahead of us and we better start thinking. I think there's going to be a lot of new ideas coming in after that first hangover of hitting the twenty-first century, because suddenly people will say, 'We don't want any more nineties, eighties, seventies, sixties revivals, what have we got that's different?'. I really feel there's going to be a generation coming up that's going to trash a lot of the stuff we're doing now, which will be great. I wouldn't worry about the past. I think the past is important now because what comics is doing is kind of taking stock of itself and saying, 'Look at the mistakes we've made, look at the things we did right, let's consolidate and make the stuff good before we start experimenting'.

MARK WAID

While Mark Waid's comprehensive knowledge of comics history — particularly as regards the workings of the DC Universe — is legendary among fans, less well known is his position as guru and godfather to two generations of comics writers. Talk to any number of today's scribes and it's Waid's name they put forward as a source of advice and encouragement; a font of comics wisdom and continuity troubleshooting. A former editor at DC, Waid first revealed his immense skill for characterisation as writer on *The Flash*, his gift for comic dialogue and timing imbuing the somewhat one-dimensional Wally West with a depth and personality that provided the series with much needed impetus. Critically lauded runs on *Captain America* (with artist Ron Garney), *Impulse* and *X-Men* helped seal Waid's reputation as one of the industry's most eminent writers, a position he cemented still further with the co-creation (with artist/painter Alex Ross) of the acclaimed *Kingdom Come* mini-series. In addition to being a cracking good read, *Kingdom Come* (and its successor, *The Kingdom*) ably highlighted Waid's faculty for believable characters and epic storytelling. His deep love for all things past resonates with a contemporary cynicism, invariably satisfying both neophyte and fan alike.

Have you always wanted to write comics?

To be honest, I never had any ambition to be a comic book writer. In fact, I really never wanted to be a writer, period. I dabbled, but there were a million other things I wanted to do, and being a writer was not one of them. I wanted to be an editor. I wanted to be the guy who sat behind the desk all day and helped make decisions about his favourite superheroes. It's why all my writer friends hate me, because I paid no dues.

Ever since I was a boy I've loved comics, and I never stopped reading them. I got involved in the fan press in the early eighties, writing articles for magazines like *Amazing Heroes* and *Comic Buyer's Guide*, and from there I was able to make inroads [into the industry]. In 1986 I became editor of *Amazing Heroes* and a year later I got a call from Dick Giordano at DC Comics asking me to fly out to be interviewed for an editor's position. I stayed at DC on staff for two years, with the intention of being an editor forever really. When I left in 1989, I needed some way to support myself, and fortunately I started to pick up the odd writing assignment here and there, mostly thanks to Brian Augustyn, who was both my editor and best friend. It was Brian who saw some potential, God bless him, and from there it's been one lucky break after another.

Did you enjoy being an editor?

Oh very much. I really figure that at some point in the future I'll be an editor again, somewhere, because I love the process. There's something about working in a very creative environment all day long and being able to multi-task. I did some consulting editing at Marvel for a few months in late 1997, early 1998, and what's important to me now is, after fifteen years or so in the business, I have a great deal of information to parcel out to a new generation of writers, artists and editors, as well as a real strong interest in learning from them. So that's something I very much want to pursue in the years to come.

Didn't you edit Grant Morrison on *Doom Patrol*?

I did indeed. And I humbly say, I was also somewhat responsible for getting Grant the job. Not that I helped pick him, but I shared an office with then editor Bob Greenberger and yelled at him every morning to please get another

Place of birth:
Hueytown, Alabama, USA
Date of birth:
21 March 1962
Home base:
Brooklyn, New York, USA
First published work:
Action Comics #572
Education:
Virginia Commonwealth
University
Career highlights:
The Avengers, Captain America, The Flash, Impulse, JLA, JLA: Year One, Ka-Zar, The Kingdom, Kingdom Come, Underworld Unleashed, X-Men

writer on *Doom Patrol*, until finally he started making some calls. Bob was Grant's first editor, and I took over after a few issues. I also edited Keith Giffen on *Legion of Superheroes* and handled *Secret Origins* [a DC anthology book], on which I got to work with dozens and dozens of writers and artists. That helped me a lot when it came to learning what I needed to know to be a writer.

What editorial skills did you transfer to your writing career?

What I learned mostly was a good work ethic; what an editor is looking for in a writer, what an editor is looking for in the material, and that it's important to be punctual and reliable. I think it was Bill Loebs who said in order to keep getting work in this business there are three factors: be on time, be good and be personable. Any two of those will get you work forever, you don't need all three. Actually, I'm not even sure you need two. I also learned a great deal working with people like Ty Templeton, John Ostrander, Neil Gaiman and Grant about story construction, and about the notion that you really have to unlock your imagination and go wild. When you do your stories anything goes; there is no such thing as an idea that is too wild.

While you were still working as a journalist you wrote a Superman story in *Action Comics*. How did that come about?

I had already talked to [then DC editor] Julie Schwartz a couple of times in my capacity as a fan press guy, and I went into his office and said, 'I've got some ideas for Superman stories, can I pitch?'. I walked out of there with an assignment, and that was the greatest day of my life. I recall it took something like two weeks to write this little eight-page story, which I look back upon now and laugh. I wrote another one for Julie which was a disaster. The first one I wrote in a very sixties-style on purpose, because I knew that was what Julie liked. But the next story I tried to drag into the modern era, and not have as many repetitive captions and as much stilted exposition, and Julie rewrote every single line. I still have his draft of my script and pull it out for a laugh every once in a while because it just drips in red ink. From there, I didn't really do anything for a while. I did a few jobs when I was on staff at DC: a *Detective Comics* annual with Brian Augustyn and a short Human Target story for *Action Comics*. But nothing to speak of, because as I've said, my ambition was not to be a writer.

You mentioned that it was Brian Augustyn who encouraged you to write. What do you think he saw in you?

We had worked together before and I was also his editor on the *Gotham by Gaslight* one-shot that Mike Mignola [drew]. Because of the way we worked on that I would like to think he saw in me a kindred spirit, telling the kind of stories he wanted to publish. That's my best guess.

Your writing has always had one eye on the big picture. Do you think that's because you were an editor?

Absolutely. It helps, as you say, look at the big picture; you start to conceive of things you can do with the comic, just little tricks, that go beyond the writing itself. I came up with this notion of indicating background chatter from characters that you're not supposed to really hear, which I used in *Kingdom Come* issues one and two. Because I wanted the background speech balloons to be readable, instead of making them smaller, we just put a greyscreen over them so they turn out a lot dimmer than the stark black and white lettering of the other balloons. It's a tiny little thing, but it's part of the storytelling process, as are other production tricks, like the blurring of colours to indicate a super-speed character.

Do you find the process of writing difficult?

Was it Dorothy Parker who said, 'No writer likes writing, but every writer likes having written'? If I sit down with too strong and stringent an idea of what I want to accomplish, what I want to say, and how I want to say it, then it just becomes typing, and is gruelling. The most frightening part of writing, and yet also the most rewarding part, is to launch into a story with as little idea of where I'm going as possible, discovering things about my story and my characters as I go. That is the only thing that keeps me going, because the rest of it is just a technical exercise and would bore me stiff.

How do you set about writing a comics script?

If I don't have a strong visual opening to start with I cannot continue. So the first part is coming up with two or three very strong visual sequences. They don't necessarily have to tie together, I just need some interesting ideas in my head. From there, I put them down on paper and very slowly start to knit them together with what has to be in the story. I try and figure out what exposition I need; what I have to accomplish in terms of getting information across from last issue to recap where we are. Clarity, I think, is probably the single most important thing in comic book writing, and it's certainly the most overlooked skill these days. I pride myself on giving readers a product they can pick up cold. The process is very much like painting. You put down a splash in that corner and a little bit up here in the middle and just start noodling with each tiny piece until it becomes a whole. I don't always write in a very linear fashion, very often I will write scenes and then start to kind of back them into each other.

Do you favour full script or the Marvel plot method?

It depends. When I'm working with someone like Andy Kubert or Ron Garney, who are both very strong visual storytellers, I do it the Marvel way. But even then, it has a lot of dialogue and frankly it's still broken down panel-by-panel. I know a lot of guys get away with writing, 'pages four through seven: big fight', but I can't do that. I have to choreograph where I'm going; I have to know what the beats are. For me, the difference between a Marvel-style plot and a full script is only a few hours of polishing. I prefer to work full script because I'm more focused that way. I get bored very easily and to me, having to write it twice takes some of the spontaneity out of it. I'd rather just focus like a laser, do one script, get it all out of my system, and then move on to the next story.

When you sit down to write, do you usually have the ending in mind?

I generally have, though the ending I have in mind is frequently not the ending I end up writing. But I do have to know to some degree where I'm going, even if it's just an image that doesn't have much of a context. I have to know that I'm going somewhere. But, as I say, the process is about discovery; that's the fun part for me. For instance, I had the image of the 'Chain Lightning' arc in mind for a year — actually for more than a year — but, much to my surprise, as I got near the end of the story (in *The Flash* #150), the ending became something completely and totally different. The story took on a power and a life of its own and said, 'I'm not going there, I wanna go here'.

With Alex Ross on _Kingdom Come_, I imagine there was an enormous amount of collaboration. What kind of relationship do you generally have with your artists?

Kingdom Come was probably the single most collaborative project I've ever worked on, because Alex was a co-plotter on the story and very invested in it, more than any other artist I've ever worked with. I can write a forty-five page script in a week and a half, while Alex would stare at those same forty-five pages every day for five months. In Alex's case, we would first talk at great

Kingdom Come

This was always going to be something special, but no one really knew just how special. Mark Waid was already firmly ensconced in the comic book writers' pantheon after an acclaimed run on *Captain America* and his attachment to one of the premier X-books, and Alex Ross's reputation was simply stratospheric after *Marvels*. Having 'done' Marvel, this was to be Ross's take on the DC Universe, and with Mark Waid at the helm, his reputation as a scholar of comics history well established, expectations were high. And, as in such cases, so was the expectation of failure. But for once the end product not only lived up to the hype, it went way, way beyond it. Set twenty years into the future, *Kingdom Come* was published in 1996 as a four-issue mini-series, under the Elseworlds banner. But so beautifully realised was this vision of the DC Universe's potentially bleak future in terms of dense characterisation, sumptuous visuals and sheer epic scope, it was decided to make it a part of ongoing DC continuity, as detailed in the sequel, *The Kingdom*. Almost exactly ten years after Miller's *Dark Knight Returns* first hit the comics scene, a worthy successor had arrived.

length about the story, then I would write down a rough breakdown of ideas and images — just a quick synopsis — and we'd fax that back and forth. Alex would talk about the images it brought to mind and I would then turn it into a script. After that, Alex would send me thumbnails, just to check his panel arrangement, to see if this was the kind of thing I was looking for, all the while making the same level of comments on my writing. We were very much in each other's heads the entire year and a half it took to do the project. Very rewarding, but exhausting.

On *The Flash*, I like to have a good strong relationship with my artists. I want to be able to talk to them; find out if they have any ideas themselves, do they have better ways of doing things, can they take my script and interpret my visuals differently in a way that makes the story stronger? That's fine, but because I've been on *The Flash* for eight years now, off and on, to some degree they're helping me execute my vision of the character and of the stories. I don't mean that to sound arrogant or dismissive in any way, because I've worked with some phenomenal people on *The Flash*, but it is much more my vision than something like *Kingdom Come* was.

On *Captain America* it's somewhere in the middle. I actually would have enjoyed both Ron [Garney] and Andy [Kubert] participating more in the storytelling process, but in both cases they were quite happy with the plots and the scripts. Ron was a little bit more interpretative of my plots and would move things around and expand or contract certain sequences. I kind of like that. Andy's attitude is, 'Man, it's your story', and I couldn't be more flattered than that.

How do you keep so many storylines running in your head?

That's the most taxing part of the job. Fortunately, I'm a very organised man, and that goes not just for my desktop, but for my brain too; it's very compartmentalised. The hardest part is not so much keeping the storyline straight in my head, it's multi-tasking and focusing, being able to block out several days in a row to work and concentrate on one specific story without having to worry about all the other assignments.

So you finish one comic before you move onto another. Do you ever mix and match?

I couldn't possibly do that, I would get completely lost. You really lose all your energy, all your intensity, if you switch back and forth. This is especially so with *The Flash*, because it's a very personal book. With a *Flash* script I often don't really know what the story is about until about page sixteen, and by story I don't mean the plot, I mean its themes and emotional context. I will invariably get to about page sixteen and go, 'Jesus, I've just realised something about my characters. I've just learned something about Wally', and it changes the whole story. I then have to go back and massage, tweak and generally fudge around with it.

CAPTAIN AMERICA #4:"Capmania" Plot for 22 Pages

PAGE NINETEEN

—tight on his feet as he kicks off the ice, using the shield as a sled—

—and BOOM! Cap, propelled across the ice, lands the finishing blow!

PAGE TWENTY

The crowd goes WILD!

Batroc, shaken and stunned, staggers to his feet. [You...you WIN, mon ami. But there will be ANOTHER day...]

As Batroc bounds away, Hawkeye readies another arrow for flight— ["He's getting' AWAY! I'LL bag him!"]

—but Cap's hand reaches in from off and grabs his bow, stopping Hawkeye from firing. Hawkeye's shocked. [Cap: "Let him GO." Hawkeye: "Are you NUTS?"]

PAGE TWENTY-ONE

Hawkeye's laughing, proud of himself. Cap, recovering his shield, is grim. [Cap says, definitively, that the fight is over. Hawkeye goes on about how they kicked Batroc's butt even with him tougher than ever, how they should be proud of themselves. Cap counters with, "What a pointless way to spend an AFTERNOON."]

Hawkeye, confused, listens to Cap speak harshly to him. LOTS of room for balloons thanks. [Cap explains to Hawkeye how stupid a fight that was, how pathetic a waste of time. He wasn't fighting for his country or fighting to protect the innocent. He was brawling because some jerk came after him. Lately, he's been thinking that he— that they all—spend too much time doing just that, and he just proved it. The world isn't any better a place now than it was an hour ago. He wants to be more proactive, less reactionary. And this wasn't either.]

They look up to the cheering crowd above. [Cap bitches about how this was just a big gladiator tournament, a wrestling match, with nothing at stake. Hawkeye counters that there was PLENTY at stake—the peoples' faith in him. Look at 'em CHEER.]

Now it's Hawkeye's turn to lecture Cap, though he does so as the happy crowd charges towards them. Hawkeye waves to the crowd. [Hawkeye points out that he gets Cap's point, but if Cap's gonna go out in a costume, that's the kind of activity he can expect to run into. Comes with the job, he *knows* that after all these years, he *must*. That suit stands for HOPE against TOUGH ODDS...it inspires COURAGE. People NEED that kinda claptrap today more than EVER. Sure, he wishes they were chantin' "HAWKEYE," but...]

Above: *Plot extract from* Captain America #4. *Courtesy of Mark Waid/Marvel Comics. Used with permission.* Captain America ™ *and* © 1999 Marvel Characters, Inc.

CAPTAIN AMERICA #14: "Turnabout" Script for 22 Pages

PAGE TEN

FULL PAGE. STREET LEVEL, IN FRONT OF THE HOTEL. A HUGE CROWD HAS GATHERED; SKULL'S IN THE THICK OF IT. EVERY-ONE'S STARING UP AT A BALCONY, CHEERING, WAVING SMALL AMERICAN FLAGS AT CAPTAIN AMERICA, WHO STANDS ON THE BALCONY, OPEN HAND OUT, ADDRESSING "HIS PEOPLE" IN A MANNER EERILY REMINISCENT OF THE NUREMBERG RALLIES. SKULL IS PAYING NO ATTENTION TO CAP; INSTEAD, HE'S EXCHANGING A MEANINGFUL GLANCE WITH A BEAUTIFUL WOMAN WHO LOOKS UPON HIM WITH KINDNESS AND INTEREST—THE FIRST PERSON WHO HAS EVER DONE SO.

1 CAPTION: When work is DONE, I attempt to rally OTHERS to the plight of my people...try to WARN them of the sin, of the HORROR, which comes from diluting ARYAN BLOOD with that of other races, other COLORS.

2 CAPTION: Always, my voice is drowned out by CHEERING. By pedagogic SINGING and insipid CHANTING.

3 CAPTION: The land of the free. One nation under God.

4 CAPTION: Indivisible.

5 CAPTION: In the visible.

6 CAPTION: Invisible.

7 CAPTION: Alone.

8 CAPTION: Alone, with no one to share my VISION.

9 CAPTION: Until a woman in the crowd turns to me and curls her lips. I stare at them.

10 CAPTION: They form a SMILE.

Above: *Original script extract from* Captain America #14. *Courtesy of Mark Waid/Marvel Comics. Used with permission.* Captain America ™ *and* © *1999 Marvel Characters, Inc.*

Do you need to identify with the characters you write?

I love Wally, and it's clear I do. He's the easiest character for me to write because essentially I shallowly impose my own voice on him. I identify with him more strongly than I do any other comic book character I've ever read. But it's not always that way, because frankly there's very little I can identify with in Captain America. The guy's much smarter than I am, he's much faster, and he doesn't have much of a sense of humour. The only thing I can identify with is, here's a guy who spends about eighteen hours a day doing his job. With all the other characters I can generally find something to latch onto. If I can't, then I'm doomed. You can tell, because the characters become flat and wooden.

I suppose there must be something more I identify with in Captain America for me to be that interested in him. If pressed, I would say it's the attitude he has under my pen of perceiving everything as a puzzle to be solved, or a challenge to be met, or an enigma to be unravelled. I would like to think that's what I can identify with, because I have a tendency to look at all situations in that light. The challenge of solving the problem is the most rewarding, delightful part.

Is it fair to say your work is characterised by a great deal of reverence for the source material?

I am very reverent towards the characters of the past, but not just because of nostalgia. It's logical; these characters, as interpreted in the forties, fifties and sixties,

The Flash Family

There's the Golden Age Flash (Jay Garrick), the Silver Age Flash (Barry Allen), Kid Flash (Wally West, a former sidekick of Barry Allen, now also just called Flash), Impulse (Bart Allen, grandson of Barry), XS (Bart's cousin Jenni), Jesse Quick, John Fox (the twenty-seventh century Flash) and Max Mercury (the 'zen master of speed'). It boils down to three key 'Flashes'; the very first Flash, who appeared in the 1940s (in what is known as the Golden Age of comics publishing, circa 1937 to 1955), his successor the Silver Age (circa 1956 to 1965) Flash, who debuted in *Showcase* #4 and died in issue #7 of *Crisis on Infinite Earths*, and Wally West, Barry Allen's wife's nephew, who was originally Kid Flash, but after Barry Allen's death took on the Flash mantle. Then Iris Allen (wife of Barry) had twins, Don and Dawn, who were born in the thirtieth century (don't ask) and became the Tornado Twins. They in turn had children, Jenni (Dawn's daughter) and Bart (Don's son), the latter of whom was hyper-kinetic, raised in a virtual reality world, and eventually sent back to the twentieth century where he became Impulse. Hhhhhh. Sometimes it's hard to keep up.

sold a hundred times more comics than we sell today. They appealed to a much wider range of readers and were targeted more towards a healthier, younger audience, which we had a potential to reach and grow with. Frankly, the guys back then knew what the hell they were doing and we don't any more. My reverence for the past is mainly a sense of respect for what's come before.

As an industry we're currently just flailing around. There are so many creators, editors and publishers who haven't a clue how to sell comics to younger readers, myself included frankly. Why not try to find something in what has gone before, and instead of dismissing it because it's old, see what was there? Not in terms of specific ideas — and this is a conversation that Grant and I have quite frequently — or specific plots or character bits, but in terms of, 'Look at that sense of wonder of these characters'. Certainly in the 1960s, when I was growing up reading comics, anything could happen. Superman, Batman, Flash and Green Lantern, they were fairy tales. There was no idea too wild, no concept too startling, there was just a barrage of new ideas and new concepts. That's certainly the foundation of Grant's work, because anybody who reads *JLA* knows that in any one issue there's five new ideas, and they come at you like shotgun shells.

I've very clearly modelled my run on *The Flash* after the Superman comics of my youth; mainly in terms of expanding the cast of characters. So there's a Supergirl and a Superboy, except in my case it's Jesse Quick and Impulse, and just as Superman had the Fortress of Solitude, Wally's got a period in the sixty–fourth century where he's thought of as a god. That is my fascination with the past. The trick is to put some sort of a modern spin on it, to make it a little less hokey for kids of today. That's the tough part of the job. I sat down as a consulting editor with a lot of the younger assistants and associates at Marvel once and they pointed out something that was very true, which is comics are written and edited almost exclusively by guys in their forties, and most of us don't even have kids. We don't have any idea how to reach this young audience.

So what do you think is the future?

Part of me thinks it's telling stories that are more accessible. While there is nothing I can do personally to control the distribution of comics and make it easier for them to be in the hands of young people, what I can do and help others do is make sure that if a comic does somehow get in the hands of a child, he understands what he's reading, that there's a story there, with heart and passion and excitement and ideas, and he's not confused, and is instead enticed to come back next month. That said, the other part of me really thinks that we're doomed, that the print comic book is hopelessly fucked.

The common wisdom that I rebel against is that we now have to compete with so many different things: video games, cable television and the internet. We've *always* had things to compete with. The problem is, we're not doing our job and competing well enough. The destruction of the industry has largely come from the fact that about twenty-five years ago it started to be run by fans instead of professionals, devotees instead of businessmen, and now the seeds of that are catching up to us. So few people in comics have ever had a real job outside comics, and they have no idea how to craft material for a new audience. All they know about is writing comics for forty year-olds like themselves.

A number of other writers have mentioned your generosity in imparting advice and ideas. Is this something that you enjoy?

It's something I not only enjoy but is integral to the process. When I sat down and wrote the twelfth issue of *Captain America: Sentinel of Liberty*, I wrote it all in one day and I cannot remember the last time I did that without at some point calling one of my friends on the phone and bouncing ideas off them, or fishing for a suggestion or, conversely, while I'm on the phone helping them with one of their stories. I don't work well in a vacuum. The best and most exciting and fun part of the process is getting on the phone with Tom Peyer or Brian or Christopher Priest or Kurt or Grant and just throwing ideas back and forth.

David Ogilvey, an advertising executive in the States, said one of the most brilliant things I ever heard about writing: he said the best ideas start as jokes, and it's absolutely true. To me, there's nothing more productive than getting on the phone and just starting to throw ideas around about Flash or Justice League, making each other laugh, trying to top the other guy. That crackling energy can manifest itself on the page. This gets back to what I said before, about how I never set out to be a writer. I would be just as happy, if not happier, telling my stories to fans at conventions, doing a stage show, because the laborious process of writing is actually the drag of it, the fun part is the ideas. The way it works is there's a fairly loose cabal of me, Grant, Mark Millar, Brian, Tom and Priest, and Kurt to some extent, and we just have each other on speed dial. It was Tom, I think, who said, 'It's always easier when it's not your story'. I can be staring at a plot development that I can't crack for three days but I can call Brian and he'll have the answer immediately, because it's not his story, there's no pressure. We constantly have our fingers in each other's pies, if you will.

You took a year's break from *The Flash* during which time Grant and Mark Millar took over, and you did four issues of *JLA* for Grant. How did that work?

I needed a year off from *The Flash* because I felt that my preceding year on the book was not particularly strong. There are a lot of writers who will stay on a book knowing they're not doing their best work, because they figure it'll get better. My feeling is, 'Why are you charging your fans two dollars a month to suffer through that with you?'. Take a break, get some perspective. Grant and Mark are the only people in the world I would have trusted to take on the book for me, because I knew we were very much on the same wavelength about what a Flash story should be.

So I thought, 'Great, I've decreased my workload by one book, I can recharge my batteries, relax a little bit'. The next thing I know I get these panic calls from Dan Raspler, the editor of *JLA*. Because Grant has taken on *The Flash* he's suddenly horrifically behind on Justice League and could I step in and help? This wasn't my plan, but I like Dan, and it is tough to resist the lure of the Justice League. I picked up the gauntlet for what was supposed to be two issues and turned into four. So it wasn't so much that we swapped, as it was just a fortuitous confluence of events.

Did you give instructions to Grant and Mark on where you wanted the story to go and where it should end up?

No, I said as long as you leave the toy box pretty much the way you found it, do whatever you want. The reason I went to them is Grant, in particular, has a million ideas, and that's what had been missing from the book: new concepts, fresh ideas. So it was like, 'Grant, please come up with a bunch of different things that we can use in the future'. As it turned out, the idea they used most often was one I gave them, which is the costume itself is actually made of speedforce energy. But they're the ones who decided Wally should propose to Linda. That came as a surprise to me, but it gave me something to launch off of on my return. It was a very productive solution to the problem of feeling burned out, because I went to the right guys and they gave me the energy I needed.

You've been writing comics for some while now. Any danger of you becoming fed up with the superhero genre?

I am getting tired after ten years of doing a comic book a week, of sitting down on Monday morning and turning on the computer and by Thursday out comes a script. I'm beginning to feel more like a machine. Frankly, I feel there's only a

---

Mark Millar

While by no means joined at the hip, British (or rather, Scottish) born Mark Millar has pooled his creative talents with fellow Scot Grant Morrison on more than one occasion. Also an alumni of the *2000 AD*/Fleetway school of comics writers, Millar cut his teeth on such strips as *Red Razors*, a *Judge Dredd* spin-off focusing on a Soviet Judge and his talking horse, and also contributed to short-lived British anthology title *Trident*. The Millar/Morrison partnership introduced America to the writer's offbeat and quirky scripts, via collaborations on *Skrull Kill Krew* (a distinctly un-Marvel extrapolation on an early Fantastic Four story), *Aztek: The Ultimate Man* (a short-lived, but generally well thought out and executed 'alternate' superhero title) and, most importantly, *Swamp Thing*. It was on the latter, where a decade earlier Alan Moore had made such an impression, that Millar really came into his own. After an introductory four-parter by Millar and Morrison, Millar went solo, taking *Swamp Thing* through to the end of its run in fine style, harking back to the emotional depth and subtle horror that had previously characterised the title. Millar's more recent work includes *The Flash*, *JLA* and *JLA: Paradise Lost.*

certain number of themes that are prevalent in any writer's work, not just comic book writers, and they have a tendency to fall back on the same ones. I've written maybe 250 comic books and I'm terrified I'm retreading the same ground over and over again. With superhero characters it begins to be difficult to explore certain themes in new ways, especially the way I envision superheroes: I see them as essentially good people who have very little in a way of a dark side. I just wonder if I need to take a break for a little while and concentrate on other genres.

Another reason is the double disappointment I experienced recently. First was issue fourteen of *Captain America* being rewritten from scratch. It was the biggest creatively-related disappointment of my career. This was a story about the Red Skull I had been looking forward to telling for a year and a half. It was a very strong story, one told from the Skull's point of view, with him narrating. Therefore I had to get into that character's head, and I couldn't wait to do it. We knew it was going to be a dangerous story, because this fellow's a racist and a Nazi, and we made sure the Marvel management was looking over our shoulder every step of the way. The story was completed, done, ready to send to the printer, and they suddenly got cold feet. I don't know why, but they got very nervous for some reason, and decided to have the entire issue rewritten in-house, *without* my input. I was just flabbergasted! I've never felt more betrayed, or had my spirit crushed more thoroughly than that.

The second blow was being told, point blank, that Grant Morrison and I, having been asked to submit a proposal, will never be allowed to write Superman. We can write one shots or special projects, but Grant and I are not welcome to do the monthly books, because we are too — quote/unquote — 'high profile'. What they're afraid of is that we are controversial and outspoken. I don't know why that precludes us from doing a monthly Superman comic book, but it was another great disappointment to be told that this job that I have been working towards ever since I was a five year-old is something that I will never be able to do. That and the Captain America thing happened within two weeks of each other, and that as much as indicated to me that perhaps it's time to re-evaluate my career.

Given all that, how do you see your future?

First off, I cannot foresee a time in my life when I will not be doing comics, at least with some of my time. That said, for the last four or five years I've had movie and television producers chasing me, asking me to do things. I've been putting them off because I've been busy doing comic books one hundred per cent of my time. The plan is to trim my workload back to a couple of comic books and spend more time in outside media. And I want to develop creator-owned projects, of which I have a plethora sitting in a drawer waiting to be dusted off. Again, I've never had the time to do them, and now it's way past time I started to develop things of my own. If I can't do Superman, which is the only other thing that is left for me to do in terms of what's already out there, it's time for me to invent things.

What kind of things?

I still think heroic adventure is my forte, but then I think that comedy is my forte also; writing *Impulse* was one of my favourite assignments of all time. There's got to be some way to marry adventure with comedy and do something a little lighter. Books like *Danger Girl*, for instance, that's not a bad way to go. Something along those lines anyway. It's still heroic adventure, but it's not traditional super-hero/supervillain cape and mask stuff. There are so many things vying for attention in my file of creator-owned projects, but the common thread is that they all have a sense of humour, and they still have to be about good people trying to do the right thing.

What would you say has been the highlight of your career to date?

The highlight was writing *The Flash* #0, which was the most intensely personal story I've ever written, because it was very much modelled after my own life. It was the moment where my life and Wally's life most intersected. Being able to tell that and have that realised so beautifully allowed me to learn things about myself. In a broader sense, the highlight is the whole run of *The Flash*, using the character of the Flash to unintentionally learn volumes about myself as a person. In that way it's been a very symbiotic relationship, and that has been the most rewarding thing that's come out of the last ten years.

Can you explain what you mean?

When I took on *The Flash* and Wally in particular, I was searching for a way to relate to the character, and I realised there were certain similarities in terms of his relationship with his parents, his attitude towards the world, and his impatience; and by that I mean the deeper reasons he is impatient, besides the fact he's just fast. I began to impart facets of my life onto him, but I also began to get things back. I realised that a lot of my own impatience stems from this idea that time is the enemy of all living things, and that Wally and I both have a tendency when the going gets tough to fall back into the past, and to live in the past. Wally wears his uncle's costume for Christ's sake! Wally thinks about his uncle all the time, and about his boyhood all the time. Well, so do I. This is a revelation that really came to me as I was writing, that we both have this bad, bad self-defeating tendency to live in the past instead of embracing the future. Things like that over the past ten years have been character revelations to me. They don't sound very earth-shattering when I speak them out loud, but they only arose after months and months of thinking and self-examination.

You mentioned that it's important to you to impart your knowledge to new writers. What can you teach them?

That the first and most important thing in this business is clarity, making sure that the very basics of your characters and the situation and the conflict are established clearly in the pages of your comic as early as possible. That way people know who the hell they're reading about and they're not confused. I think people are looking for reasons not to read comics, and every time we confuse a reader we run the risk of them tossing the book across the room and not bothering with it again. It doesn't mean we have to write simple, or we have to be stupid, but it does mean we have to be clear and not introduce characters without telling the reader who they are or what they can do. It's just simple stuff that's true in every medium; in films, television, comics. Because we are fans, we assume that because we know who Gorilla Grodd is we don't have to give him a name and don't have to explain who he is. Well, that road leads to doom.

Beyond that, it's a matter of trying to impart the knowledge that you can only write effectively about the things you're passionate about yourself. Stop writing stories you think other people want to read, and instead write about the things that move you. So many times I see people wrestling with fight scenes or typical superhero/supervillain battles because they feel it incumbent upon them to put them into a story. They assemble the comic books all wrong. They're trying to please others instead of their own muse. Those are the two most important things I keep yelling at people and pounding into their heads.

Are there any new, young writers who impress you?

Joe Kelly impresses the hell out of me. Joe, I think, has a real strong balance between adventure and motion picture technique, and knowing what can and can't fit in a comic book story in terms of visual stuff. Devin Grayson impressed me even before I met her as someone with a real strong sense of dialogue and very highly developed sense of character. And Joe Casey I think has a lot of potential too. He has a nice, witty snap to his scripts. Those are the ones who stand out. We need to have a lot more people coming into comics who aren't comic book geeks, to show us new things. A lot of them will do a bad job because they don't know how a comic book is done, but even if you get five guys who suck, if that sixth guy can show me something new, it was worth it.

*　　　　　　*　　　　　　*

Check out:
Captain America: Operation Rebirth
Captain America: Man Without a Country
The Flash: The Return of Barry Allen (collects issues #74–79)
The Flash Terminal Velocity (collects issues #95–100, #0)
Impulse: Reckless Youth
JLA: Year One
Kingdom Come (with Alex Ross)
The Life Story of the Flash
Underworld Unleashed

FOR THE LATEST NEWS, INFO AND PRICES ON COMIC BOOKS AND ACTION FIGURES, READ

HOW TO DRAW & SELL
COMIC STRIPS

By Alan McKenzie

This book will teach you not only how to master the art of creating
exciting comic strips, but also how to get them published.
Alan McKenzie and other professional comic strip creators share their
inside trade secrets, including:

- what equipment to buy

- how to write a script and break it down into panels

- how to draw the human figure in convincing poses

- the pencilling, inking, lettering and colouring processes

- how to present and pitch your work to publishers

Plus — a special appendix of US and UK comic publishers and syndicates,
complete with addresses, gives you the contacts you need to get started.

HOW TO DRAW COMICS
THE MARVEL WAY

By Stan Lee and John Buscema

Two of the biggest names in modern comics reveal the secrets of their craft in this accessible and highly illustrated guide to drawing comics... the Marvel way.

Stan Lee, the man who created Spider-Man, the Fantastic Four and the Incredible Hulk (to name but a few), takes us through every aspect of crafting a comic strip in the inimitable and much loved Marvel style. Using examples from countless classic Marvel comics and a featuring numerous new illustrations from acclaimed artist John Buscema, the reader is graphically guided from rough sketch to finished illustration, covering foreshortening, perspective, proportions, basic figure drawing, action poses and much, much more.

How to Draw Comics the Marvel Way is essential reading for every kid who ever wanted to illustrate his or her own comic strip.

Also available from TITAN BOOKS

CONTEMPORARY/ ADULT-THEMED GRAPHIC NOVELS

Also available from TITAN BOOKS

CONTEMPORARY/
ADULT-THEMED GRAPHIC NOVELS

THE SANDMAN: BRIEF LIVES
Neil Gaiman/Jill Thompson/
Vince Locke

**THE SANDMAN: THE DOLL'S
HOUSE**
Neil Gaiman/Mike Dringenberg/
Malcolm Jones III

**THE SANDMAN: DREAM
COUNTRY**
Neil Gaiman/Various

**THE SANDMAN: FABLES AND
REFLECTIONS**
Neil Gaiman/Various

**THE SANDMAN: THE
KINDLY ONES**
Neil Gaiman/Various

**THE SANDMAN: PRELUDES
AND NOCTURNES**
Neil Gaiman/Sam Kieth/Various

**THE SANDMAN: SEASON
OF MISTS**
Neil Gaiman/Various

THE SANDMAN: THE WAKE
Neil Gaiman/Various

THE SANDMAN: WORLDS' END
Neil Gaiman/Various

**DUST COVERS — THE
COLLECTED SANDMAN
COVERS 89–96**
Dave McKean/Neil Gaiman

SIN CITY
Frank Miller

SIN CITY: THE BIG FAT KILL
Frank Miller

**SIN CITY: BOOZE, BROADS
& BULLETS**
Frank Miller

**SIN CITY: A DAME TO
KILL FOR**
Frank Miller

SIN CITY: FAMILY VALUES
Frank Miller

**SIN CITY: THAT YELLOW
BASTARD**
Frank Miller

STARDUST
Neil Gaiman/Charles Vess

VIOLENT CASES
Neil Gaiman/Dave McKean

Also available from TITAN BOOKS

SUPERHERO GRAPHIC NOVELS

BATMAN: ARKHAM ASYLUM
Grant Morrison/Dave McKean

**BATMAN: THE DARK KNIGHT
RETURNS 10th ANNIVERSARY
EDITION**
Frank Miller

BATMAN: THE KILLING JOKE
Alan Moore/Brian Bolland/
John Higgins

**BATMAN: KNIGHTFALL:
PT1 - BROKEN BAT**
Doug Moench/Various

**BATMAN: KNIGHTFALL:
PT2 - WHO RULES
THE NIGHT?**
Doug Moench/Various

BATMAN: KNIGHTSEND
Chuck Dixon/Alan Grant/
Various

**BATMAN: THE LONG
HALLOWEEN**
Jeph Loeb/Tim Sale

**DC vs MARVEL: SHOWDOWN
OF THE CENTURY**
Various

HITMAN
Garth Ennis/John McCrea

JLA: AMERICAN DREAMS
Grant Morrison/Howard Porter

JLA: NEW WORLD ORDER
Grant Morrison/Howard Porter

JLA: ROCK OF AGES
Grant Morrison/Howard Porter

**JLA: STRENGTH
IN NUMBERS**
Grant Morrison/Mark
Waid/Howard Porter

**JLA: WORLD WITHOUT
GROWN-UPS**
Todd Dezago/Various

KINGDOM COME
Mark Waid/Alex Ross

SPAWN: ANGELA
Todd McFarlane/Neil Gaiman

SPAWN: CREATION (1)
Todd McFarlane

SPAWN: EVOLUTION (2)
Todd McFarlane

Also available from TITAN BOOKS

SUPERHERO GRAPHIC NOVELS

SPAWN: REVELATION (3)
Todd McFarlane

SPAWN: ESCALATION (4)
Todd McFarlane/Grant
Morrison/Greg Capullo

SPAWN: CONFRONTATION (5)
Todd McFarlane/Greg Capullo

SPAWN: RETRIBUTION (6)
Todd McFarlane/Greg Capullo

**SPAWN:
TRANSFORMATION (7)**
Todd McFarlane/Greg Capullo

SPAWN: ABDUCTION (8)
Todd McFarlane/Greg
Capullo/Alan Moore

SPAWN: SANCTION (9)
Todd McFarlane/Greg Capullo

SPAWN: DAMNATION (10)
Todd McFarlane/Greg Capullo

SPAWN: CORRUPTION (11)
Todd McFarlane/Greg Capullo

SUPERGIRL
Peter David/Gary Frank

**THE DEATH OF
SUPERMAN**
Dan Jurgen/Various
ISBN: 1 85286 480 X

**WORLD WITHOUT A
SUPERMAN**
Dan Jurgens/Various
ISBN: 1 85286 495 8

**THE RETURN OF
SUPERMAN**
Dan Jurgens/Various
ISBN: 1 85286 514 8

**SUPERMAN FOR ALL
SEASONS**
Jeph Loeb/Tim Sale
(Autumn 99)

SUPERMAN: TRANSFORMED
Dan Jurgens/Various

WATCHMEN
Alan Moore/Dave Gibbons

Titan Books are available through all good bookshops and comic shops.

All titles available in UK & Eire only, unless otherwise stated.